Jeremiah Travis

A law treatise on the constitutional powers of Parliament and of the local legislatures

Under the British North America act, 1867

Jeremiah Travis

A law treatise on the constitutional powers of Parliament and of the local legislatures
Under the British North America act, 1867

ISBN/EAN: 9783337153793

Printed in Europe, USA, Canada, Australia, Japan

Cover: Foto ©Suzi / pixelio.de

More available books at **www.hansebooks.com**

A LAW TREATISE

ON THE

CONSTITUTIONAL POWERS OF PARLIAMENT,

AND OF THE

LOCAL LEGISLATURES,

UNDER THE

British North America Act, 1867;

BY

J. TRAVIS, Esquire, LL. B.;

OF THE NEW BRUNSWICK BAR; ANNOTATOR OF PARSONS ON PARTNERSHIP; FIRST PRIZE LAW-ESSAYIST OF HARVARD UNIVERSITY OF 1866; AUTHOR OF LEADING LAW EDITORIALS IN THE AMERICAN LAW REGISTER, (PHILA. 1866 and '67; HON. CHIEF JUSTICE REDFIELD, AUTHOR OF "LAW OF WILLS;" "LAW OF RAILWAYS," &c., EDITOR), ON ORIGIN AND HISTORY OF THE COMMON LAW: JURISDICTION OF THE UNITED STATES FEDERAL COURTS; COMMON LAW CRIMINAL JURISDICTION OF THE STATE COURTS, &c., &c.

" *Nothing extenuate,*
Nor set down aught in malice !"
SHAKSPEARE.

" *Of course, recognising as I do that the Bishop possesses a discretion in this matter, I most fully admit that he is vastly more capable of exercising it well than I am. But the way he does exercise it is subject to criticism, even by those less competent than himself; in the same way as the opinion and sentences of this Court*, MAY AND OUGHT TO BE, AND ARE, *criticised by laymen."*
Per BRAMWELL, L. J., *in Regina v. Bishop of Oxford*, 4 Q. B. Div., 556; IN COURT OF APPEAL OF ENGLAND.

SAINT JOHN, N. B.:
PRINTED BY THE SUN PUBLISHING CO., CANTERBURY STREET.
——
1884.

INTRODUCTION.

So much confusion and contradiction have grown up in connection with the Constitutional Law of Canada, that it has become very desirable that some attempt were made to overcome and remove it.

On the one hand, we have the extreme views of Mr. *Blake*, Mr. *Mowat*, Judge HENRY, the Supreme Court of New Brunswick, and others, laying down principles of construction, which, carried to their logic result, would virtually deprive Parliament of all legislative power; while, on the other hand, we have judgments from Justices STRONG, TASCHEREAU and GWYNNE, and from the Supreme Courts of British Columbia and New Brunswick, which, carried to their ultimate consequence, would denude the Local Legislatures of all legislative power. Neither of these sets of views is right. It was to demonstrate this fact, and to make an attempt to bring Order out of Chaos, that this treatise has been written.

The Author had previously, for another purpose, made an exhaustive analysis of all the Constitutional cases in the Supreme Court of Canada, and of all decided by the Judicial Committee of the Privy Council, down to the Citizens' Insurance Co. *v.* Parsons, inclusive; and felt that he was prepared to grapple with the difficulties of construction that were in his way. With this view, at the beginning of the treatise, he confronted himself with three questions, covering the whole ground, which he proposed making the whole discussion answer. In proceeding with the discussion, at quite an advanced stage of the work, he was *astounded* to find, in two later cases decided by the Privy Council; viz, Dobie *v.* The Temporalities Board, (the Presbyterian case); and Russell *v* The Queen, (The Canada Temperance Act case); principles of construction laid down, which, as he looked upon them, if logically applied as sound principles—if, from their peculiar unsoundness, it were not really impossible to practically apply them as governing principles—would sweep away the whole legislative power of the Local Legislatures.

As this fact forced itself more and more strongly on his mind, three questions as to his course arose, viz :—

First,—In this new element of confusion being introduced, should the work be abandoned as impracticable?

Second,—Should the original design of the treatise be carried out, and be confined to meeting only the difficulties that were then foreseen? or

INTRODUCTION.

Third,—Should the new difficulties be grappled with, and an attempt be made to show that false principles, even when sustained by high authority, are not the less false?

After much hesitation and deliberation, this last course has been thought the most manly, the wisest and the best. A Second Part has, therefore, been added to this treatise; some necessary modifications and qualifications made in the First Part, to more closely harmonize it with the author's views, as expressed in the new and unlooked-for investigation; and the work launched.

Some readers will be startled, no doubt, at the boldness with which these new difficulties are met; but the author has the satisfaction of feeling that in meeting palpable error "fearlessly and faithfully," and boldly confronting it, whether found in the utterance of politicians; among our own courts and judges, or even with so august and authorative a body as the Privy Council Board, he has not only performed his duty; but, that, he but anticipates the judgment of his intelligent readers when he entertains the hope that he has done so with success.

St. John, N. B., April, 1884.

CANADIAN CONSTITUTIONAL LAW.

Incomparably the most interesting and important legal questions for the consideration of the people, whether lawyers or laymen, of this Dominion, are those in connection with the construction of the B. N. A. Act, 1867, relative to the rights of legislation of Parliament, and of the Local Legislatures, respectively.

In the speech of the Lieut. Gov. of N. B., in opening the recent session of the N. B. Legislature, is the following :—

"The judgment of the Supreme Court of Canada, affirming the right of the Province in the Fisheries, and other judicial decisions recently rendered upon questions involving the powers of the Local Legislature, justify the hope that we may rely upon the court of final resort preserving the political autonomy of the Provinces against the dangers which threaten it from Federal encroachments."

Numerous articles, mainly from a political standpoint, have appeared in the leading political papers, in which the subject has been discussed, and in which such language as " Federal usurpation", &c., is common. Recently, out-Heroding-Herod, a pamphlet has been issued from the " *Morning Chronicle,*" Quebec press, purporting to be by " *The Honorable Mr. Justice T. J. J. Loranger,*" in which the most extraordinary and utterly untenable positions in the matter are taken. In a later portion of this treatise, we may direct attention to some of the crude absurdities in which that pamphlet abounds, in which the author makes the most ludicrous efforts to " darken counsel with words without knowledge." Just now, we propose to make, entirely independent of any political bias whatever, an honest, and we trust, intelligent examination and analysis of a number of the decided cases, with a view of making much clearer than at present is the case, the relative powers of Parliament, and of the Legislatures, (as for convenience we will designate them), under the B. N. A. Act. We propose with other cases, to examine a number of cases that have been decided in the Supreme Court of N. B., not because that Court, since it lost the benefit of the presence of its late Chief Justice, (the present Sir WM. J. RITCHIE), to give shape, with his great legal knowledge, to its judgments, is of any very high authority, for it must be frankly admitted that it is not ; but rather because we find a variety of cases there well fitted for examination, in connection with the decisions of the Supreme Court of Canada, and of the Privy Council Board, to enable us to come to an intelligent conclusion as to what is the law on the vexed, and confessedly, intricate, questions, involved in the cases decided under the not very clear language of the Act.

THE DIFFICULTIES STATED.

Perhaps, except for lawyers already familiar with the leading points in the discussion, it would be plunging *in medias res*, to a greater extent than might be judicious, to take up those cases without some preliminary explanation, which we will, therefore, first make, as briefly as possible ; reserving a fuller discussion of the points involved until the cases which we shall cite shall come under examination.

The Constitutional difficulties which have arisen, have mainly been under the 91st and 92nd sections of the Act, which are within that division of the Act providing for the " Distribution of Legislative Powers." And the difficulties which have arisen have been from two causes : *first*, that the subjects named in the 92nd section of the Act, as the subjects within the " *Exclusive* Powers of Provincial Legislatures", are very largely in direct conflict with many of the subjects named in the 91st section, as within the " Powers of Parliament." Thus, while it is declared in the 92nd section of the Act, under the head too of " *Exclusive Powers of Provincial Legislatures*," that " In each Province the legislature may *exclusively* make laws in relation to matters coming within the classes of subjects next hereinafter enumerated, that is to say ";—naming sixteen different " classes" of subjects, among which are, for instance,—

" 9. Shop, saloon, tavern, auctioneer, and other licenses, in order to the raising of a revenue for provincial, local, or municipal purposes.

" 12. The solemnization of marriage in the Province.

" 13. Property and civil rights in the Province ; "

under the 91st section, under the heading of " Powers of the Parliament," are given as among the subjects or matters, within

" the *exclusive* legislative authority of the Parliament of Canada," such, for instance, as—

" 2. The regulation of Trade and Commerce.
" 10. Navigation and Shipping.
" 12. Sea Coast and Inland Fisheries.
" 21. Bankruptcy and Insolvency.
" 26. Marriage and Divorce."

Here, clearly, it is obvious, that if Parliament has the exclusive right of legislating, for instance, on *all* matters connected with the regulation of trade and commerce; shop, saloon and other licenses, as named, as subjects, would come within the wide field of all matters relating to the regulation of trade. So, again, legislation on Trade and Commerce; on Navigation and Shipping; on Sea Coast and Inland Fisheries, and on Bankruptcy and Insolvency, would be not only virtually, but absolutely, impossible, without interfering with Property and Civil Rights, or one or other of these subjects. And, on the other hand, if the Legislatures could *exclusively* legislate on all matters within Property and Civil Rights, they would be able to legislate exclusively, on about *all* matters; and Parliament would be unable to legislate at all. So, again, if all matters connected with Marriage were within the legislative power of Parliament, that, necessarily, would include the Solemnization of Marriage as well. To have left the powers of the two legislative bodies in such an utterly irreconcileable state of antagonism, would have been quite too absurd; and to obviate this, there were certain provisions made at the beginning and end of the 91st section of the Act. It is in the somewhat involved language used in these provisions, and in the failure to give due force to that language that

THE SECOND DIFFICULTY

in the construction of the Act has arisen.

It will be necessary now to examine these clauses.

We will first consider the language at the close of the 91st section, and which has been the subject of misapprehension by very many; among whom, as hereafter will be more specifically shown, may be mentioned, *Mr. Loranger* in his pamphlet; *Judge* FISHER in two cases; *Mr. Blake* in the Mercer-Escheat case; and, still more surprising, by the Privy Council; SIR MONTAGUE E. SMITH delivering the judgment, in Parsons v. The Citizens Insurance Co., L. R., 7 App. Cas., at p. 108.

The language of the clause referred to, is:—

" And any matter coming within any of the classes of subjects enumerated in this section shall not be deemed to come within the class of matters of a local or private nature comprised in the enumeration of the classes of subjects by this Act assigned exclusively to the Legislatures of the Provinces."

This clause, alone, is very indefinite, and it is not singular that in many cases, it has been misunderstood. As a matter of relief from an excess of heavy discussion, which we will have directly, one difficulty in it might be illustrated by

THE SMART BOY'S JOKE.

" How many legs has a horse?" he asked of his less brilliant companion.

" Four," was the reply.

" Suppose you called its tail a leg, how many would it have?"

" Why five, to be sure!"

" No, it wouldn't, you goose! *Calling its tail a leg, wouldn't make it a leg, would it?*"

When the clause says then, that matters arising within the classes of subjects in the 91st section, shall *not be deemed* to come within the classes of matter in the 92nd section, they do so, notwithstanding, whether "deemed" to do so or not. And it is the very fact that they *do* come within them, that makes all the difficulty. And in what sense, when they actually do so come within those classes, they are not to be *deemed* to come within them, the clause leaves indefinite, and open to construction, or—mis-construction! There are two senses in which the language may be taken : one, that they shall not come within the classes of subjects named in the 92nd section, so as to interfere with the right of the Legislatures to legislate with reference to the subjects-matter in that section. This is the view taken of it by Mr. Justice FISHER in the two cases, Robertson v. Steadman, 3 Pugs., at p. 637, and in Steadman v. Robertson, 2 P. & B., at p. 594. But if this were the meaning, the words " *be deemed to* " would not have been inserted in the clause at all, and the language then expressly would have been, " shall not come within," &c. And, in fact, Mr. Justice FISHER in quoting the language from the Act in the cases above named, does misquote the language in that way,— " Shall not come within," &c. If this had been the language, and there had been nothing else in the Act to have modified it, the Act, then, *would* have been perfectly clear and simple, and the absurdities which now fill up Mr. *Loranger's* pamphlet, would not have been absurdities at all; but the Legislatures would, in very deed, have been the dominant legislative bodies, and the power of Parliament would have been almost as unsubstantial " as a vision faded !" For, if Parliament could only legislate on the regulation of trade and commerce; on navigation and shipping; on bankruptcy and insolvency, &c. &c., so as to be entirely outside and clear of " Property and Civil Rights," it could not legislate at all; for not a particle of legislation on the subjects named could be had which would not relate to Property or Civil Rights, or to both of these subjects.

THE OTHER INTERPRETATION.

But the other and the correct interpretation involves no such absurdities. It is this: "Shall not be deemed to come within," &c., so that " no matter how much it may appear to do so," (to quote in effect, the language of SIR WILLIAM RITCHIE, C. J; TASCHEREAU and GWYNNE JJ., &c.,) or, to use our own language, *how much it may actually do so*, it shall not be deemed to do so, so as to interfere with or prevent such legislation by Parliament. The term "deemed" too, is always thus used in Acts of Parliament, to provide that when a thing does something particularly named, it shall not be " deemed " to do so; always implying that it *may* do that particular thing without being " deemed" to do it. But, with this undoubtedly correct construction of the language in the clause we have been considering; and which enables us to avoid the monstrous absurdities in which we would be involved if the first named construction were adopted; and if Parliament had indeed no greater power and authority than Mr. *Loranger* in his pamphlet, and others who are talking so much about " Federal usurpation," &c., try to establish; there are still

THREE FURTHER POINTS

which require to be made much plainer than they at present are. These are :—

First, What is the power of the Legislatures to legislate in the first instance, (that is before Parliament has legislated on any of the subjects-matter in the 91st section that though not " deemed" to come within those in the 92nd section, actually do so,) on the subjects-matter named in the 92nd section?

Second, What is the limit of the power of Parliament to legislate with reference to matters named in the 91st section which do come within or interfere with those in the 92nd section? and

Third, How are the Acts of the Legislatures, and their powers to legislate, affected by such legislation, as named, by Parliament?

It is with the object of making, as intimated, these confessedly difficult questions much clearer than they now are, that we propose grappling with them, and, as far as we can, honestly clearing away " without any political bias whatever," much of the doubt and uncertainty that, mainly through the perversions of political writers, (*apropos* of which we might say, parenthetically, that Mr. *Loranger's* pamphlet is rather a political essay than a legal argument), has been cast about these questions ; confessedly difficult to deal with even as mere questions of law. We would first however, make still clearer, (as so much depends upon establishing what some very high authorities think should not, in connection with questions coming up under this Act, be attempted, namely, " a hard and fast" rule of construction), that the construction named, of the clause at the end of the 91st section, is the correct one. And, if correct, is as a rule of construction " a hard and fast" one. This *is* made much clearer by—following the rule in Coke's Institutes, *first,* p. 381, thus : " It is the most natural and genuine exposition of a statute to construe one part by another of the same statute, for that best expresses the meaning of the makers, and such construction is *ex visceribus actus*,"—making, as we now shall do, an examination of

THE FIRST CLAUSE OF THE 91ST SECTION,

as has already been done by SIR WM. J. RITCHIE, C. J. ; by Justices TASCHEREAU and GWYNNE and by others. The clause is as follows :

" 91. It shall be lawful for the Queen, by and with the advice and consent of the Senate and House of Commons, to make laws for the peace, order and good government of Canada, in relation to all matters not coming within the classes of subjects by this act assigned exclusively to the Legislatures of the Provinces ; and for greater certainty, but not so as to restrict the generalty of the foregoing terms of this section, it is hereby declared that (notwithstanding anything in this act) the legislative authority of the Parliament of Canada extends to all matters coming within the classes of subjects next hereinafter enumerated, that is to say :—" enumerating, then, twenty-nine classes of subjects.

It is astonishing how strangely, and how frequently, this clause has been misconstrued. In many cases the last portion of it, which is the part that really shows how the conflicting subjects given to Parliament and to the Legislatures are to be treated and reconciled, is entirely omitted, or treated as though it were utterly meaningless. Thus, Mr. *Loranger* in the pamphlet to which we have already made reference, on page 15, and again on page 50, quotes the first portion only of the clause, as though that were the whole of it, ending his quotations with the word "Provinces;" and thus, leaving out of sight the very essence of the clause, "Playing Hamlet with the part of Hamlet omitted!" So, also, as we shall see, does Mr. JUSTICE HENRY.

The first part of the clause is clear. By it, Parliament has the power "to make laws for the peace, order and good government of Canada in relation to all matters not coming within the classes of subjects by this act assigned exclusively to the Legislatures of the Provinces." Here, then, Parliament is allowed to legislate, only, for the purposes named, on the matters that *do not come within* the classes of subjects assigned to the Legislatures. So far, that is clear. But that is by no means, as it has so often been, most singularly, treated to be, the whole of it.

The next part of the clause provides, that, "for greater certainty, but not so as to restrict the generality of the foregoing terms of this section, it is hereby declared that (*notwithstanding anything in this Act*) THE EXCLUSIVE LEGISLATIVE AUTHORITY of the Parliament of Canada extends to all matters *coming within the classes of subjects next hereinafter enumerated*, that is to say,"—enumerating them.

The clause in whole, then, simply says that "for the peace, order and good goverment of Canada," Parliament may make laws "in relation to all matters" by the Act "*not assigned exclusively to the Legislatures*"; and, also, without interfering with the general right of Parliament to legislate as above, on all matters not so assigned to the Legislatures; it shall also have the power, *notwithstanding anything in the Act*, to *exclusively legislate* on all matters coming within the enumerated classes of subjects, (naming them;) and, then, by the passage at the close of the section, which we have already examined, it is further provided, as in effect we have seen, that no matter how much the classes of subjects enumerated in the 91st section may come within the class of matters named in the 92nd section, they shall not be deemed to do so, so as to prevent legislation by Parliament, on the subjects enumerated in the 91st section, no matter how much such legislation may *appear* to interfere, or may *actually* interfere with the subjects named in the 92nd section; or with the legislation of the Legislatures, or with their right to legislate, with respect to such subjects, so named in the 92nd section.

This is the only construction of the language to which it is fairly open; and, with such construction, the clauses at the beginning and end of the 91st section are entirely consistent and intelligible.

The effect of this, of course, is altogether different from what it would have been, if the latter part of the opening clause of the 91st section, (which is so often ignored in the misconstruction of the Act), and the clause at the close of the section, had been omitted. Then, Parliament would have had the right to have legislated only on such matters as were not given to the Legislatures; and any legislation by Parliament within the subjects assigned to the Legislatures, would have been *ultra vires* and invalid. And the Legislatures, as regards these subjects-matters, would have been the superior bodies, and Parliament the inferior body. But now all this is reversed; and, on all the subjects-matter named in the 91st section, all *proper and bona fide legislation by Parliament, within the fair scope and effect of such subjects-matter* is *intra vires* and valid, no matter how much it interferes with, overrides, or renders abortive, the legislation of the Legislatures with respect to the subjects-matter named in the 92nd section of the Act.

This, we claim, is the only possible construction of the language of the Act; and it is also claimed that the Act thus gives us what it has been said more than once, by the very high authorities to which we have referred, we should not attempt to get, "a hard and fast" rule of construction in the matter, but that every question as it comes up, should be treated on its own individual facts and merits. We respectfully submit, that in the face of the Act, there is no escape from this "hard and fast" rule of construction, and that we are not to be left entirely at sea in the matter. And further, that carrying this construction to its legitimate result, and the legislation of Parliament being shaped thereby, is not as has been alleged by one of the political writers on the subject:— "A most unjustifiable usurpation of the rights of our Local Legislatures!"

The very construction claimed here as the only proper construction, is not either a fanciful or accidental result. Whether Parliament has too much power or not, it has only just such powers as the framers of the Canadian Constitution—leading men on both sides of politics—designed to give it. While, we claim, there is no escape from "the hard and fast rule of construction" which the express language of the Act gives us, we would also add that the language of Lord Carnarvon, in introducing the Bill into the House of Lords, shows how thoroughly well considered the whole matter had been by the framers of the Act; Sir John A. Macdonald, Sir Etienne Cartier, the Hon. George Brown, &c., &c.; and how deliberately they had concluded with reference to the "Distribution of Legislative Powers," as provided by the Act. After commenting on the distribution of powers, Lord Carnarvon added:—

"In closing my observations on the distribution of power, I ought to point out that *just as the authority of the Central Parliament will prevail wherever it may come into conflict with the Local Legislatures*, so the residue of Legislation, if any, unprovided for in the specific classification, which I have explained, will belong to the Central body." British Col. "Case," in the Supreme Court of Canada, p. 54, line 3,737, &c.

"JUDGE" LORANGER'S PAMPHLET DISPOSED OF.

As we have made reference already to a very pretentious and utterly absurd pamphlet by "*The Honorable Mr. Justice Loranger*," in which he fairly runs to death the doctrine of the dominant power of the Local Legislatures; and as we do not wish, uselessly, to take up time and space with any further consideration of that dreadfully weak production, we would dismiss all consideration of it, with merely this statement. Whether that pamphlet has been written by one who is, or who is not a Judge, if the author knows anything whatever about Law, so that he may be properly designated *a Lawyer*, he should know, that, as by the language of even that portion of the 91st section of the Act he has three times quoted, all that is retained to the Legislatures is, only, what is expressly, "*by this Act*," assigned to them, and, that, therefore, they possess no other than certain limited and defined powers; even without any consideration whatever, of the manner in which these are liable to be affected and over-ridden by the dominant powers of Parliament, as provided for, as we have shown, by the latter part of that clause, and by the clause at the end of the 91st section.

ANOTHER PROVISION.

We have seen what the proper construction of the language in the two explanatory clauses of the 91st section, is. Very much the same effect that is produced by those clauses in reference to the subjects named in the 91st and 92nd sections, is also produced by somewhat different language in the 95th section, relative to the subjects of "Agriculture and Immigration." Here it is provided that the Legislatures may legislate on these subjects for the respective Provinces, and that Parliament may do the same, but it is further provided that the legislation of the Legislatures on these subjects " shall have effect in and for the Province *so long and so far only as it is not repugnant to any Act of the Parliament of Canada.*" This, as has been shown, is very much the same effect as is designed to be produced, and as is produced by the explanatory language at the beginning and end of the 91st section.

FURTHER CONSIDERATION AS TO CONSTRUCTION.

While we have shown, that, under the express language of the Act, Parliament is the dominant power; and that the rule of construction is, that Parliament has the right *bona fide* to legislate on all the subjects-matter named in the 91st section, no matter how much these may interfere with, or come within, or override the subjects-matter named in the 92nd section, and that this is " a hard and fast rule of construction " ; we would now state, that, while we think there can be no question (notwithstanding the numerous discussions on the point that have taken place), of the correctness of this position, there is another point closely allied to it, that should be made equally as clear. And that is this, that the subjects-matter legislated on by Parliament, must *bona fide* come within the classes of subjects named in the 91st section, and that it is here that the statement that there can be no " hard and fast rule of construction," applies; and not to those portions of the 91st section, where we get a rule of construction, that, absolutely, admits of no departure from it whatever.

But whether certain legislation by Parliament is, or is not, fairly and *bona fide*, within those subjects-matter; or whether the legislation of the Legislatures is within the subjects-matter of the 92nd section ; and, if so, whether such legislation is, also, within the subjects-matter of the 91st section, which are *exclusively* within the powers of Parliament, are nicer questions, that have to be dealt with by the Courts as they arise, and with reference to which it is perfectly clear, that " no hard and fast rule of construction," applicable to all cases, can be adopted. But, every such case, so decided, is a step towards establishing " a hard and fast rule " of construction, and is an aid in the construction of other questions, more or less analogous, that thereafter arise. As an instance, we beg to say, although we have never yet seen the point adverted to, that the decision of the Privy Council on

THE CONSTITUTIONALITY OF THE CANADA TEMPERANCE ACT, carries the doctrine of the dominant power of Parliament to legislate, *very much farther than it has ever been carried before;* and very much farther, notwithstanding the attacks in the matter made, on that point, on the Supreme Court of Canada, (one of such attacks being contained in the pamphlet to which we have alluded), than the Supreme Court of Canada, had, previously, in any of its decisions, thought of approaching. This, we think we will be able to show, when

IN THE EXAMINATION OF THE CASES,

which we now propose to make, we shall have reached Russell *v.* The Queen, L. R., 7 Ap. Cas. 829.

THE QUEEN *v.* CHANDLER, (A. D. 1869),

1 Han. (N. B. R.) 556, is the first case for consideration in our attempt to test all the rules of construction applicable to the questions we are discussing. The question in this case was whether an Act passed in 1868 by the N. B. Legislature, for the relief of Insolvent confined debtors was *ultra vires.* It was claimed that the Act was of no force or effect, as being an Act relating to Insolvency, which the Local Legislature had no right to pass; that being one of the subjects assigned to the exclusive legislative authority of Parliament. It was claimed in reply, that the B. N. Act makes procedure in civil matters in all Provincial Courts a matter within the exclusive control of the Legislatures; and that the arrest and discharge of debtors were clearly proceedings in civil matters, and controlled by the Courts where the proceedings are had; neither arrest of a person nor his discharge relating to Insolvency. RITCHIE, C. J., in delivering the judgment of a Court, which by his ability, he sustained in the high position of respectability as to the value of its decisions, which it has ever since lacked, in holding that the Act in question was *ultra vires,* said, *inter alia* :—

"By section 91 it is declared, that, *notwithstanding anything in the Act,* (the italics are his own), the exclusive legislative authority of the Parliament of Canada is extended to all matters coming within the classes of subjects next thereinafter enumerated, of which No. 21 is Bankruptcy and Insolvency. And, after enumertion of all classes of subjects thus exclusively assigned to the Parliament of Canada, it is at the end of the enumeration enacted that any matter coming within any of the classes of subjects enumerated in this section, shall not be deemed to come within the class of matters of a local or private nature, comprised in the enumeration of the class of subjects by this Act assigned exclusively to the Legislatures of the Provinces. Thus, the exclusive right to legislate on the subjects enumerated is affirmatively vested in general terms, as all matters not coming within the class of subjects assigned exclusively to Legislatures of the Provinces," (this is not strictly critically accurate, "and for greater certainty but not so as to restrict the generality of such terms, the exclusive right is specifically extended in the enumeration of the subjects; and, finally, by unequivocal words, it is declared that any matter coming within any of the enumerated classes of subjects shall not be deemed to come within the class of matters assigned exclusively to the Legislatures of the Provinces."

And, again,—"That branch of the Insolvent system which the Local Legislature has attempted to alter is, it is true, exclusively applicable to Insolvent confined debtors; but it is not the less a matter relating to Insolvency, and we are at a loss to understand how it can be argued that it is not a matter coming within that class of subjects, viz., Bankruptcy and Insolvency, enumerated in the British North America Act as assigned exclusively to the Parliament of Canada."

The entire change that the B. N. A. Act has made in the powers of the Legislatures to legislate, is fully shown in this case. It will be noticed, too, that this decision was on the invalidity of an Act by a Local Legislature passed prior to Parliament having legislated at all on the same subject-matter.

TWO RAILWAY CASES.

The next N. B. cases to which we will refer, are the E. & N. A. R. Co., v. Thomas, 1 Pugs. 42, and the Queen v. Dow, *Ibid.*, 300. In the former it was held that legislating with reference to a railway in N. B., which was part of a scheme for a continuous railway, extending into the State of Maine, was not *ultra vires* the Local Legislature, as coming within the exception of lines "extending beyond the limits of the Province" under the 10th sub-section of section 92. In the Queen v. Dow, it was held, FISHER, J. dissenting, that an Act of the N. B. Legislature, providing for the issue of debentures to assist in the construction of a railway from the State of Maine into N. B., was *ultra vires*, as being legislation as to a railway extending beyond the Province. In the former of these cases, it seems that Judge FISHER was *dubitante*. If so, there would seem to be good ground for his doubts; for if the exception did not apply to the railroad in question, it would be impossible to find a road to which it would apply, and the clause would be meaningless. In the latter of these two cases, the dissenting opinion of Judge FISHER was well founded. The ground upon which he put it, that that was not, within the meaning of the Act, legislating as to a railroad ; but as to a mere local assessment for a beneficial purpose to the locality, was clearly correct, and in this view he was sustained by the Privy Council, where the case, *nominatim* Dow v. Black, L. R., 6 P. C. 272, went on appeal. *Notice, particularly, the point in this early case.* In delivering judgment in this case, the Privy Council fully sustain the " hard and fast rule of construction," which, as shown, the Act itself furnishes ; and also show that, in the construction of the Act, the real import and intent of the legislation, is matter for very nice consideration. Thus their opinion is, that the Act in question was clearly "a law relating to a matter *of a merely local or private nature* within the meaning of the 9th article of sect. 92 of the Imperial Statute, and therefore, one which the Provincial Legislature was competent to pass, *unless its subject-matter could be distinctly shown to fall within one or other of the classes of subjects specially enumerated in the 91st section.*" And, as a mere local matter, and one not within the 91st section, the Act of the Local Legislature was sustained. Thus, in this early case in the Privy Council, while fully sustaining the dominant power of Parliament under the B. N. A. Act, where, under the 91st and 92nd sections, there is conflicting legislation ; the doctrine which has been thought to be a new one, established in Parsons v. The Citizens Insurance Co., and in Hodge v. The Queen, is merely an affirmation of the clear principle *established long before, in Dow v. Black* ; the question decided in the Mercer-Escheat case coming under other sections of the Act.

ANOTHER PRIVY COUNCIL CASE.

The same questions, in effect, had been previously decided by the Privy Council in L'Union St. Jacques de Montreal v. Belisle, *Ibid*, p. 31. This was a case where an Act had been passed, by the Quebec Legislature, for the relief of a Benefit Society in embarrassed circumstances. A majority of the Court of Queen's Bench of that Province held, that, in so doing, the Legislature had legislated on a matter coming within the class of "Insolvency," which belonged, under the 91st section of the B. N. A. Act, to the exclusive authority of the Parliament of Canada ; and, that, therefore the Local Act was invalid. We make the following important extracts, applicable to the general questions we are considering. Says LORD SELBORNE, in delivering the judgment, holding that the Act was not one relating to Bankruptcy and Insolvency; and, therefore, being legislation with reference to merely local and private matters within the 92nd section, was not invalid :—

"Clearly this matter is private; clearly it is local, so far as locality is to be considered, because it is in the Province, and in the City of Montreal; *and unless, therefore, the general effect of that head of section 92 is for this purpose qualified by something in section 91*, it is a matter not only within the competency, but within the exclusive competency of the Provincial Legislature. *Now, sect. 91 qualifies it, undoubtedly, if it be within any one of the different classes of subjects there specially enumerated*; because the last and concluding words of sect. 91, are : ' And any matter coming within any of the classes of subjects enumerated in this section shall not be deemed to come within the class of matters of a local or private nature, comprised in the enumeration of the classes of subjects by this Act assigned exclusively to the Legislatures of the Provinces.' *But the onus is on the Respondent to show that this, being of itself of a local or private nature does also come within one or some of the classes of subjects specially enumerated in the 91st section.*"

LORD SELBORNE, having considered the power of Parliament to pass a general law relating to "Bankrupty and Insolvency," continues :—

" Well, no such general law concerning this particular association is alleged ever to have been passed by the Dominion. The hypothesis was suggested in argument by Mr. *Benjamin* of a law having been previously passed by the Dominion Legislature, to the effect that any association of this particular kind throughout the Dominion, on certain specified conditions assumed to be exactly those which appear upon the face of this Statute, should thereupon *ipso facto*, fall under the legal administration in bankruptcy or insolvency. *Their Lordships are by no means prepared to say that if any such law as that had been passed by the Dominion Legislature, it would have been beyond their competency ; nor that, if it had been so passed, it would have been within the competency of the Provincial Legislature afterwards to take a particular association out of the scope of a general law of that kind, so competently passed by the authority which had power to deal with bankruptcy and insolvency.* But no such law ever has been passed ; and to suggest the possibility of such a law as a reason why the power of the Provincial Legislature over this local and private association, should be in abeyance, or altogether taken away, *is to make a suggestion, which if followed up to its consequences, would go far to destroy that power in all cases.*"

These are very important extracts in the matter. Their importance will be shown more fully hereafter, when we come to state summarily, the principles which these cases so clearly establish.

SEVERAL OTHER NEW BRUNSWICK CASES,

which we will now examine, all tend to make clear the principles applicable to the questions we are considering. In McAlmon v. Pine, 2 Pugs. 44, the absurd claim was made, that an Act altering the law establishing gaol limits, was *ultra vires* as relating to Insolvency. The Court held *contra* without calling on the other side. Yet, within the idea thrown out in the Privy Council, in the previous case we considered, there is no doubt that Parliament, in legislating on Insolvency, could legislate *bona fide*, and within its power, to affect gaol limits.

Regina v. McMillan, *Ibid.*, 110, almost identical in principle with the more celebrated recent case of The Queen v. Hodge, was a question under a License Act. It was there held that an Act of the Legislature imposing fines and penalties for selling liquor without license, was not *ultra vires*.

In Whittier v. Dibble *Ibid.*, 243, the validity of a section in a Dominion Act, (32 Vic. c. 29, sec. 134), making provision as to costs in suits against Justices of the Peace, was questioned on the ground that it related to procedure in a civil matter, which, it was claimed, was entirely within the jurisdiction of the Local Legislature. RITCHIE, C. J., thought it " worthy of all consideration," but as the question did not really arise in the case, it was not further considered.

FURTHER CASES RELATING TO INSOLVENCY.

Armstrong v. McCutchin, *Ibid.*, 381, was a case where it was objected that an act passed in N. B. in 1874, abolishing imprisonment for debt, was *ultra vires*. The Court held otherwise, as far, at least, as it affected the defendant who was not a trader, and was not subject to the Insolvent Act of 1869. The learned Chief Justice, (RITCHIE) delivered the judgment of the Court, holding that the case was distinguishable from Regina v. Chandler, stated *supra*. As this class of cases, including Regina v. Chandler, is so valuable in settling the law as to relative powers; and as the judgment states the law, admirably, we quote largely from it.

B

"By the Imperial Act," says the learned CHIEF JUSTICE, "legislation on Bankruptcy and Insolvency is confined exclusively to the Dominion Parliament; and, in like manner, legislation, on 'Civil Rights,' and, 'Procedure in Civil Suits,' belongs to the Local Legislature. Legislation on Bankruptcy and Insolvency necessarily involves an interference, to a certain extent, with Civil Rights and Procedure in Civil Suits; *and, so far as such is necessary for, and incident to legislation on Bankruptcy and Insolvency, it is within the power of the Dominion Parliament to deal with these subjects; and when the Local Legislature deals directly with Bankruptcy and Insolvency, or the legislation of the Dominion Parliament and the Local Legislature conflicts,* so much of the legislation of the Local Legislature as so deals, or interferes, or is in conflict with the legislation of the Dominion Parliament, when legislating within the limits of Bankruptcy and Insolvency, is ultra vires."

That is the law, beyond any question; and nowhere can it be found more clearly and succinctly stated. It is as admirable a summary of the law on the question as can be conceived; complete and yet not redundant. There is not one *well considered case*, from the Queen *v.* Chandler to the latest Privy Council case of Hodge *v.* The Queen, that is in antagonism with it; though some of the Privy Council cases, improperly, it is claimed, go much further than this. The rest of the judgment is so applicable to the last named case, and to others that have been greatly misunderstood, as though, in accordance with the view expressed by the Lieut. Gov. of N. B., as quoted *ante*, the law in the matter relating to the rights of the Local Legislatures, to legislate, within the defined limits under the Act, had been by recent decisions at all, and radically, changed, so as more plainly to establish *their claim of enlarged powers,*—we quote still further from that judgment.

"But," added *then*, the learned Chief Justice, "while legislation on the subject of imprisonment for debt, may be, under some circumstances, involved in legislating on Bankruptcy and Insolvency, and therefore fit matter to be dealt with by the Dominion Parliament, it by no means follows that, under no circumstances, can the Local Legislature legislate with reference thereto. On the contrary, there may be many cases where the abolishment or regulation of imprisonment for debt is in no way mixed up with, or dependent on insolvency. In this case in which application has been made for discharge under the Local Act, the party does not appear by the affidavits to be in any way amenable to the Insolvent Act of 1869, nor a person who could be brought within the operation of that Act; nor, so far as he is concerned, or as applicable to his case, are the clauses of the Local Act, under which he seeks his discharge, in any way in conflict with that Act. The defendant simply appears in the position of a person not subject to the Insolvent Act of 1869, and whom the Legislature has declared shall not be proceeded against for recovery of a debt by imprisonment, without reference to any question of solvency or insolvency; and, therefore, there is no reason why he should not receive the benefit of an Act passed by the Local Legislature, for regulating the procedure in civil suits in relation to the civil rights of parties in the recovery of debts. So far, therefore, as the defendant is concerned,—and we limit our decision to the particular circumstances of this individual case—there is no reason why the Act should not have full force and effect."

The correctness of the decision cannot be questioned; nor, on the other hand, can it be questioned that Parliament has full power, in legislating on Bankruptcy and Insolvency, to make perfectly valid regulations as to imprisonment, as applicable to cases coming within the subject of Insolvency. The distinction in this case applies admirably, also, to the conflicting questions that have come up in matters relating to the Fisheries, as we shall see when we come to examine the cases where these questions are involved.

In marked contrast with that able judgment of RITCHIE, C. J., is the dissenting judgment of WETMORE, J. in McLeod v. Wright, 1 P. & B., 68, delivered after the ability of the N. B. Supreme Court had left it, by RITCHIE, C. J. having gone on the Bench of the Supreme Court of Canada.

By the 89th section of the Insolvent Act of 1869, it was *inter alia*, declared, that all transfers of property by any person in contemplation of insolvency, by way of security to a creditor where an unjust preference was obtained over other creditors, was null and void. WETMORE, J. delivered a dissenting judgment in which he held that this section, as it affected property transferred by the Insolvent to a creditor, was *ultra vires*. He sets forth the opening and closing clauses of sec. 91, of the meaning of which, he, obviously, has not the most remote conception, italicising the words in the first clause, "*not coming within the classes of subjects by this Act assigned exclusively to the legislatures of the Provinces*," as though that settled the whole question; and actually says,—"The

Dominion Parliament, doubtless had ample power to legislate upon bankruptcy and insolvency, *but it had no right to legislate upon property and civil rights in the Province;*" and much more equally as nonsensical. How, in the world, Parliament *could* legislate on Bankruptcy and Insolvency and not legislate on either Property or Civil Rights was a difficulty, that, evidently, never presented itself to the mind of Mr. Justice WETMORE. And it is from just such absurd judgments that so much confusion has been produced in connection with the subject we are considering, as has now involved it; and, which, by this thoroughly fair and candid examination of the cases and of the *ratio decidendi* thereof, we trust to be able, to some extent, to clear away.

In *Ex parte* Ellis, *Ibid.*, 593, where a question was raised as to the validity of a N. B. Act, providing for imprisonment of a debtor in certain cases, one of the points taken was that it was legislating on Insolvency. ALLEN, C. J., in delivering the judgment of the majority of the Court, holding that the Act was not *ultra vires*, said,—" Admitting that the debtor might be entitled to be discharged under the Insolvent Act, which he probably would be if he was subject to the provisions of that Act; does it follow that this proves the Act of the Provincial Legislature to be *ultra vires?* Might not his imprisonment, under the latter Act, be perfectly legal up to the time that he proved himself entitled to be discharged under the provisions of the Act? . . In the case of imprisonment under this Act if a person subject to the provisions of the Insolvent Law, *his imprisonment would be legal until it came in conflict with the Insolvent Act,* by his obtaining an order for his discharge; and then the latter Act would prevail, because the Dominion Parliament alone can deal with the subject of Insolvency. Armstrong *v.* McCutchin, (*supra*). There may also be cases of imprisonment under this Act, of persons not subject to the provisions of the Insolvent Act. In such cases, no conflict would arise; therefore the two Acts are not necessarily inconsistent."

That is stating the law on the points very clearly and very correctly.

AN IMPORTANT CASE

on this question is the case of Cushing *v.* Dupuy, in the Privy Council, 5 App. Cas. 409. This case which shows the absurdity of arguments such as we have had in such abundance, like that, for instance, of Mr. Justice WETMORE, in McLeod *v.* Wright, holds that,—

"The British North America Act, 1867, in assigning to the Dominion Parliament the subjects of bankruptcy and insolvency, *intended to confer and did confer on it legislative power to interfere with property, civil rights, and procedure within the Provinces, so far as these latter might be affected by a general law relating to those subjects.* Consequently the Dominion enactment amending the Canadian Insolvent Act, and providing that the judgment of the Court of Appeal in matters of insolvency should be final, *i. e.*, not subject to the appeal as of right to Her Majesty in Council allowed by the *Civil Procedure Code,* is within the competency of the Canadian Parliament, and does not infringe the exclusive powers given to the Provincial Legislatures by sect. 92 of the Imperial Statute."

In this case it was contended by Mr. *Davidson,* of the Canadian Bar, that the Appeal could not be taken away by a Dominion enactment; that, if it could be interfered with at all by Canadian authority it must be by the Provincial Legislature, which had the exclusive right of dealing with the matter; being one of civil procedure.

SIR MONTAGUE E. SMITH, in refuting this contention, as well as that, that as the Act was an interference with Property and Civil Rights in the Province, subjects "*exclusively*" within the jurisdiction of the Local Legislatures, it was, therefore, *ultra vires,* exposed the fallacy of this contention, which has so foolishly, and, notwithstanding the language of the B. N. A. Act, and the decisions under it, is still, to this day, so persistently urged; said,—

"It was contended for the Appellant that the provisions of the Insolvency Act interfered with property and civil rights, and was therefore *ultra vires.* This objection *was very faintly urged,* but it was strongly contended that the Parliament of Canada could not take away the right of appeal to the Queen from final judgments of the Court of Queen's Bench, which, it was said, was *part of the procedure in civil matters exclusively assigned to the Legislature of the Province.*

"The answer to these objections is obvious. It would be impossible to advance a step in the construction of a scheme for the administration of insolvent estates *without interfering with and modifying some of the ordinary rights of property, and other civil rights, nor without providing some mode of special procedure for the vesting, realization, and distribution of the estate,* and the settlement of the liabilities of the insolvent. Procedure must necessarily form an essential part of any law dealing with insolvency. It is therefore to be presumed, indeed it is a necessary implication, that the Imperial Statute, in assigning to the Dominion Parliament the subjects of bankruptcy and insolvency, intended to confer on it legislative power to interfere with property, civil rights, and Procedure within the Provinces, *so far as a general law relating to those subjects might affect them*. Their Lordships therefore think that the Parliament of Canada *would not infringe the exclusive powers given to the Provincial Legislatures, by enacting that the judgment of the Court of Queen's Bench in matters of insolvency should be final, and not subject to the appeal as of right to Her Majesty in Council, allowed by art. 1178 of the Code of Civil Procedure.*"

Taking that case as a connecting link, we will now examine some cases closely akin to those, relating to

ACTS AFFECTING PROCEDURE IN THE PROVINCIAL COURTS.

This is a matter, which, as far as "Procedure in Civil Matters in those Courts," is concerned, is assigned, "exclusively," by the 14th article of the 92nd section, to the Local Legislatures.

The case of Valin v. Langlois, in the Privy Council, 5 App. Cas., 115, puts a limitation on the so-called "exclusive" rights of the Legislatures as against Parliament and carries the matter a step further than the cases we have been examining. In this case it was held that under sec. 41 of the B. N. A. Act, giving Parliament power to provide for an Election Court, Parliament had power to use the Provincial Courts as Election Courts, notwithstanding the so-called exclusive power of legislation given, as above named, to the Local Legislatures.

On an application to the Privy Council, for leave to appeal from the judgment of the Supreme Court of Canada, it was broadly claimed that Parliament had no power to make laws in relation to the administration of justice in the Province of Quebec, or to the constitution of any Provincial Courts, or to procedure in those Courts; that, consequently, it had no power to confer any new jurisdiction upon the Superior Court, or to effect its procedure, or to impose new duties on its judges; and, that, therefore, the Canadian Controverted Election Act of 1874, was *ultra vires* and inoperative.

In refusing this leave to appeal, while the Privy Council laid down the doctrine, broadly, that "*If the subject-matter is within the jurisdiction of the Dominion Parliament, it is not within the jurisdiction of the Provincial Parliament;*" then, using language, which, clearly, would be both applicable and correct, where the power in Parliament to legislate is sought under the Act, outside of the subjects-matter named in the 91st section—in this case under the 41st section—they showed, that, even as regards that, " that which is excluded by the 91st section from the jurisdiction of the Dominion Parliament, is not anything else than matters coming within the classes of subjects assigned exclusively to the Legislatures of the Provinces." Then, acting on this doctrine, as applicable to the case in question, they say,—." The only material class of subjects relates to the administration of justice in the Provinces, which read with the 41st section, cannot be reasonably taken to have anything to do with election petitions. There is therefore nothing here to raise a doubt about the power of the Dominion Parliament to impose new duties upon the existing Provincial Courts, or to give them new powers, as to matters which do not come within the classes of subjects assigned exclusively to the Legislatures of the Provinces;" and, accordingly, they held the Act in question within the powers of Parliament; sustaining the judgment of the Supreme Court of Canada.

In the case in the Court below (3 S. C. R. 1), it was claimed, as it is in effect to this day, in political articles in the newspapers; in speeches in Parliament; in the Legislatures, and elsewhere, that "The Federal principle has for its end to preserve and protect the autonomy of the Provinces, and the B. N. A. Act has enumerated the rights and duties of every one of them. By the 92nd section of the Act, in each Province the Legislature has an *unlimited authority and a power beyond control* to make laws in relation to the constitution, maintenance and organization of Provincial Courts, both of civil and criminal jurisdiction, and including procedure in civil matters in these Courts. If so, the Federal Parliament cannot add to, take from, or extend the jurisdiction of Provincial tribunals." That is not, by any means a bad summary of the positions taken in the pamphlet to which we have before referred.

The Court, unanimously refused to assent to such positions, and held that the Dominion Parliament has the right to interfere with civil rights, when necessary for the purpose of legislating generally and effectually in relation to matters confined to the Parliament of Canada.

In the judgment of the learned Chief Justice, (SIR WM.

RITCHIE), he, again, sets forth the law clearly as it has been established in the first well decided case, under the Act; and as it is still, we claim, and think we will be able distinctly to show, notwithstanding the view that has been entertained that the later cases have at all changed the doctrine, (so as to greatly increase the powers of the legislatures, as established in all the earlier well-decided cases, down to Valin v. Langlois, inclusive. The following extracts state the law, succinctly:—

"In determining the question of *ultra vires* too little consideration, has, I think, been given to the constitution of the Dominion, by which the legislative power of the Local Assemblies *is limited and confined* TO THE SUBJECTS *specifically assigned to them, while all other legislative powers, including what is specially assigned to the Dominion Parliament* is conferred on that Parliament; differing in this respect entirely from the constitution of the United States of America, under which the State Legislatures retained all the powers of legislation which were not expressly taken away."

And, with reference to the claims, under the terms, "property and civil rights," for exclusive legislation in the Provincial Legislatures, is the following statement of principle, which, as we shall see, is wide enough to cover, on that point, all the cases decided down to Hodge v. The Queen, inclusive, so far as, on that point, they are correctly decided:—"The terms 'property and civil rights' must necessarily be read in a restricted and limited sense, because many matters involving property and civil rights are expressly reserved to the Dominion Parliament, of which the first two items in the enumeration of the classes of subjects to which the exclusive legislation of the Parliament of Canada extends, are illustrations, viz.:—'1. The Public Debt and Property;' '2. The regulation of Trade and Commerce;' to say nothing of beacons, buoys, light-houses, &c., 'navigation and shipping,' 'bills of exchange and promissory notes,' and many others directly affecting property and civil rights; that neither this, nor the right to organize Provincial Courts by the Provincial Legislatures was intended in any way to interfere with, or give to such Provincial Legislatures, any right to restrict or limit the powers in other parts of the statute conferred on the Dominion Parliament; that the right to direct the procedure in civil matters in those Courts had reference to the procedure in matters over which the Provincial Legislature had power to give those Courts jurisdiction, and did not, in any way, interfere with, or restrict, the right and power of the Dominion Parliament to direct the mode of procedure to be adopted in cases over which it has jurisdiction, and where it was exclusively authorized and empowered to deal with the subject-matter ; or, take from the existing Courts the duty of administering the laws of the land ; *and that the power of the Local Legislatures was to be subject to the general and special legislative powers of the Dominion Parliament."*

The following additional paragraph covers, explicitly, what are supposed to be modifications of the rule, (claimed in this treatise, to be a true, uniform, " hard and fast rule,) as contained in some of the latest cases, but which we claim, are no modifications of the rule whatever; but, rather, simply make clear what the rule is, thus, — " But while the legislative rights of the Local Legislatures are in this sense subordinate to the right of the Dominion Parliament, I think such latter right must be exercised, so far as may be, consistently with the right of the Local Legislatures ; and, therefore, *the Dominion Parliament would only have the right to interfere with property or civil rights, in so far as such interference may be necessary for the purpose of legislating generally and effectually in relation to matters confided to the Parliament of Canada."*

That, we allege, will cover all the supposed exceptional cases, such as the Fishery case ; the Parsons Insurance case ; the Mercer-Escheat case, and the Ontario License case. This, we will make clearly appear, when, in detail, we examine these cases.

The following brief extracts from the judgment of Mr. Justice TASCHEREAU, in the same case, are apt. The learned Judge says,—

"I see in the B. N. A. Act many instances where Parliament can alter the jurisdiction of the Provincial Civil Courts. For instance, I am of opinion, that Parliament can take away from the Provincial Courts all jurisdiction over bankruptcy and insolvency, and give that jurisdiction to Bankruptcy Courts, established by such Parliament. I also think it clear, that Parliament can say, for instance, that all judicial proceedings on promissory notes and bills of exchange, shall be taken before the Exchequer Court, or before any other Federal Court. This would be certainly interfering with the jurisdiction of the Provincial Courts. *But, I hold that it has the power to do so quoad all matters within its authority."*

And, again,—

" The authority of the Federal power, it seems to me, over the matters left under its control is exclusive, full and absolute ;

whilst as regards at least, some of the matters left to the Provincial Legislatures by sect. 92, the authority of these Legislatures cannot be construed to be as full and exclusive, when, by such construction the Federal power over matters specially left under its control would be lessened, restrained or impaired. For example, civil rights, by the letter of sub-sect. 13 of sect. 92, are put under the exclusive power of the Local Legislatures, yet this cannot be construed to mean all civil rights, *but only those which are not put under the Federal authority by the other parts of the Act.*"

That, intelligently applied, is the principle to this day, governing *all the rightly decided cases*, down to Hodge v. The Queen, inclusive, nothwithstanding all the vapid declamation to the contrary, in Parliament, or elsewhere!

THE OTHER EXTREME.

In our examination of the absurd dissenting judgment of WETMORE J., in McLeod v. Wright, we exposed the silly reasoning there, the *rationale* of which is, followed to its legitimate issue, that Parliament has, virtually, no power to legislate at all. We come now to a case, which errs in the opposite direction, and, if it were law, would leave the Legislatures denuded of substantially, all *their* legislative powers. The case to which we allude is the somewhat celebrated case known as

"THE THRASHER CASE,"

decided by the Supreme Court of British Columbia. The judges in this case,—SIR MATTHEW BEGBIE, C. J., and CREASE and GRAY, JJ., in most elaborate judgments, held, entirely mistaking the holding in Valin v. Langlois, just examined, that the Supreme and County Courts of the different Provinces are not the "Provincial Courts" within the meaning of sub-sec. 14, of sec. 92, with reference to the "Procedure in Civil Matters," in which, the Legislatures have the "*exclusive*," right to legislate; and that, therefore such legislation by the Legislature, relating to the Supreme Court of British Columbia, was *ultra vires.*

Their reasoning from the term "exclusive," is very much, in the opposite direction, like the reasoning of those, who *entirely ignoring all the rest of the Act, particularly those governing clauses in sect.* 91,—because it is provided, in sect. 92, that "In each Province the Legislature may *exclusively* make laws in relation to matters coming within the classes of subjects next hereinafter enumerated, that is to say," (enumerating them),—foolishly jump to the conclusion, ignoring as named, because it is stated that the

Provincial Legislatures may "*exclusively*" legislate in reference to such matters, that that term "exclusively" *excludes* Parliament from legislating on such matters at all; notwithstanding the sweeping, over-riding nature of the clauses in sect. 91, which we have examined. This explanation covers an immense amount of absurd judicial reasoning in many cases, and a great many very foolish political articles in the Press, and speeches in Parliament, and in the Local Legislatures.

Having previously written to some extent, articles on the proper construction of the B. N. A. Act; when the judgments in the "Thrasher Case" were delivered, an early copy was sent the writer by some parties interested in the question, and who were carried away with the judgments, requesting that they should be reviewed; assuming that they were unanswerable, and that this was without question. After a careful reading of the judgments, we wrote the following in reply to such request:—

"An honest review of the judgments, would, in the main, be an attempt, (I think an easy and successful one) to refute the many fallacies the judgments contain. . . . When, entirely mistaking the holding in Valin v. Langlois, it is argued that the Supreme Court and County Courts of the Provinces are not the 'Provincial Courts' within the scope and effect of the 14th sub-sec. of the 92nd sec. of the Act; the 'Procedure' of which 'in civil matters,' the Local Legislatures have the '*exclusive*' right to regulate, I think a position is taken that is entirely untenable, and, that, on that point, are against it, the whole Act itself; judicial decisions under it, and the uniform legislation of all the Provinces with reference to those Courts. . . .

"Let me, now, within the necessarily limited space of a letter, meet one of the views, put, in the different judgments, with a considerable apparent logical force, and, with reference to which I marked the word '*exclusive*,' above, in italics and quotation marks. The argument in the different judgments, is, that, clearly, by Valin v. Langlois, it is decided that the Dominion Parliament has the right to regulate procedure in the Supreme Court of one of the Provinces. But, it is claimed, where the Dominion Parliament has the right to legislate at all, it has the 'exclusive' right to do so; therefore, it is insisted, that, having the right to legislate with reference to the Procedure in those Courts, it has the 'exclusive' right to do so; hence, it is concluded, that the Provincial Legislatures cannot legislate with reference to such Procedure, being *excluded* by the 'exclusive' rights of the Dominion Parliament. That is putting the argument fairly. Let us test it, now, for instance, by the 13th sub-sec., and see where we would land. By this, the '*exclusive*' right to legislate in matters relating to 'Property and Civil Rights in the Province,' is in the Local Legislatures. But, in connection with 'The Regulation of Trade and Commerce,' 'Navigation and Shipping,' 'Sea Coast and Inland Fisheries,' 'Bills of Exchange and Promissory Notes,' 'Bankruptcy and Insolvency,' 'Naturalization and Aliens,' 'Marriage and Divorce'; &c., &c., &c.; the 'exclusive' right to legislate with reference to which is in the Dominion Parliament, Parliament has a right to legislate with reference to Property or Civil Rights, or to both of these subjects. Then, having the right to legislate with reference to Property and Civil Rights, pursuing the same argument as before, it has the 'exclusive' right to do so; hence the Local Legislatures have no right to legislate with reference to Property and Civil Rights; their right to do so being *excluded* by the 'exclusive' rights of Parliament; and, therefore, the 13th sub-sec. goes with the 14th, and all the rest of the sub-secs. follow suit, and the Local Legislatures have no power at all.

"In fact, the term 'exclusive,' in both sections, does not absolutely mean '*exclusive*.' In each section it simply means, '*exclusive*' *subject to, &c.* The right in the Dominion Parliament is to legislate *exclusively* subject to certain limitations; and, in the Legislatures, subject to others.

"I presume that your reason for wishing me to review the judgments was because you honestly felt that the positions were so strong that they could not be successfully attacked. With equal honesty, I am forced to a different conclusion; and as I think, that, in fairly reviewing the judgments, I could show the correctness of this conclusion, *unanswerably*, I shall not comply with your request to review them, unless, after your receipt of this, and with a full knowledge of my views in the matter, you should still wish me to do so, *as a pure matter of science*; in which case, on hearing from you again to that effect, I will do so, meeting the arguments simply as arguments, utterly irrespective of those who used them, and dealing with the judgments as mere matter for critical examination, exactly as I did with the absurd judgment of our own Court on the Constitutionality of the Canada Temperance Act, and a copy of which review I sent you."

The letter was written on the 27th March, 1882. The request was not repeated. The CASE was submitted to the Supreme Court of Canada, by the Governor-General in Council, under sec. 52 of the Supreme Court Act, and the Court, on the 18th June, 1883, by their answers, held the judgments unsound, and sustained the construction of the B. N. A. in accordance with the contention in the letter from which we have quoted.

GANONG *v.* BAILEY, 1 P. & B., 324, forms a connecting link between the class of cases we have just been considering, and that, including the *casus celebre*, the Mercer-Escheat case, which has given birth to two quite elaborate pamphlets, and the simple point decided in which is greatly misunderstood.

In Ganong *v.* Bailey it was decided, by a majority of the Court, that a Local Act to establish Parish Courts, the commissioners to preside in which were to be appointed by the Lieut. Gov. in Council, was valid. It was claimed by *Weldon*, Q. C. (M. P.,) that the Act was *ultra vires*, inasmuch as the Court established by the Act was a Provincial Court within the meaning of the sub-section (14), we have been considering; and, that, therefore, the appointment was in the Dominion Government, under sec. 96 of the B. N. A. Act. The holding of the majority of the Court that these Parish Courts were not within the terms of the 96th section, relating to " *Superior, District and County* Courts" in the Provinces, the judges of which the Gov. General was to appoint, is too clearly correct for doubt.

In the dissenting judgment of ALLEN, C. J. and DUFF J., delivered by the learned CHIEF JUSTICE, there is a great amount of stilted nonsense, as regards the position of the Provinces under the B. N. A. Act, such as is found in the *Mercer* case, and in some of the other cases, about " The Queen, as the fountain of justice ;" " the undoubted prerogatives of the Crown," &c., &c.

The fact really is, that the whole Executive and Legislative power that the Provinces now possess is simply such as by the express language of the B. N. A. Act, or by necessary implication from that language, is, *by that Act*, conferred on them. The whole of the rest of the power to make " laws for the peace, order and good government of Canada," is vested in Parliament *in relation to all matters not coming within the classes of subjects* BY THE ACT, *assigned to the Legislatures of the Provinces*. The word " exclusively" has tended to mislead ; without, to the slightest extent, affecting the proper construction of the Act.

In the case of Ganong v. Bailey there was but a question of the construction of one or two plain and simple passages in the Act, and all the mystery that was cast about the case goes, literally, for nothing.

"THE CROWN," AND THE PROVINCES.

In the last case considered, "The Crown" was made an important factor in it. This "Crown" business is being fairly run to death. In a speech, the other day, by the Attorney General of N. B., in the House of Assembly of that Province, the power of the "Crown" was strongly descanted upon, and it was declared as unquestionable that "The Crown has the right, in itself," to build a bridge across the St. John River, at Fredericton—Act or no Act. This is carrying "the political autonomy of the Provinces against the dangers which threaten it from Federal encroachments," idea, even beyond that in connection with which it was so grandiloquently used in Lieut.-Gov. Wilmot's speech! What perfect nonsense such utterly unfounded pretensions cover!

This Crown question came up, squarely, in Lenoir v. Ritchie, 3 S. C. R. 575, where the question was as to the regulation of precedence of Queen's Counsel, in which it was claimed that "In all matters that are under the exclusive jurisdiction of the Local Legislatures, the Lieutenant-Governor represents the Queen, and all powers enjoyed by him prior to Confederation in relation to the organization of the Courts and the administration of justice were confirmed by the B. N. A. Act," and, *semble*, that the power to appoint Queen's Counsel, or to regulate precedence among them, was vested in the Lieutenant-Governors, either *ex officio* as representing the Queen, or by virtue of Acts of the Local Legislatures.

In reply it was alleged that similar claims of the Lieutenant-Governors to exercise powers as representatives of the Crown had been made ; in one case by the Lieut.-Gov. of N. B., who claimed to exercise the pardoning power ; and, in another, where the question arose as to the amnesty claimed to have been promised by the Lieut.-Gov. of Manitoba in the *Lepine* case. In both cases the pretension was refuted and ignored.

In the principal case itself, the Court held that it was simply a question of authority under the B. N. A. Act, and that that Act had not given any such power as was claimed ; and that the N. S. Act relating to the matter, was *ultra vires*, and void.

TASCHEREAU J., in his very able judgment, pertinently remarks,—

"Indeed, there is not a single clause, a single word of the B. N. A. Act upon which it can be seriously contended that the Lieut.-Governors are vested with *Her Majesty's* prerogative rights of conferring such honors and dignities."

And, after examining the different sections of the Act relating to the powers of Lieut.-Governors, adds further,—

"In fact, no where in the Act, can a single expression be found to sustain the contention that the Lieut.-Gov. has such a power. Well, if he has not this power in virtue of the B. N. A. Act, how can the Provincial Legislatures give it to him? In what clause of the Act can it be found that these Legislatures have such a right? What part of section 92, *where the subjects left under their control and authority are enumerated*, gives them the power to legislate upon Her Majesty's prerogatives?"

The answer to these questions was rather a difficult one, but it were easier to find that, than to find 'that the Province so far represents "The Crown," and, as such, by exercise of the prerogative, simply, without any claim, whatever, to any other power, can build a bridge across a public navigable river; let the jurisdiction over such be never so much in Parliament! The unreasoning advocates of the "Provincial autonomy" idea, are fairly running mad!

Mr. Justice GWYNNE, in the same case, says,—

"As to the appointment of Queen's Counsel, nothing is said, nor is there any subject placed under the exclusive control of the Provincial Executive or Legislative authorities, which, by the most forced construction, can, in my opinion, be said necessarily to involve the right to appoint Queen's Counsel. The result must therefore be, that the right still continues to form, as it ever has formed, part of the Royal Prerogative vested in Her Majesty (who still retains her Supreme Executive authority over the Dominion of Canada equally as over the British Isles), to be exercised by her at her pleasure, either under her sign manual, or through the high officer, the Governor-General of the Dominion, who alone within these Confederate Provinces fills the position of Her Majesty's representative."

And, again,—

"Now, if it has been and is lawful for the Lieut.-Governor to make Queen's Counsel, *it can only be so by the provisions of the B. N. A. Act.* If that Act does confer the power upon the Provincial Executive, no doubt the Lieut.-Governor has it, and a Provincial Act can add no force to the Imperial Act; *but if the*

Imperial Act does not confer the power, then the Lieutenant-Governor has it not, nor can any Act of the Provincial Legislature effectually declare that he has, or by enactment pointing to the future, confer it upon him."

That is clearly the law. The questions as to whether the Local Legislatures have certain powers; or whether the Acts of Parliament are an infringement or not on rights vested in the Provinces, under the Act; or whether, under the powers in the Act, Parliament can, and to what extent, over-ride the legislation of the Legislatures, are simply questions of construction of the Act itself; and all else that has been dragged into the discussion, is entirely extraneous, and has led to unnecessary confusion and complication in connection with many of the questions that have arisen under the Act.

One of these cases into which so much superfluous matter has been brought, is the somewhat celebrated, but extremely simple

MERCER-ESCHEAT CASE.

This was a case,—Mercer *v.* The Attorney General for Ontario, 5 S. C. R. 538,—where the simple question that was involved in it, was, as to whether under the B. N. A. Act, where lands escheated for want of heirs, the lands so escheated went to the Province or to the Dominion. The discussion of this really simple question took a wide range; the report of the case occupying in the official reports not less than one hundred and seventy-five pages; and the result of which was that a majority of the Court wrongly held, misconstruing the Act, that the lands vested in the Dominion. SIR WM. RITCHIE, C. J., and STRONG J., dissented.

The whole matter depended on the proper construction of sections 102 and 109 of the B. N. A. Act; the first of which provided that "All duties and revenues over which the respective Legislatures," &c., "before and at the Union had and have power of appropriation *except such portions thereof as are by this Act reserved to the respective Legislatures of the Provinces, or are raised by them in accordance with the special powers conferred on them by this Act*," shall, in effect, belong to the Dominion.

And section 109, as follows,—

"All lands, mines, minerals and royalties belonging to the several Provinces," &c., "at the Union, and all sums then due or payable for such lands," &c., "shall belong to the several Provinces in which the same are situate, or arise," &c.

The simple reason of the case is this: The ungranted lands,

called "Crown" lands, at and prior to the Union, were all vested in the several Provinces in which they were situated, with all the incidents attached, including escheat. So thoroughly was this the case that the Legislatures passed Acts relating to escheat, the same as they did to any other incident of the land. The Provinces controlled their lands; licensed them; rented them; sold them. In the very ownership of the "Crown" lands, was implied that all the incidents of such ownership in the lands were in the "Crown land" owners; such as the right to rents; to license fees; to the proceeds of sales; to the reversion, and, clearly, prior to Confederation, to escheat.

The Privy Council held that, under the term "royalties," escheat went to the Provinces. SIR WM. RITCHIE, in his dissenting judgment, held, that the escheat went to the Provinces, under the term "lands," in the above section, as one of the incidents in the land.

We take it, notwithstanding the judgment of the Privy Council, and with, of course, every deference to that Board; which deference, however, we must admit, oozes out very considerably before we get through this independent investigation; the holding of the learned CHIEF JUSTICE of the Supreme Court of Canada, on the question, is the better one. When it was declared that the lands *belonging to the several Provinces*, were to remain theirs, it was an express declaration, or, at least, a very clear implication, that they were to own them, exactly as they did before, with all their incidents. To give them the lands, and then to claim under the 102d section of the Act, that the "Revenues" from those lands went to the Dominion, would be a construction of the Act, utterly ridiculous. SIR WM. RITCHIE well pointed out that an exception to the "duties and revenues vesting in the Dominion under the 102d section, were those that "are by this Act reserved to the respective Legislatures of the Provinces, *or are raised by them*," under the Act; and, clearly, vesting the lands in the Provinces would "raise" with them all the revenues derivable from their continued ownership in those "Crown" lands.

The Privy Council found, as named, under the use of the word "Royalties," a reason for holding that escheat as a "Royalty" inured to the Provinces; but, as that term was more immediately connected with mines and minerals, and, in Nova Scotia, was used to cover the "Royalties" derived from them; as the Act was, very largely, framed by Provincialists, and from a Provincial point of

view, the holding would not impress us as favorably as though the
Act had been the exclusive production of the English law officers.
But, under either holding, it will be observed that it is simply a
question as to the proper construction of sections 102 and 109, of
the Act; and, in the case in the Privy Council, 8 App. cas., 767,
the Counsel for Ontario, *Davey*, Q. C., and *Mowat*, Q. C., rested
their case entirely on that ground ; thus (p. 769),—" The question
at issue turns on sects. 102 and 109 of the Act of 1867. Escheated
lands are within sect. 109." How absurd, then, for one who when
arguing that case before the Supreme Court of Canada, which he
did very indifferently, and who, then, arguing with reference to
sections 91 and 92, (which had in fact nothing substantially to do
with the points involved,) claimed that " in the distribution of
powers made by these two sections, whatever be their wording, the
general rule is the Provincial jurisdiction, and the exception the
Federal ; " to claim that the decision of the Privy Council, in the
Mercer case, sustains any such utterly unfounded doctrine ! This
is exactly what " Judge " *Loranger* does.

RIDICULOUS CONSTRUCTION !

The attempts of some of the Counsel in the Mercer case to
construe the clauses in sections 91 and 92, to carry out this so
called " general rule " of dominant Provincial jurisdiction in cases
of conflict, under the two sections, between the different legislative
bodies, are, decidedly, more original than successful. The following is one of them, by Mr. *Loranger*, Q. C., whose ideas and language seem to be appropriated wholesale by " The Honorable Mr.
Justice" *Loranger*, the author of the pamphlet, to which reference
has been made. Says *Mr. Loranger*, (5 S. C. R. 616),—

" Sections 91 and 92 *might, perhaps, as well have been
couched in the following terms:* ' The competence with respect to
matters of a local or private nature, including the powers specially
enumerated in section 92, *which shall always be considered as
local powers,* shall belong to the Legislatures, AND THE REMAIN-
DER of the legislative powers necessary for the peace, order and
good government of Canada, including the special powers enumerated in section 91, shall be considered as general powers and
shall belong to Parliament.' "

Well, it is quite clear that if the sections had been couched in
such language, and Parliament had only the power to legislate with
such " remainder " of powers, it could scarcely be claimed that
Parliament was the dominant power ; and LORD CARNARVON'S

speech, from which we have quoted, would have had to have been most materially altered. But, how in the world, Parliament could exercise "the special powers enumerated in section 91," and legislate, for instance, on Trade and Commerce; on Bankruptcy and Insolvency, &c., &c., &c., if it were excluded from touching or interfering with, for instance, Property or Civil Rights in either of the Provinces, would puzzle, certainly, one much more able than Mr. or "*Judge*" *Loranger* to decide. There would then, certainly, be difficulties in construction in the way that a dozen Supreme Courts and Judicial Committees might try in vain, to struggle with!

But the "learned" Counsel, not satisfied with that attempt at Constitution making, tries again. He says, (*Ibid.*),—

"I cannot overlook the difficulties in interpretation occasioned by a phraseology so intricate and so confused," (he is struggling now, with the language in the clauses in section 91, which will not yield to the distorted construction of them that has been so often attempted), "and in order to understand it better, we might again *further alter the wording of these articles*," (that is refreshingly cool!) "which might be summed up as follows:—'*With the exception of the matters enumerated in section* 92 *and of all which are of a local or private nature, which shall be within the competence of the Provinces, Parliament shall have power to make laws necessary for the good government of Canada, upon all matters, including those enumerated in section* 91.'"

If such a ridiculous clause as that had been in the B. N. A. Act, while it would be clear that Parliament could not touch the subjects in section 92, how it could make laws on the subjects in section 91, would be as difficult to answer as under Mr. *Loranger's* previous misconstruction of the Act; or, under the equally foolish construction of the Act put upon it by Mr. Justice WETMORE, in the case of McLeod *v.* Wright, previously examined.

Mr. *Blake's* attempts at dealing with these sections,—in order to get over the only possible construction to which they are open, as already shown; and, which, as shown by the quotation from LORD CARNARVON'S speech, was, on the part of the framers of the Act, their studiously designed intention,—are as bad as those very weak attempts of Mr. *Loranger*, and of Mr. Justice WETMORE.

The very profound Mr. *Blake* has been caught napping! He says, (*Ibid.*, 580),—

"True, it is provided that the particulars of section 91 shall over-ride the particulars of section 92, but, it is nowhere provided that if the two conflict, the latter shall be superseded. This section has been wrongly interpreted, for it is not said matters enumerated in section 91 shall exclude matters enumerated in 92."

If the particulars of section 91 "over-ride" the particulars of section 92, how they can *over-ride* them, without superseding or excluding them, in the sense in which Mr. *Blake* uses these words, would be as puzzling as the questions that the foolish construction of, for instance, *Mr. Loranger*, would involve. If the powers in section 91, do, as they undoubtedly do, and as Mr. *Blake* confesses they do, "over-ride" those in section 92 ; the powers in section 91 are the dominant powers, and, being the dominant powers, *over-riding*, necessarily "exclude," or "supersede," the powers in section 92, so far as is necessary to give effect to the confessedly over-riding powers in section 91. In fact, Mr. *Blake* himself, though using the term "over-ride," as in some fanciful way, not synonymous with "exclude," or "supersede," immediately thereafter, with the most refreshing "innocence," substitutes the very word "over-ride," ("over-ridden",, to express *exclusion* or *superseding*. He says, (*Ibid.* 581),—

"In section 95 there is a concurrent power over emigration. This is the only subject-matter over which there is a concurrent power, and therefore it is the only case in which a law within the jurisdiction of the Local Legislature can be *over-ridden* by the Parliament of Canada."

And, in that section, 95th), the express language is—"Any law of the legislature of a Province relative to Agriculture or to Immigration shall have effect in and for the Province *as long and as far only as it is not repugnant to any Act of the Parliament of Canada.*"

As the "over-riding" effect of the power in this section is to *supersede or exclude* the legislation of the Legislatures as far as such legislation on the subjects named is repugnant to the legislation of Parliament, Mr. *Blake* clearly uses *over-ride* as a synonym for *supersede* or *exclude*. So, according to his logic, the powers of Parliaments, under the 91st sect. over-ride, and yet do not over-ride ; supersede, and yet do not supersede ; exclude, and yet do not exclude, the conflicting powers of the Legislatures, under the 92nd section. To just such pitiful straits are they all brought, who attempt to get clear of the one proper construction of these sections, as named in the Act, and as established, as we have shown, by a long list of well decided cases.

It is, on the other hand, submitted that the learned Judge, (Mr. Justice GWYNNE), whose generally clear expositions of the law, have done so much towards showing the absurdity of those ignorant and fanciful constructions of the Act, such as those of Judge WETMORE, Mr. *Loranger*, &c., to which we have referred; in the *Mercer Case*, lays down a proposition, the effect of which is to too greatly narrow the powers of legislation in the Provincial Legislatures. The learned Judge says, (*Ibid.*, 701),—

" Now, that the British North America Act places under the absolute sovereign control of the Dominion Parliament, all matters of every description not by the Act *in precise terms* exclusively assigned to the Legislatures of the Provinces, which by the 5th section of the Act are carved out of *and subordinated to the Dominion*, cannot, in my judgment, admit of a doubt."

" Definitions are," proverbially, " dangerous things ;" and the above partakes, very greatly, of the *definition* character. It strikes us that the errors into which, we submit, that very able, painstaking Judge, has fallen, in the Mercer case ; the Parsons Insurance case, and in the Fishery case, arise from his having held, in those cases, too closely to the proposition as above laid down. We submit that the insertion of the words, "*or by necessary implication*," after the words " in precise terms," will make the proposition correct, and make it accord with all the properly decided cases from Dow *v.* Black to Hodge *v.* The Queen, inclusive.

THE FISHERY CASES

come next, naturally, in order for consideration. These are others of that class of cases, which it has been claimed, with the cases last considered, and those remaining to be considered, have caused a change in the construction of the opening and closing clauses of the 91st section.

As is to be expected with reference to a Court, in connection with which Truth and Candor compel the admission, without doing them a particle of injustice, that, since RITCHIE, C. J., left it, it has not contained, nor does it now contain, among its judges, a single lawyer possessing anything like thorough scientific legal knowledge ; its decisions, now still further to be examined, in this connection, show anything else than sound legal knowledge; but, in some respects, Truth compels the statement, are supremely ridiculous. Still, they answer admirably, by their very mistakes, as aids to us in reaching a correct conclusion on the points we are considering.

By the 91st section, article 12, of the Act, it is provided that the legislative authority over the subject of "Sea Coast and Inland Fisheries," shall be in Parliament. By 31 Vic. c. 60, sec. 2, power was given to the Minister of Marine and Fisheries, to grant fishery leases and licenses, "*where the exclusive right of fishing does not already exist by law.*" This shows, clearly, both the knowledge, and an admission, that there were cases where the right of fishing did already exist by law. A lease or license for fishing having been granted for fishing in non-tidal, and virtually, non-navigable, waters, the question came up in Robertson v. Steadman, 3 Pugs. 621, whether the lease was good. *Weldon*, Q. C. (M. P.) differing radically from his political leader, Mr. *Blake*, as to the construction of sections 91 and 92 of the Act, alleged that "It is true civil rights and rights of property are reserved to the Local Legislatures, *but wherever the Acts of the two Parliaments are in conflict, that of the Local must be read subject to that of the Federal Legislature;*" so far, he should have added, as the legislation of Parliament is within the legitimate scope and effect of the subjects named in the 91st section; or else, as decided by Russell v. The Queen, 7 App. Cas. 829,—assuming that to be law, a point which we discuss, very fully, at a later stage of this discussion—is not an Act so within the scope and effect of the subjects enumerated in section 92, as that it might be passed by the Local Legislatures. His not having so added, making just the mistake which Mr. Justice GWYNNE, we claim, has also made, as we have pointed out, Mr. *Weldon's* next position that "The Fisheries being given to Canada, this necessarily carries with it as an incident whatever powers the Federal Parliament may deem it necessary to exercise for the proper management and control of the fisheries, *whether by granting leases or otherwise*," was too large a claim, and unwarranted by a fair construction of the language of the Act.

This case presents a combination of fallacies, not easily to be equalled—except, perhaps, in some of the other judgments of the same Court. We have in this case, in fact, a very

COMEDY OF ERRORS.

On the one hand, as one absurd extreme, and as one instance of fallacious reasoning in one direction, we have Mr. CHIEF JUSTICE ALLAN "reasoning," in his struggle with that word "exclusive," and without a correct appreciation of the apparently conflicting language in the two sections, as follows,—

"If the Dominion Parliament has the *exclusive* power of legislation over the fisheries, how can the Provincial Legislature have *any* power over the same subject-matter? Again, the Dominion Parliament is to have this exclusive power, *notwithstanding anything in the Act,*" (all the italics are his own.) " How is it possible to give effect to these words if we deny the power of Parliament to legislate regarding the fisheries? Can the plain, clear, positive and unambiguous language of the 91st section, declaring that the Parliament shall have the exclusive power of legislation over the fisheries, be taken away or controlled by the general words of the 92nd section, declaring that the Provincial Legislatures shall have the exclusive power of legislating respecting property and civil rights?"

With the same mixture of truth and error, and the same failure properly to appreciate the effect of whole Act on the different sections, Mr. CHIEF JUSTICE ALLEN continues,—

"I understand the Imperial Parliament to say, in effect, in the 92nd section, that all matters affecting property and civil rights in the Province, shall be under the control of the Provincial Legislatures, *unless they relate to some of the matters over which the exclusive legislative authority has been given to the Dominion Parliament by the 91st section;*" (these italics are ours); " that notwithstanding the use of the words 'Property and Civil Rights,' or any terms in the Act of a similar character, which, uncontrolled, would vest the right of legislation in the Local Legislature, the exclusive power of legislation in certain matters is vested in the Dominion Parliament, though such matters may affect property and civil rights in the Province. Where such exclusive power of legislation is given to the Dominion Parliament, the general power given to the Provincial Legislatures must yield to the particular power given to the Dominion Parliament. In no other way, that I can see, can full effect be given to the positive and unambiguous words of the 91st section, and the two sections be made consistent."

This is reasoning very much as the British Columbia Judges reasoned in the "Thrasher Case." If the Legislatures were excluded from legislating on matters which "relate to the matters over which the legislative authority has been given to the Dominion Parliament by the 91st section," on some of the subjects in the 92nd section, they could not legislate at all. For instance, legislation on the " Solemnization of Marriage" is legislation on matters relating to Marriage. Legislating on *Trade* Licenses is legislating on matters relating to Trade. And legislating on Property and Civil Rights in the Provinces may involve legislation that "relates" to nearly every subject in the 91st section, and yet be perfectly good legislation within the powers of the Local Legislatures. The fallacy, which is by no means an unimportant one; for it is a fallacy, on one side of the question, which would sweep away, virtually, all the powers of legislation on the part of the Legislatures; as would have been the case if the British Columbia "Thrasher Case" had been law; is still better shown by the next paragraph. Mr. CHIEF JUSTICE ALLEN continues,—

"There are numerous other subjects besides the fisheries over which the exclusive control is given to the Dominion Parliament, and by which either the property or the civil rights, or both, of the people of this Province are affected; such as trade and commerce; navigation and shipping; bankruptcy and insolvency; marriage and divorce; and yet it has never been contended that the Local Legislatures would have any power to legislate upon any of these subjects. Indeed, this Court has already decided in the case of Reg. v. Chandler, (1 Han. 548), that the Legislature of this Province has no authority, since the union, to pass an Act relating to Insolvent Confined Debtors, because it related to insolvency— a matter over which the Dominion Parliament had the exclusive control under 'The British North America Act'—though it was contended, in that case, that the Act in question merely affected the civil rights of debtors in respect to their discharge from prison. The effect of that decision is, that the Local Legislature *has no right to deal with any subject which, even indirectly, relates to a matter over which the Dominion Parliament has the exclusive power of legislation*. I cannot distinguish this case, in principle, from Reg. v. Chandler."

In one of a series of articles written by the writer in October, 1879, and published in the *Globe*, (St. John,) where we undertook to show that the unanimous judgment of the Supreme Court of N. B. in *Ex parte* Grieves, as to the Canada Temperance Act being *ultra vires*, was wrong, and which view was subsequently sustained, and on the ground we took, by the Supreme Court of Canada; we then claimed that the positions taken as above, by Mr. CHIEF JUSTICE ALLEN, were wrong, and that he then erred, in going too far in an opposite direction, from the views enunciated by the Court on the validity of the Canada Temperance Act. The decisions since, in the Parsons Insurance Case; the Fishery Case; the British Columbia Case; the Mercer Escheat Case, and the Ontario License Case, sustain the view expressed by us, as above, before any of these cases were decided.

In the case of Robertson *v.* Steadman, (*ante*), WELDON and
DUFF, JJ., concurred with the judgment of ALLEN, C. J. FISHER,
J., delivered a dissenting judgement, in which, making a mistake
in the opposite direction from the rest of the Court, he states, that,
in the 91st section it was declared that none of the classes of subjects enumerated in it "*should come within* ' the class of matters of
a local or private nature comprised in the enumeration of the
classes of subjects assigned to the Local Legislatures, and especially
stated in the last paragraph of the 92nd section.' " This statement
is incorrect in two particulars. First, the provision in the section
is not that they *shall not come within*, &c.; as stated; but that they
shall not be deemed to come within, &c.; the one expression being,
as we have seen, the exact opposite of the other; and, exactly, reversing the construction of the Act on the points named. The
other mistake is, that the words " and especially stated in the last
paragraph of the 92nd section," although treated as part of the
clause, and included within the quotation, is an interpolation.
Eliminating this from Mr. Justice FISHER'S dissenting judgment,
and the judgment otherwise, is, in the main correct; altho' it contains some other passages too broadly stated. The following are
apt quotations in the matter:—

"All the power possessed by the Legislature of New Brunswick still exists as potential as ever, but it is distributed between
the Parliament and the Local Legislature, and it is exercised in
each according to the limitations of the constituting Act. . . .
Now, what is the meaning of the words 'Sea Coast and Inland
Fisheries' in the 91st section? By the employment of this language, what power of legislation is conferred on the Parliament?
Looking at the objects sought to be attained by the union of the
Provinces, and the state of legislation in the different Provinces at
the time of the union, I think it must be inferred that the intention was to confer upon the Parliament the same power that the
Legislatures had been accustomed to exercise; that is, *the power to
provide for the regulation and protection of the fisheries.*"

And, again,—

"If the authority to legislate upon 'Sea Coast and Inland
Fisheries,' empowered the Parliament to interfere with private
rights, and deal with the property in the fish, upon the same
principle, by the authority to legislate upon 'Navigation and Shipping,' it would be enabled to deal with the property in the ships
of ship-owners." (So, in fact, it can; for instance, when the ques-

tion of ship-ownership, as property, comes, *bona fide*, within either of the subjects-matter of the 91st section; 'Bankruptcy and Insolvency,' for instance. As a reference, however, by Judge FISHER, to ships, as property, not, in its most extended sense, *bona fide* coming within the subject of 'Navigation and Shipping,' it is not, at all, an objectionable one). "The right in the ship is no higher or more sacred to the ship-owner than the right in the fish to the riparian proprietor."

In the following, Mr. Justice FISHER, clearly, (as is shown by different portions of his judgment; for instance, by that one corrected by us above, showing that there were distinctions, and qualifications, and extensions, in the matter, that had not entered into his mind), wrote " wiser than he knew ":—

"In conferring upon the Local Legislatures the power to legislate upon property and civil rights, I am of opinion it was the intention *that their power should only be trenched upon to the extent required to enable the Parliament to exercise the authority to legislate upon the different subjects assigned to it, and the Parliament, in legislating upon the subjects within its competency, can only so far interfere with property and civil rights as is necessary to work out the legislation upon the particular subjects specially delegated to it.* The authority to deal with the fish, the property of individuals, and to appropriate that property, is not necessary to the working out of the powers relating to Sea Coast and Inland Fisheries."

That, on the branch of the subject to which it relates, is the law, well expressed, as established by the well-decided cases bearing on it. And, yet, in the very next sentence of Judge FISHER'S judgment, he reasons as though, under no circumstances, and in no case, has Parliament the right "to trench" upon any of the subjects-matter named in the 92nd section. There, and where he misquotes the closing clause of the 91st section, and in other instances, as wrong in the one direction, as CHIEF JUSTICE ALLEN, and those concurring with him, were, in the other.

A RATHER UNCERTAIN COURT.

Here, now, comes a feature in the case almost unique—except, always, of course, in the same Court, since A. D. 1875. That was the case of Robertson v. Steadman, 3 Pugs. 621 ; the judgment in which was delivered by ALLEN, C. J.; WELDON and DUFF JJ., concurring ; and FISHER J., delivering a dissenting judgment; " WETMORE J. taking no part, being related to one of the parties in the cause." Subsequently, *the same question, came up before the same Court*, and between some of the same parties, and in Steadman *v.* Robertson, 2 P. & B. 580, ALLEN C. J., whose judgment, assented to by WELDON and DUFF, JJ., was to be over-ruled, took no part : and, now, FISHER J.'s judgment, including even the mistakes pointed out, that was the dissenting judgment in Robertson *v.* Steadman, is re-delivered, and is the only judgment delivered, in Steadman *v.* Robertson ; WELDON J., with a new inspiration,— ." I have had the opportunity of reading the able judgment of my brother FISHER, and I entirely agree with him." WETMORE J. concurred. And DUFF J.—" I have not been able to consider this matter as fully as I would desire to do. I am not able to concur, but I do not wish to be considered as dissenting. I therefore take no part."

It was well that there was another Court where the question could be more authoritatively disposed of.

In Steadman *v.* Robertson the claim of Counsel for the Plaintiff was substantially established ;—" That, in non-tidal waters, in the Province, the right of fishing is in the riparian owner where the lands through which the rivers run have been granted, and, where not granted, the right is in the Crown, represented by the Local Government, and exists for the benefit of all the inhabitants of the Province : That the Local Legislature could not regulate the fisheries, but that it could legislate as to the right of property in the fish in non-tidal waters. Clearly the Parliament of Canada may regulate the fisheries, that is, the time and manner of fishing, but they cannot interfere with private property." To which latter clause, to make it correct, we would add :—They cannot do it in the instance named, simply because *bona fide* legislation on the fisheries, does not, in the particular case named, involve interference with the private property of either individuals, or of the Province. But, holding this doctrine, does not at all interfere with that; that Parliament may legislate upon all the subjects-matter named in the 91st section, no matter how much these may over-ride, exclude or supersede the powers of the Local Legislatures with reference to any of the subjects-matter named in the 92nd section. This latter is "the hard and fast rule ; " but what does fairly and *bona fide* come within the classes of subjects named in the 91st section, is, as in the case of legislating on the subject of the fisheries, a question for consideration, as it arises. To decide that, due consideration has to be given to such parts of the Act as relate to the subject-matter ; and it is then a question of construction as to what does, or does not, come within such subject-matter.

The question next came up in the Exchequer Court, on the petition of Robertson, before Mr. Justice GWYNNE. That learned Judge, in steering clear, as he has been so careful to do, in so many judgments, of the Scilla of entirely ignoring the effect of the controlling clauses in section 91, on which the barques of so many judges of little erudition have been wrecked; gets into the Charybdis of giving too much effect to those clauses, by which he would, in all such cases as these Fishery Cases; the Parsons Insurance Case, and the Mercer Escheat Case, deprive the Local Legislatures of their power, legitimately and *bona fide* to legislate on different items of the subjects-matter left within their legislative power, by a proper reading of the Act. To avoid, for instance, Mr. *Blake's* blunder, that the power under the 91st section, cannot be exercised so as to *over-ride*, or *supersede*, or *exclude*, (which ever, or all, of these it was he really meant), any of the rights of the Local Legislatures to legislate on the subjects-matter in section 92, the learned JUDGE falls into the opposite mistake that "nothing is placed under the exclusive control of the Local Legislatures unless it comes within some or one of the subjects specially enumerated in the 92nd section, *and is at the same time outside of the several items enumerated in the 91st section, that is to say, does not involve any interference with any of these items.*" This learned JUDGE has been consistent throughout in acting on this rule, strictly, as a "hard and fast" one. If the rule were true, he would, of course, be correct in doing so. But, if false; then, necessarily, when the cases arise with reference to which the rule is a false one, the learned JUDGE's unsound rule—as it is claimed that it is—leads him astray; and, therefore, his judgments in such cases as those named have not been sustained. To mention instances, named before, where, under such a rule, legislation on subjects-matter named in section 92 could not be had at all, reference might be made to the 13th sub-section,—" The Solemnization of Marriage in the Province," which, of necessity, " involves an interference " with the subject of " Marriage," in the 26th sub-section of section 91. Again, legislating with reference to trade licenses, ("Shop, Saloon, Tavern, Auctioneer and other licenses"), necessarily involves some interference with the subject of " Trade."

To show that we are not at all mis-stating the positions of the learned Judge, we quote from The Queen v. Robertson, 6 S. C. R. 52, at page 64, where, in the judgment delivered in Exchequer, the learned JUDGE says,—

"To secure an uniformly consistent construction of this our Constitutional Charter, it is necessary that some certain and sufficient canon of construction should be laid down and adopted, by which all Acts passed as well by the Parliament as by the Local Legislatures may be effectually tested upon a question arising, as to their being or not being *intra vires* of the legislating body passing them. Such a canon appeared to me to be that formulated by me in the City of Fredericton *v.* The Queen, 3 S. C. R., 505, and it still appears to me to be a good and sufficient rule for the required purpose, namely,—' All subjects of legislation of every description whatever are within the jurisdiction and control of the Dominion Parliament to legislate upon, *except such as are placed by the British North America Act under the exclusive control of the Local Legislatures,* and nothing is placed under the exclusive control of the Local Legislatures, unless it comes within some or one of the subjects specially enumerated in the 92nd section, *and is at the same time outside of the several items enumerated in the 91st section, that is to say, does not involve any interference with any of those items.*"

It seems, also, clear to us, that the first part of this rule is not accurate. The exception seems to us to be too large. According to that rule there is either nothing placed within the power of the Local Legislatures, at all events as regards some of the sub-sections of sec. 92, under the latter part of the rule ; or, else, under the first part of the rule, with reference *to the same sub-sections,* there are powers in the 92nd section that Parliament cannot over-ride. Both of these positions, we claim, are wrong. The Local Legislatures may legislate on the subject of licenses, so as *bona fide*, on that subject, to affect trade, or " to involve an interference" with trade. And, against the first part of the rule, then, Parliament can legislate on trade so as to interfere with tavern or other licenses, and so as to over-ride the local legislation, as was done under the Canada Temperance Act. When we get fairly through with the preliminary examination of the cases, we will try if, from them, we cannot evolve better rules than these.

It is also submitted, that, in the next of the learned JUDGE's clauses there is a repetition of his mistake. The passage is as follows,—

"The effect of the closing paragraph of the 91st section, namely : 'And any matter coming within any of the classes of subjects enumerated in the 91st section shall not be deemed to come within the class of matters of a local or private nature comprised in the enumeration of the classes of subjects by this Act assigned exclusively to the Legislatures of the Provinces,' in my opinion, clearly is to exclude from the jurisdiction of the Local Legislatures the several subjects enumerated in the 92nd section, in so far as they relate to or affect any of the matters enumerated in the 91st section."

This position is open to precisely the same objection and criticism as the learned JUDGE's rule. The next paragraph in the learned JUDGE's judgment is much more cautiously written, and comes much nearer the truth. We give it entire, void in all its sentences but one which we italicise, of what we think are the mistakes of the previous paragraph ; which we have quoted above in full. We submit that *residuum* is not the correct idea, as, according to what we claim is the correct construction of the Act, some, at least, of the sub-sections of the 92nd section may entirely cease to be operative. For instance, that as to the granting of Tavern Licenses in order to the raising of a revenue, by an Act, clearly within the power of Parliament to pass, and beyond even such an over-riding, excluding Act, as the Canada Temperance Act ; viz. an absolute prohibitory Act. And, not only so, but as we have already clearly shown, the Local Legislatures may legislate on some matters that may be brought within different clauses of section '92, although, by *bona fide* legislation in Parliament, under the legitimate meaning of the language of the Act, subsequent legislation by Parliament may entirely destroy the previous legislation of the Legislatures. For instance, on licenses, as affected by the Canada Temperance Act, or by an absolute prohibitory law. So, that, in the first instance, the Legislatures had power to legislate upon matters that were absorbed by the legislation of Parliament, and that which was the *residuum* before, is now no *residuum* at all. So, the residuum idea in the following is clearly wrong ; the rest, we submit, as far as it goes, not inaptly states the law. We quote the paragraph in full as a valuable one :—

" Now, among the items enumerated in section 92, there is nothing which could give to the Local Legislatures any jurisdiction whatever over Sea Coast and Inland Fisheries, unless it be the item ' Property and Civil Rights in the Province,' but inasmuch as 'Sea Coast and Inland Fisheries' are enumerated specially in the 91st section as placed under the exclusive control of Parliament, this enumeration carries with it exclusive jurisdiction over property and civil rights in every Province in so far as whatever is comprehended under the term 'Sea Coast and Inland Fisheries' is concerned, and the Local Legislatures have no jurisdiction whatever over this subject; the jurisdiction therefore which is given to the Local Legislatures over 'property and civil rights in the Province' is not an absolute but only a qualified jurisdiction, *and must be held to be limited to the residuum of such jurisdiction not absorbed by the exclusive control given to the Dominion Parliament over every one of the subjects enumerated in the 91st section:* while the jurisdiction of Parliament over every subject placed under its control is as absolute and supreme as the jurisdiction of the Imperial Parliament over the like subject-matter in the United Kingdom would be: the design of the B. N. A. Act being to give to the Dominion of Canada a constitution similar in principle to that of the United Kingdom. It is of course, in every case, necessary to form an accurate judgment upon what is the particular subject-matter in each case as to which the question arises, for the extent of the control of Parliament over the subject-matter, may possibly be limited by the nature of the subject; for example the first item enumerated in the 91st section as placed under the exclusive control of Parliament is the Public debt and property, and by section 108 the Provincial Public Works and property are declared to be the property of Canada. The jurisdiction of Parliament over such property is in virtue of the subject-matter being the property of Canada, but if Parliament should so legislate as to dispose absolutely by sale of portions of this property from time to time, it may well be that the property so sold, when it should become the property of individuals, should be no longer subject to the control of the Dominion Parliament any more than any other property of any individual should be; but over most of the subjects enumerated in the 91st section, the right of the Dominion Parliament to legislate is wholly irrespective of there being any property in the several subjects vested in the Dominion of Canada, and over those subjects the right of legislation continues forever, no matter who may have property or civil rights therein. There is nothing strange in this provision; on the contrary, it is in perfect character with the whole scheme of the Act, that the jurisdiction of the Dominion Parliament should be supreme over all subjects which are of general public interest to the whole Dominion in whomsoever the property in such subject may be vested."

And, yet, after all, where, under the Act of Parliament, the power to grant fishing leases was given only where the exclusive right did not already exist by law; and where it was declared under the B. N. A. Act that the lands belonging to the several Provinces should "belong" to them: as with the lands went also the riparian rights as an incident, the same as,—as other incidents— went the revenues, rents, proceeds of sales, reversions and escheat; applying Mr. Justice GWYNNE's own language, as quoted above, and forming "an accurate judgment upon what is the particular subject-matter" in the case, it surely was not difficult to decide that giving the right to legislate on such a matter, merely, as "the fisheries," while the land and all its incidents with it were given (and, that, by the way not under the 92nd section at all, but under one entirely different, the 109th), to the Provinces, that that could not vest in the Dominion which, expressly, or by necessary implication, vested in the Provinces, viz.—the riparian rights as a property!

Mr. Justice GWYNNE held that the leases were inoperative as to the waters flowing by granted lands; but good as to the waters flowing by ungranted lands. But, with reference to the lands and their incidents, the Provinces had the same rights in the ungranted lands and their incidents, as the owners of the granted lands had in theirs. And, further, as regards the subject-matter of fisheries, Parliament, in legislating on that, had the same right to legislate on it as respects the fisheries in waters flowing through or past granted lands as through or past ungranted lands. As regards, properly, the *bona fide* subject of the "fisheries," the rights and powers to legislate effectually on it, involved the one right quite as much as the other. Mr. Justice GWYNNE was over-ruled in that part of his judgment where his reasoning led him astray, and sustained in the other. And, fairly, without at all interfering with the rule with which we are supplied by the express language in section 91, there seemed to be no other possible result.

So far, in the examination of the cases, no difficulty of construction has presented itself; nor, in any of the properly decided cases so far examined, is there anything at all militating against the rule of construction furnished in section 91 itself, and referred to, approvingly, by LORD CARNARVON, as quoted *ante* p. 11. The Mercer case, as has been seen, (notwithstanding the amount of mystification thrown about it, in the lengthy arguments and judgments in that case, and in very much that has been said and written about it), was a perfectly simple case. It was not a case of conflicting legislation at all ; nor was it one arising out of the 91st and 92nd sections of the Act. It was really a question whether under secs. 102 and 109 of the Act, (and that was all that was involved in it), escheat went to the Provinces under the term "lands," or under the term "royalties;" and whether the revenue from it was, or was not, within the revenues that were reserved to the Provinces. The holding of SIR WM. RITCHIE, C. J.,—and, as we have intimated, what we think was the sounder view—was that escheat as an incident of the ownership by the Provinces in the " Crown " (that is to say, *the ungranted*) lands, went to the Provinces. The holding of the Privy Council, giving an English construction to the local Nova Scotia word, "royalties," used there in connection with the words "mines and minerals ;" that, under it, the benefit of the escheat inured to the Provinces, was the other holding.

In the Fisheries case that we have just been examining, again there was no question in it of conflicting legislation. The Federal Act, as we have seen, expressly recognized a right of fishing by law, not in the Dominion. Again, the construction turned on the effect of the provision that the lands of the different Provinces were to belong to them ; when it was, clearly, properly held, that, with the lands, the riparian rights went as an incident, the same as did the escheat. In this case, there were additional attempts made at manufacturing rules or canons of construction, but they were quite unnecessary, and, as regards the case, are *obiter dicta*. It was claimed, that, under the right to legislate as to the Fisheries under the 91st section, the property in the Fisheries vested in the Dominion. But the obvious absurdity of this has been seen and well illustrated by the position, that, under the right of legislating as to the Fisheries, the property as against the riparian owners, no more vested in the Dominion, than, by the right of legislating as to shipping did the property in the ships so vest. And there is this further analogy in the two cases, with reference to the powers of legislating as between secs. 91 and 92 ; that, while the Dominion has the right to legislate as to shipping so as to affect property and civil rights in the ships, so far as such legislation as to shipping *bona fide* comes within that subject, in the sense in which it is used, as a subject-matter of legislation, or within any of the other subjects-matter enumerated in section 91; no matter how much such legislation may interfere with property and civil rights, or with any other of the subjects-

D

matter named in sec. 92 ; so is the same statement equally true as regards the right in Parliament to legislate as regards the Fisheries ; no matter how much such *bona fide* legislation, on that subject-matter, may affect property and civil rights, or any other of the matters in the different clauses of sec. 92. In each case, the *bona fide* legislation of Parliament, on each of those subjects-matter— Shipping and the Fisheries—will over-ride, or exclude, or supersede the legislation of the Provinces on any of the subjects-matter of sec. 92, to the extent to which, under the Act, they have been so legitimately affected by such *bona fide* Parliamentary legislation. Thus, notwithstanding the correct decision of the Supreme Court of Canada, that the riparian rights, as an incident of the land, go to the owners of the land, whether these are private individuals or Provinces, and carry with them the right in the Local Legislatures to legislate as to land and its incidents, within the terms " property and civil rights," outside of what is contained *bona fide* in the subject-matter of the Fisheries ; so, under the hard and fast rule in the 91st sec., Parliament in legislating, *bona fide* on the Fisheries, can interfere with both property and civil rights ; and over-ride, and supersede, and exclude the Provincial right to legislate on these subjects-matter, so far as they come within or are affected by, legitimate, *bona fide* legislation, by Parliament on the Fisheries. Thus, Parliament, as all admit, in legislating on the Fisheries, can interfere with civil rights, in legislating as to the time of fishing ; and, equally so, with any other civil right that may *bona fide* come within legislation on the Fisheries. Equally so, too, as regards affecting property. Thus, clearly, Parliament, in legislating on the Fisheries, can legislate with reference to mill-dams, so as to require them to be built with fish-ways ; and in legislating, legitimately, on the Fisheries, can declare that the property in all nets wholly across streams, or that have meshes below a certain size, shall be forfeited.

So far, then, it is again suggested, as our examination has yet extended, not a case has presented itself outside of the hard and fast rule, which, we submit, is the clear and unquestionable rule under the Act; that, when the legislation of the two bodies under sections 91 and 92—both being legitimately followed—comes in conflict, the dominant power is in Parliament ; the subordinate in the Local Legislatures.

We now propose taking up other cases for examination, the most of which, including the Parsons Insurance Case ; the Canada

Temperance Act Case, and the case of Hodge v. The Queen, will rank themselves under the general heading of

THE LICENSE CASES.

Ex parte Fairbairn, 2. P. & B. 4. In this case it was held that a Local Act, applicable to Commercial Travellers, authorizing the Mayor of Fredericton to grant to any persons wishing to engage in any trade, profession, &c., in the City, a license to engage therein, is not *ultra vires*, as being an interference with Trade and Commerce.

ALLEN, C. J., in delivering the judgment said,—

"It was contended that the Act was *ultra vires*, as interfering with Trade and Commerce, the regulation of which is assigned exclusively to the Parliament of Canada, by the 91st section of the B. N. A. Act. We think, however, that the right to require licenses for the purposes mentioned in the several Acts referred to is clearly within the power of the Provincial Legislature, under the 92nd section of the B. N. A. Act, which gives the Provincial Legislature the exclusive power to make laws in relation to various matters enumerated; and, among others, (sub-section 9), Shop, Saloon, Tavern, Auctioneer, and other licenses, in order to the raising of a revenue for Provincial, local or municipal purposes.

"The object of requiring Commercial Travellers, (so called), to take out licenses to enable them to carry on their business, is that they shall contribute to the local revenues in like manner as the residents of the place contribute to the revenues by the payment of taxes. We cannot see how this is any greater interference with Trade or Commerce than the requiring a person to take out a license to sell liquors, or a license to sell goods as an auctioneer. In either case the statute says the person shall not carry on that particular business unless he obtains a license to do so; and, therefore, it may be said that indirectly such an Act interferes with trade; but if so, it is just such an interference as the 92nd section of the B. N. A. Act allows."

In Severn v. The Queen, 2 S. C. R. 70, a variety of questions came up, but the case really turned upon the question whether Brewers' licenses were included in the words "and other licenses," in section 92, sub-sec. 9 of the Act, and it was held that they were not; and, that, therefore, an Ontario Act requiring a Brewer to take out a license, who had been licensed under a Dominion Act, was *ultra vires*, as in conflict with a Dominion Act regulating Trade.

RITCHIE and STRONG JJ., dissented, on the ground that the term "Brewers" came fairly within "other licenses" in the sub-section. The latter learned Judge, however, went a good deal farther than this, in meeting the objection that, holding that the allowance of such legislation would conflict with the right of Parliament to legislate ; and laying down what we think is another incorrect rule in the construction of sections 91 and 92, said,—

"The objection, that the wider construction which I have attributed to sub-section 9 brings that provision into collision with sub-section 2 of sec. 91, which confers the power of regulating trade and commerce on the Parliament of the Dominion, is, I think, fully answered *by reading the subjects enumerated in section 92 as excepted from section* 91. It is, I conceive, the duty of the Court so to construe the B. N. A. Act as to make its several enactments harmonize with each other, and this may be effected, without doing any violence to the Act, by reading *the enumerated powers in section 92 in the manner suggested, as exceptions from these given to the Dominion by section* 91. Read in this way, *sub-sec.* 2 *must be construed to mean the regulation of trade and commerce save in so far as power to interfere with it is, by sec.* 92, *conferred upon the Provinces*. . . . The words 'other licenses' must either be silenced, altogether, or else, whatever they may mean in conjunc- tion with the preceding specific words, *they must be read as an exception to sub-section* 2 *and every other enumeration of section* 91, *with which they would conflict* if otherwise construed."

While it might have been held in this case that the term "Brewers" came within the words "other licenses," without, as between, merely, sections 91 and 92, coming any more in conflict with sub-section 2 of section 91, than it would in the case of any of the licenses named ; or than it did in the previous case to which we have referred, (*Ex parte* Fairbairn), in sustaining the right of licenses to Commercial Travellers ; the learned Judge (Mr. Justice STRONG), going beyond that in laying down the rule he did, not only contravenes the express language of the Act and the rule of construction there given, but furnishes a rule as bad as are those of Mr. *Loranger* in the Mercer Case, or either of the numerous rules that are offered in lieu of that which the Act itself expressly supplies. For, if, reading the clauses in section 92, as "exceptions from," the right of legislation in Parliament, under section 91, while, clearly, all difficulty is got over, very easily, as to the right and power of the **Legis-**

latures to legislate, what becomes, in their turn, of the rights and powers of Parliament? If Parliament can, on that rule, only legislate on the Regulation of Trade and Commerce; the raising of Money by any mode or system of Taxation; Navigation and Shipping; Sea Coast and Inland Fisheries; Bills of Exchange and Promissory Notes; Bankruptcy and Insolvency; Copyrights; Naturalization and Aliens; Marriage and Divorce, and even the Criminal Law, excepting from all these the matters of Property, and Civil Rights; it is difficult to see what kind of legislation on those different subjects there could be; allowable only on the terms of making Property and Civil Rights exceptions from such legislation. In fact, the rule, like those that have been examined which have been offered in connection with the "Provincial autonomy" idea, is so utterly and palpably unsound that it was only with some difficulty, that we were able to come to the conclusion that we had not mistaken the meaning of the learned JUDGE. But the idea is too plain, and too often repeated, (four times, as italicised by us), to allow us any such aperture for escape. So, it is only left for us to point this out as another impracticable rule introduced in lieu of that which the Imperial Parliament has given us in the Act.

The same contestation, in another shape, was made by counsel in the case, Mr. *Mowat*, (*Ibid.* 81), and it is to-day the claim made by many politicians; but, as we have seen, it is utterly unsound. Mr. *Mowat* stated his claim, and that of many others with him, thus broadly,—

"Section 92 of the B. N. A. Act, 1867, confers upon the legislature of each Province the jurisdiction of making laws *so as to exclude the authority of the Parliament of Canada in relation to matters coming within the classes of subjects enumerated in that section.*"

This is open to the same criticism as Mr. Justice STRONG's rule, as it, in effect, expresses but the same thing in a somewhat different way. "Exclude the authority of the Parliament of Canada in relation to all matters coming within" section 92; and not only do you controvert the rule of construction in section 91; but the whole force of the section itself is destroyed, AND PARLIAMENT CANNOT LEGISLATE AT ALL! The "Provincial autonomy" would swallow up everything!

Mr. *Crooks*, if possible, holds still stronger views. According to him,—assuming that he was really in earnest—" In each Province a *plenum imperium* was constituted and not a subordinate authority, or one with only such powers as were specially conferred. Once jurisdiction is given over a subject-matter, the power is absolute." *Ibid.* 84. This is reasoning very much, in the opposite direction, like the British Columbia Court reasoned in the "Thrasher Case;" and, in the opposite direction, leads to about the same absurd result. And, it is such views as these, that, it is claimed, the Mercer-Escheat case; the Fisheries case; the Parsons Insurance case, and Hodge v. The Queen, sustain! "The force of folly can no farther go!"

In Regina v. McMillan, 2 Pugs. 110, it was held that an Act of the Local Legislature passed since Confederation, imposing fines and penalties for selling liquor without license, was not *ultra vires*, as within the right to make laws relating to licenses and to impose penalties for enforcing such a law. Hodge v. The Queen, in principle, goes not one step further than this properly decided case.

The case of Regina v. The Justices of Kings, 2 Pugs. 535, is quite an important case in the matter. It was an application for a mandamus to compel the sessions for the County to grant a license for the sale of spirituous liquors, the Justices having refused to grant licenses on the ground that a local act vested a discretion in them whether to do so or not. RITCHIE, C. J. thus lays down the law,—

"To the Dominion Parliament of Canada is given the power to legislate exclusively on 'the regulation of trade and commerce, and the power of raising money by any mode or system of taxation.' The regulation of trade and commerce must involve full power over the matter to be regulated, and must necessarily exclude the interference of all other bodies that would attempt to intermeddle with the same thing. The power thus given to the Dominion Parliament is general *without limitation or restriction*," (it is questionable if SIR WM. RITCHIE would use just these terms now; and, if he would, whether in some senses, he would be strictly accurate), "and therefore must include traffic in articles of merchandise, not only in connection with foreign countries, but that also which is internal between different Provinces of the Dominion, as well as that which is carried on within the limits of an individual Province. . . If, then, the Dominion Parliament authorize the importation of any article of merchandise into the Dominion, and place no restriction on its being dealt with in the due course of trade and commerce, or on its own consumption, but exacts and receives duties thereon on such importation, it would be in direct conflict with such legislation and with the right to raise money by any mode or system of taxation if the Local Legislature of the Province, into which the article was so legally imported and on which a revenue was sought to be raised, could so legislate as to prohibit its being bought or sold, and to prevent trade or traffic therein, and thus destroy its commercial value, and with it all trade and commerce in the article so prohibited, and thus render it practically valueless as an article of commerce on which a revenue could be levied."

And the learned CHIEF JUSTICE discusses the matter, in the same judgment, from another point of view, thus,—

"Under the B. N. A. Act, 1867, *the Local Legislatures have no power except those expressly given to them,* and with respect to the granting of licenses affecting trade they are expressly confined to 'shop, saloon, tavern, auctioneer and other licenses, *in order to the raising of a revenue,* for Provincial, Local or Municipal purposes,' a provision under which a revenue may be derived from the sale and traffic, but which the prohibition of the sale or traffic would entirely destroy, and which would be in direct antagonism with the privilege thereby conceded.

"We by no means wish to be understood that the Local Legislatures have not the power of making such regulations for the government of Saloons, Licensed Taverns, &c., and the sale of spirituous liquors in public places, as would tend to the preservation of good order and prevention of disorderly conduct, rioting or breaches of the peace. In such cases, and possibly others of a similar character, the regulations would have nothing to do with trade or commerce, but with good order and Local Government, matters of municipal police and not of commerce, and which municipal institutions are peculiarly competent to manage and regulate;'* but if, outside of this, and beyond the granting of the licenses before referred to, in order to raise a revenue for the purposes mentioned, the Legislature undertakes directly or indirectly, to prohibit the manufacture or sale, or limit the use of

---

* This is exactly the doctrine which is established by the Privy Council in Hodge v. The Queen; the holding in which case has been entirely misunderstood. It is a mistaken idea to suppose, as many seem to do, that Hodge v. The Queen, has introduced a new principle in the construction of the B. N A. Act. The leading point established by it accords, exactly, with the law as above laid down by RITCHIE, C. J.

any article of trade and commerce, whether it be spirituous liquors, flour, or other articles of merchandise, so as actually and absolutely to interfere with the traffic in such articles, and thereby prevent trade and commerce being carried on with respect to them, we are clearly of opinion they assume to exercise a legislative power which pertains exclusively to the Parliament of Canada, and in our opinion the Act of the Local Legislature declaring 'that no license for the sale of spirituous liquors shall be granted or issued within any Parish or Municipality in the Province when a majority of the ratepayers, residents in each Parish or Municipality, shall petition the Sessions or Municipal Council against issuing any license within such Parish or Municipality,' is *ultra vires* the Local Legislature."

This case was followed by *Ex parte* Mansfield, in the same Court, 2 P. & B. 56, when it was again held by the whole Court, that the Local Legislatures have no power, directly or indirectly, to prohibit the sale of spirituous liquors, "*such power belonging exclusively to the Parliament of Canada.*" ALLEN, C. J., delivering the judgment of the full Court, constituted, then, of himself, and WELDON, FISHER, WETMORE and DUFF, JJ., said,—

"This case cannot be distinguished from that of the Queen *v.* The Justices of King's County, where, under precisely similar circumstances, the sessions of King's County refused to grant a tavern license to one McManus, and this Court granted a mandamus, on the ground that the Local Legislature had no power, directly or indirectly, to prohibit the sale of spirituous liquors, *such power belonging exclusively to the Parliament of Canada. We adhere to that decision, and to the reasons on which it was founded,* which may be considered as incorporated in this judgment, and, therefore, we shall make the rule absolute for a mandamus, as applied for."

And, yet, this very Court, constituted exactly as above, which had, unanimously, held,—"adhering to the decision and the reasons on which it was founded," in Regina *v.* The Justices of Kings,—that, "*directly or indirectly to prohibit the sale of spirituous liquors*" belonged "*exclusively to the Parliament of Canada,*" held in *Ex parte* Grieves, (not, in that name, reported on this point), that—

THE CANADA TEMPERANCE ACT, OF 1878,

was *ultra vires*. The judgments, particularly of WELDON, FISHER, and WETMORE JJ., were, probably, the most ridiculous of all the judgments that have yet been delivered on this *ultra vires* question, and we notice, that, in Regina *v.* Taylor, 36 U. C., Q. B., 183, the deduction is there stated, from the holding in that case, that the exclusive power given in the 91st section to the Dominion Parliament is not exclusive as against the Local Legislatures, *but as against the Imperial Parliament!* That was rather an extraordinary provision in the " Distribution of Legislative Powers" certainly! but even that pales before the absurdities in the judgments which we shall now examine, in *Ex parte* Grieves.

Thus, while on the one hand, stating the law exactly as it is, they say,—

"Under the B. N. A. Act, 1867, section 91, sub-section 2, the powers of Parliament extend to the regulation of Trade and Commerce; *and if this Act is within the powers of this section,* NO OBJECTION AS TO ITS CONSTITUTIONALITY CAN BE SUSTAINED."

And, again,—

"If the provisions of this section (the 99th section of the C. T. Act), are necessary for the regulation of the trade in intoxicating liquors in the different Provinces, then *though they may appear to trench upon property or civil rights, or to limit the power of the Local Legislature to raise a revenue from saloon, tavern, or other licenses, they must be deemed to be within the power of Parliament; if* they are not necessary they are *ultra vires.*"

Right in the very teeth of these thoroughly correct statements of the law, then, as though they had not the slightest idea in the world of the meaning or effect of what they had just been saying, as quoted above, they go on with such nonsense as the following :—

"The power to legislate by this section (the 91st of the B. N. A. Act,) is expressly confined to matters not coming within the classes of subjects assigned exclusively to the Legislatures of the Provinces; so that, however plausible an argument might be raised upon the previous part of the section, *where the matter comes within the classes of subjects assigned exclusively to the Local Legislatures, Dominion legislation must be stayed.* . . What right has the Dominion Parliament to declare what shall be the law, and what a breach of it, in reference to the very class of subjects so withheld from the Dominion Parliament, and exclusively given to the Provincial Legislature, and to impose a penalty for the violation? . . The Provinces had the right to the making and enforcement of municipal regulations for the purposes mentioned in sec. 92, and *the Dominion Parliament had no power to interfere with such Provincial rights.*"

And the climax of absurdity is fairly reached in the following quotation from Mr. Justice WETMORE'S judgment:—

"*Then as to property and civil rights these are exclusively under the control of the Local Legislatures.* The law authorises the importation and manufacture of liquors on payment of certain duties. When legally imported or manufactured, liquor is the subject of property as much so as a horse or any other description of personal property. The owner has just the same right in and to it, as he can have to or in any other personalty, and he has a right to use it and dispose of it at his own will, and pleasure, *subject to any local enactment or regulation, and the Dominion Parliament has no right or power to interfere in the slightest degree with it, simply because the Imperial Act has declared* THAT IN REFERENCE TO PROPERTY AND CIVIL RIGHTS IN EACH PROVINCE, THE LEGISLATURE MAY EXCLUSIVELY MAKE LAWS IN RELATION THERETO."

If Parliament had "*no right or power to interfere in the slightest degree,*" with property or civil rights, how in the world it was going to legislate in reference to Bankruptcy and Insolvency, or to the numerous other subjects in sec. 91 that had property or civil rights for their very essence, never occurred to those sapient judges; who, really, until the utter absurdity of their judgments was publicly exposed, actually were priding themselves on their judgments as wonderful achievements; and *wonderful achievements* they really are! but in a sense entirely different from their views of them when they were first delivered. Of course with *such* reasoning, and ignoring all that was stated in their judgments as to the dominant power of Parliament in case of conflict arising as between the subjects-matter in the 91st and 92nd sections, they declared that the Canada Temperance Act was *ultra vires*, on the ground of its interference with the subjects-matter in Nos. 9, 13, and 16 of the clauses of sec. 92.

And, really, aside of their absurd self-contradictions, and utter ignoring of the powers of Parliament on the subjects-matter enumerated in section 91; if the question simply were as to whether the Canada Temperance Act did interfere with the Provincial right to legislate as to Licenses; to Property and Civil Rights in the Province, or to matters of a local or private nature in the Province, it would be very difficult, and we see no escape from it, very absurd, to hold, (notwithstanding all that there may be in the Privy Council case of Russell v. The Queen, 7 App. Cas. 829, yet to be examined), that the Canada Temperance Act did not interfere with all those things; and, if that of itself were sufficient to make the Act *ultra vires*, that it, unquestionably, was so.

But, inasmuch, as it had been very clearly decided by, as we have seen, the Supreme Court of N. B. itself, over and over again; by the Supreme Court of Canada, and by the Privy Council Board, that legislation by Parliament, within the legitimate scope and meaning of the various subjects-matter in section 91, is perfectly valid; then it became clear, that, if the Canada Temperance Act were within the regulation of Trade and Commerce or any other of the subjects-matter enumerated in section 91, it was valid, *tho' it did interfere with Property and Civil Rights; the granting of Licenses, or matters of a local or private nature in the Province.*

Mr. Chief Justice ALLEN, though not less wrong in his judgment, (with which DUFF J. concurred), than his brother judges, was, at least, much more consistent in his judgment than they.

Thus, while we see him laying down the law, properly, very much as did his brother judges at the outset of *their* judgments, thus,—

" If the Act was a regulation of Trade and Commerce within the words of the 91st section, the fact that it affected Property and Civil Rights would not be sufficient to establish its unconstitutionality. No doubt this Act does affect Property and Civil Rights; but there are many subjects over which the Dominion Parliament has undoubtedly the exclusive right of legislation, which also affect Property and Civil Rights in the Province, *e. g.* Bankruptcy and Insolvency; Navigation and Shipping; the Fisheries and others. In these cases where the exclusive power is given to the Dominion Parliament, *the general powers given to the Local Legislature by section 92 must yield*, Robertson v. Steadman, 3 Pugs. 621.

"*In cases where the Dominion Parliament has the exclusive right to legislate its power is supreme and it would be no valid objection to an Act so passed, that it interfered with private rights;* and if the Act in question related to a subject-matter which was within the provisions of section 91 of the B. N. A. Act, it could not be objected that the effect of it was to prevent persons from selling as they thought proper, property which they had acquired before the Act passed ; "—

he took, at least, the more consistent, if equally unsound position, that the Canada Temperance Act, which is an Act regulating the traffic in intoxicating liquors, is not, within the meaning of the 91st section, an Act regulating Trade; and joined with his brother judges in holding the Act *ultra vires* as being an interference with the right of the Local Legislatures to legislate on the subjects-matter named in clauses 9, 13 and 16 of section 92.

Those judgments seemed to us so utterly absurd, that, in a lengthy review of them, published in St. John, N. B., in Oct., 1879, we pointed out, very plainly, the transparent fallacies with which they abounded; and, after a very exhaustive examination of the authorities in that Province bearing on the questions involved, we claimed to have established the following propositions :—

" *First,*—That the Dominion Parliament and the Local Legislatures, have not, as has been claimed, concurrent powers, but that Parliament has the dominant, and the Local Legislatures, the subordinate power.

" *Second,*—That subject to this dominant power, the rights of the Local Legislatures, whether as to the granting of licenses; to Property and Civil Rights, or to matters of a local nature, have to yield; not less in this case than in the analogous cases where Parliament legislates as to Bankruptcy and Insolvency; to Navigation and Shipping, and other similar subjects—classes of questions decided in our own Courts; and

"*Third,*—That an Act regulating the traffic in Intoxicating Liquors, for the promotion of temperance; or for the peace, order, and good government of Canada is within the powers of section 91 of the Act, and is *intra vires* Parliament."

We then added,—

" We can see no reason why the Supreme Court of Canada should not sustain these three propositions, and, we do not hesitate to say that we have not the slightest doubt whatever that they will be sustained by that Court."

It is scarcely necessary to say that this statement proved to be correct.

The question came up again after this in the same Court, in The Queen, *v.* The Mayor, &c., of Fredericton, 3 P. & B. 139, when the same judgments as were delivered in *Ex parte* Grieves, were, with some slight modifications, adhered to. PALMER J. who had become a sixth member of the Court, delivered a dissenting judgment, which is very loosely reasoned; rambling, and incoherent. Following the position previously taken by Mr. *Thomson* in Regina *v.* The Justices of Kings, 2 Pugs. 535, Mr. Justice PALMER rested his judgment very largely on the claim that the Act was criminal legislation; and, therefore, was within the exclusive power of Parliament. But this would no more give the power to Parliament than would the clause as to the Regulation of Trade and Commerce; and that the Act comes within this clause is much clearer than the other view of it. The Supreme Court of Canada rest their judgment on the Act being within the Regulation of Trade and Commerce, and place no stress on the position taken by Judge PALMER. The Privy Council, while not denying that the Act was within the Regulation of Trade and Commerce, make scarcely any reference whatever to the Criminal Law view, but find a new basis for their judgment.

Mr. Justice PALMER ridicules one of his brother Judges for his reference to the interference with the Civil Rights of individuals, by the Act; as preventing the use of intoxicating liquors for various domestic purposes. References to those instances of interference with Civil Rights, which, clearly, made out that there was such an interference, may be necessary when we examine the judgment of the Privy Council in the matter.

IN THE SUPREME COURT OF CANADA.

We will now proceed to consider the important and interesting questions we are examining, as they are next presented to us in the case on appeal to the Supreme Court of Canada, in the City of Fredericton v. The Queen, 3 S. C. R. 505, where the judgment of the Court below was reversed. It will be necessary to examine the views of the learned Judges in this case at some considerable length.

Two propositions by *Mr. Lash*, Counsel for the Appellants, read together, are not, in themselves, in one sense, unsound. Thus,—" That the Provincial Legislatures have only such legislative powers as have been specially conferred on them by the B. N. A. Act, and that the whole balance of the legislative power over the internal affairs of Canada and the Provinces composing it, rests with the Parliament of Canada;" and, that, "When the powers specially conferred upon the Dominion Parliament clash with the powers of the Provincial Legislatures, the latter must give way." Yet, at the same time, the first of these propositions, as an independent one, is open to the criticism that the B. N. A. Act assumes, in its "Distribution of Legislative Powers," to specify the powers given to each; and the description of the powers given to Parliament is quite as special as it is in relation to the powers given to the Legislatures. The position, therefore, taken by the learned Counsel in the first of these propositions, does not, except in one sense to which we shall hereafter advert, assist us in the construction of the Act. Even the *general* language used, whether as to Parliament or the Legislatures, is *special* as to the powers of the one relatively with, or as against, those of the other. Other quite different principles than that certain specific powers are given to the Legislatures and all else to Parliament, are required to be considered in meeting the difficulties that arise when the subjects-matter legislated upon are within, or conflict with, the special powers given to each of the legislative bodies, as it is claimed that the Canada Temperance Act does. Before we leave the matter, we hope to make clearer, than, from the public statements now being made, it at present is, what is, really, on the questions now vexing the Dominion, the *ratio decidendi* of all the well decided cases.

In answer to an enquiry of the learned CHIEF JUSTICE, SIR WM. RITCHIE, Mr. *Maclaren*, Counsel with Mr. *Lash*, observed,—

"Our answer is that Parliament has power to regulate trade and commerce in such a way as to promote the good government of the country. Then also it is said that this Act interferes with the exclusive control given to the Local Legislatures over municipal institutions in the Province, and matters affecting civil rights and property. My contention is that the Dominion Parliament has full power to legislate upon all matters strictly within its jurisdiction, no matter what effect it may have on classes of matters comprised in those assigned by sec. 92 to the Legislatures of the Provinces; and I base my contention on the concluding lines of sec. 91. The Court below has not given full force to the words 'shall not be deemed to come within the class of matters of a local, &c.'"

This statement of the claim in the case covers exactly what the case in the Supreme Court of Canada decides. The learned CHIEF JUSTICE virtually assented to it, with the observation that "The Dominion Parliament can deal with shipping, and can it not do so irrespective of the power given to the Local Legislatures as to the civil rights over the subject?"

And in reply to a question by Mr. Justice HENRY, Mr. *Maclaren* stated this sound position:—"Where there is an apparent conflict, in so far as it is a *bona fide* regulation of trade and commerce, the local interest must give way. I think this is a fair construction to put on the concluding words of section 91."

Mr. *Kaye's* position for the Respondent, was, broadly, that, in the distribution of legislative powers, the B. N. A. Act assigns exclusively to the Provincial Legislatures the power of legislation in relation to all matters coming within the classes of subjects named in sec. 92, excluding any like power in the Parliament of Canada with respect to these matters; thus giving no force whatever to the over-riding power in the over-riding language, particularly, of the opening clause of sec. 91.

The learned CHIEF JUSTICE, states, very clearly, the effect of the language in secs. 91 and 92, thus,—

"If the Dominion Parliament legislates strictly within the powers conferred in relation to matters over which the B. N. A. Act gives it exclusive legislative control, we have no right to enquire what motive induced Parliament to exercise its powers. The statute declares it shall be lawful for the Queen, by and with the advice and consent of the Senate and House of Commons, to make laws for the peace, order and good government of Canada, in relation to all matters not coming within the class of subjects by this Act assigned exclusively to the Legislatures of the Provinces, and, notwithstanding anything in the Act, the exclusive legislative authority of the Parliament of Canada extends to all matters coming within the classes of subjects enumerated, of which the regulation of trade and commerce is one; and any matter coming within any of the classes of subjects enumerated, shall not be deemed to come within *the classes* of matters of a local or private nature comprised in the enumeration of the classes of subjects by the Act assigned exclusively to the Legislatures of the Provinces."

Unless it can be denied that this is a correct summary of the Act, relating to the matter, then, unless by judicial decision,— "Judge-made law"—*the Act is repealed*, the above quoted passage settles, clearly and unmistakably, the law on the question, beyond a peradventure. That it is, as to the question in dispute, a correct statement of the very language; the essence; the very letter and spirit, of the Act, is, absolutely, unquestionable. Then, it is not a question of political bias at all; but a plain statement of the clear law of the case, *on this point;* that, with respect to all *bona fide* legislation of Parliament on the subjects-matter named in the 91st section, such legislation is good, no matter how much it over-rides, excludes, supersedes or interferes with the power of the Local Legislatures to legislate with respect to the *classes* * of local or

---

* This, advisedly, mark, (as, perhaps inadvertently, but, it is claimed correctly, has been done by SIR WM. RITCHIE, in the italicised passage above), does not strictly follow the language of the Act, in using the plural word "classes" instead of the singular word "class." In so using the word, there is a marked disagreement with SIR MONTAGUE E SMITH, who, in the Parsons Insurance Case, misconstrued the closing clause of the 91st section, where the language occurs; as will be hereafter shown.

private subjects enumerated in the 92nd section. Beyond this principle laid down, so clearly, by the learned CHIEF JUSTICE, there is still another correct principle of construction to which we shall require to direct attention in connection with the examination of the case we are now considering; which, from the Privy Council's view, assuming it to be right, may, possibly, still further enlarge the power of Parliament under the Act, as against the right of the Local Legislatures to legislate as to mere local or private matters in the Province. That other rule of construction we will consider when we reach the case in the Privy Council.

The following additional paragraph from the judgment of the learned CHIEF JUSTICE, on the point, is equally clear, and we submit, equally indisputable:—

" It has been likewise very strongly urged that the Dominion Parliament cannot have the right to prohibit the sale of intoxicating liquors, as a beverage, because to do so would interfere with the right of the Local Legislatures to grant licenses and to deal with property and civil rights and matters of a purely local character, and so interfere with the right of the Local Legislatures to raise a revenue by means of shop and tavern licenses. I fail to appreciate the force of this objection. If substantial it would prohibit to a great extent the Dominion Parliament from legislating in respect to that large branch of trade and commerce carried on in intoxicating beverages, and so take away the full right to regulate alike foreign and internal commerce. If they cannot prohibit the internal traffic because it prevents the Local Legislatures from raising a revenue by licensing shops and taverns, the same result would be produced if the Dominion Parliament prohibited its importation or manufacture. For, by the same process of reasoning, it must follow, that they could not prohibit its importation or manufacture, or in any way regulate the traffic, whereby the sale or traffic should be injuriously affected, and so the value of licenses be depreciated or destroyed. In my opinion, *if the Dominion Parliament, in the exercise of and within its legitimate and undoubted right to regulate trade and commerce, adopt such regulations as in their practical operation, conflict or interfere with the beneficial operation of local legislation, then the law of the Local Legislature must yield to the Dominion Law,* because matters coming within the subjects enumerated as confided to Parliament, are not to be deemed to come *within the matters of a local nature,*" (this, as we shall see, is not the way SIR MONTAGUE

E. SMITH and the Privy Council would erroneously put it), " comprised in the enumeration of subjects assigned to the Local Legislatures. In other words, the right to regulate trade and commerce is not to be over-ridden by any local legislation in reference to any subject over which power is given to the Local Legislature."

Mr. Justice TASCHEREAU, also, puts the matter very clearly, and very correctly, in the latter part of the following paragraph; which paragraph covers another important ground in addition to the position taken by the learned CHIEF JUSTICE; as shown in the extracts we have made above. The additional point named by the learned JUDGE is the one to which we intend referring more particularly when examining the judgment of the Privy Council in the case. We make the following important extract from the judgment of Mr. Justice TASCHEREAU :—

"Section 91 of the Imperial Act is clear on this : It expressly authorizes the Federal Parliament to make laws in relation to all matters not exclusively assigned to the Provincial Legislatures, and enacts in express terms, that the enumeration given of the classes of subjects falling under the control of the Federal Parliament is given for greater certainty, but not so as to restrict the rights of the Federal Parliament generally over all matters not expressly delegated to the Provincial Legislatures. If this Temperance Act would be *ultra vires* of the Provincial Legislatures, because the B. N. A. Act does not give them the power to enact it, I fail to see why it is not *intra vires* of the Dominion Parliament. Then, it seems to me, that under the words 'regulation of trade and commerce,' the B. N. A. Act expressly gives the Dominion Parliament the right to this legislation. It may, it is true, interfere with some of the powers of the Provincial Legislatures, but sec. 91 clearly enacts that, *notwithstanding anything* in this Act; *notwithstanding* that the control over local matters, over property and civil rights, over tavern licenses for the purposes of raising a revenue, is given to the Provincial Legislatures, the *exclusive* legislative authority of the Dominion extends to the regulation of trade and commerce, and this Court has repeatedly held, that the Dominion Parliament has the right to legislate on all the matters left under its control by the Constitution, though, in doing so, it may interfere with some of the powers left to the Local Legislatures."

We would, respectfully, submit, that the latter part of this paragraph, is a clear, honest statement of the law as the statute itself gives it to us. It is a difficulty inseparable from written Constitutions, as with codes, that, in their practical operation, conflicts and difficulties arise not previously anticipated, involving construction, and very often leading to misconstruction; very much of which latter has already, in different decisions of the Provincial Courts, accumulated about the B. N. A. Act, 1867. The first part of the paragraph we will examine more fully at a later stage of this investigation, as already intimated.

It is also respectfully submitted that the following paragraphs from the judgment of that able and usually accurate Judge, Mr. Justice GWYNNE, (*Ibid.*, 564), do not furnish a reliable rule of construction in the matter. Thus, says the learned JUDGE,—

"All that is necessary, therefore, in order to determine whether any particular enactment is *intra* or *ultra vires* of the Parliament, is to enquire: does or does not the enactment in question deal with, or legislate upon, any of the subjects assigned exclusively to the Provincial Legislatures? If it does, it is *ultra*, if it does not, it is *intra vires* of the Dominion Parliament."

If this were law, then, as Parliament, in passing the Canada Temperance Act, "dealt with," or "legislated upon,"—as was not down to this stage of the case seriously and intelligently questioned at all—Property and Civil Rights and Licenses, then, according to that rather singular statement of Mr. Justice GWYNNE, such legislation was *ultra vires*. But if so, so also was all the legislation of Parliament with reference to trade and commerce, bankruptcy and insolvency, and hosts of other subjects, the legislation in reference to which, *ex necessitate rei*, involved *dealing with* or *legislating upon* some one, or other, or others, of the subjects-matter assigned "exclusively to the Provincial Legislatures."

It is difficult to conceive that Mr. Justice GWYNNE could have laid down so unsound a proposition as the above. But he has not only done so, but repeats the error. After setting forth the opening and closing clauses of section 91, the learned JUDGE again erroneously repeats the unreliable, and, really, unsound "test;" thus, (p. 565),—

"Here, then, to dispel all doubts, if any should perchance arise in certain cases, and to remove all excuse for any encroachment by the Dominion Parliament upon the jurisdiction of the Local Legislatures, or for any assumption by the latter of the sovereign power and authority of the former, two tests are given by our charter for the ready determination in every case of the question, whether a particular enactment is or is not *ultra vires* of the Dominion Parliament, or of the Local Legislatures; namely:—

"First,—if to the question 'does the particular enactment deal with any of the particular subjects, assigned exclusively to the Local Legislatures?' a plain answer in the affirmative or negative can be given free from any doubt, that settles the point. If the answer be in the affirmative, the enactment in question is beyond the jurisdiction; if in the negative, it is within the jurisdiction of the Dominion Parliament."

This is open to the same observations as were made with reference to the first quotation from Judge GWYNNE's judgment. It is unsound, as has been shown. And, not only is it unsound, but it is directly opposed to what the learned JUDGE calls "the second test," which, unlike the other, is a real test in the matter; and agrees with the statements in the valuable extracts from the judgments of the CHIEF JUSTICE and Mr. Justice TASCHEREAU. Judge GWYNNE says,—

"But to remove all doubts, in case the enactment under consideration should be of a nature to raise a doubt, whether it does or not deal with one or other of the matters particularly enumerated in the 92nd section, the second test may be applied, namely: 'does the enactment deal or interfere with any of the subjects particularly and for greater certainty enumerated in the 91st section?' If it does, then, (notwithstanding that it otherwise might come within the class of subjects enumerated in the 92nd section), it is within the jurisdiction of the Dominion Parliament, for the plain meaning of the closing paragraph of the 91st section is, that, notwithstanding anything in the Act, any matter coming within any of the subjects enumerated in the 91st section shall not be deemed to come within the class of subjects enumerated in the 92nd section, however much they may appear to do so."

This is so well, and so accurately stated, that it makes the previous incorrect paragraphs appear the more remarkable. Following this, the general reasoning of the learned JUDGE agrees with his position in the paragraph just quoted. But, as he proceeds, carrying his argument in this new direction rather far, the learned JUDGE, it is submitted, limits to too great an extent the power of legislation in the Local Legislatures, and deprives them of powers that legitimately belong to them; at least as regards some of the subjects-matter in section 92. The following is the passage,—

"All subjects of whatever nature, not exclusively assigned to the Local Legislatures, are placed under the supreme control of the Dominion Parliament, and no matter is exclusively assigned to the Local Legislatures, unless it be within one of the subjects expressly enumerated in section 92 *and is at the same time outside of all of the items enumerated in section* 91, by which term 'outside of' I mean does not involve any interference with any of the subjects comprehended in any such items."

Right in the very teeth of this rule, stands the fact that the solemnization of marriage, (one of the subjects in sec. 92), is not "outside of," but is right inside of, and does involve an interference with the subject of marriage—one of the subjects of sec. 91. So, too, is the legislating on Trade licenses right inside of, and involves an interference with, to a certain extent, the subject of Trade. The learned JUDGE evidently saw the difficulty as regards his last named rule, (which, again, is not a sound one), as regards the first named subject, (solemnization of marriage), and has fought hard, (p. 566, &c.), to get over the difficulty in his way; but is not successful. After we get through with the examination of the cases, and we come to answer the questions stated at the commencement of this treatise, we will see, if, on this last named point, (i. e. as to the rights of the Local Legislatures to legislate), we cannot furnish a more correct rule.

The same question of solemnization of marriage, to which we have referred, has, more than once, been thought to present a difficulty in the way of our accepting, as the rule of construction in all cases, the plain, simple rule that the statute itself gives us. We may as well deal with that now. Take the rule laid down in the statute, and as a test, apply it specially to the two subjects-matter, and see what is the *clear, legal effect;* which is that, carry us where it will, which we are seeking in the matter. If the provision is an unwise or injurious one; the remedy is by its legal repeal by the necessary legislation; not by construing away that which is the express law in the matter.

The Act gives the " Exclusive Power" for the Provincial Legislatures to legislate on the subject of " The Solemnization of Marriage in the Province," but it provides, that, " for the peace, order and good government of Canada," Parliament—notwithstanding that it is provided in the Act that the Local Legislatures may exclusively legislate on the subject of the solemnization of marriage in the Province—shall have the exclusive legislative authority to legislate on the subject of marriage, and any matter coming within the subject of marriage, shall not be deemed to come within the subject of solemnization of marriage, no matter how much it may appear to do so, or how much it may actually do so, so as to prevent or interfere with Parliament legislating effectually and *bona fide* on the subject of marriage. This, as we have seen, over and over again, is the only construction that the language in sections 91 and 92 is fairly open to. It is, alike, the construction of the Privy Council in all their well decided cases ; of the Supreme Court of Canada, and of all the well decided cases in the matter, in the Provincial Courts.

This, then, in this most extreme case, is the result, that legislation by Parliament on marriage is good, no matter how much it may interfere with the subject of solemnization of marriage in the Province. It may be said that this is begging the question. Not by any means. It is simply making a clear, plain, honest application of the Statute within its express language. It is but another application of the Privy Council Case, which, under precisely the same inexorable rule in the Act, holds that legislation by Parliament on Insolvency, is good, no matter how much it interferes with the so-called "exclusive" legislative power of the Legislatures on Property and Civil Rights; procedure in the Provincial Courts, or with any other of the "exclusive" powers of the Local Legislatures.

As an instance, perhaps not inapt, of the power of Parliament to legislate on marriage so as to effect solemnization of marriage in the Province. Suppose Parliament passed a general act legalizing marriage with a deceased wife's sister; but, with the provision that it would require, before the marriage could be solemnized, that a special license should be obtained from the Governor of the particular Province, and, (to meet the objections of some clergymen), that it be solemnized before a Justice of the Peace. This would be legislating on marriage, and, at the same time, with reference to the solemnization of marriage in the Province; and, not only would it be good within the express terms of the Act; but, unless good, then, on neither the ground on which the Canada Temperance Act has been sustained in the Supreme Court of Canada, nor, on the very different, and much stronger ground, as we shall see, on which it was sustained by the Judicial Committee of the Privy Council, could that Act have been held *intra vires*. We name these questions of marriage and solemnization of marriage, because they have been steered clear of so often ; or else have been met by the most fanciful treatment in the attempts to get clear of the difficulties that they seemed to present to any "hard and fast rule or canon of construction." For an extremely fantastic way of treating this subject, see, in the case we are considering, per Mr. Justice GWYNNE, 3 S. C. R. 568.

The most satisfactory way to test the correctness of "hard and fast rules" is with extreme cases.

It is respectfully submitted that the learned JUDGE, (Mr. Justice GWYNNE, is again wrong when he says, (p. 571),—

"*The unerring test to determine whether the power to pass the Act is, or is not, vested in the Dominion Parliament is to enquire, under the application of the rule, as I have stated it, is, does it, or does it not, deal with a subject jurisdiction over which is given exclusively to the Local Legislatures? for, if not, it is vested in Parliament."*

As before intimated, that is no test at all; as there are many things that would come within property and civil rights, (classes of subjects declared to be within the "exclusive" jurisdiction of the Local Legislatures), that, as being within trade and commerce; insolvency; the fisheries, and many others of the subjects named in section 91, would not be within the jurisdiction of the Local Legislatures at all.

A better rule—at least to test the powers of the Local Legislatures—is one furnished by the Privy Council, SIR MONTAGUE E. SMITH delivering the judgment, in the Citizens Insurance Co. *v.* Parsons, 7 App. Cas. 109, thus,—

"The first question to be decided is, whether the Act impeached falls within any of the classes of subjects enumerated in sect. 92, and assigned exclusively to the Legislatures of the Provinces; *for if it does not, it can be of no validity, and no other question would then arise. It is only when an Act of the Provincial Legislature prima facie falls within one of these classes of subjects*" that the next question arises; viz., *whether, notwithstanding this is so, the subject of the Act does not also fall within one of the enumerated classes of subjects in sec.* 91, *and whether or not,* (the *ratio decidendi* of the case), *it so falls within the class in sect.* 91 *as to be thereby* "over-borne," ('an equivalent for "over-ridden"), *by the power of the Dominion Parliament?* We will further, hereafter, consider the point with the case from which we take the rule.

Mr. Justice HENRY's dissenting judgment, on the validity of the Canada Temperance Act, in which he differs with all the rest of his brothers of the Supreme Court of Canada, was as fallacious as the judgments of WELDON, FISHER and WETMORE, JJ., in the Supreme Court of N. B. It is observable in Valin *v.* Langlois, 3 S. C. R. 63, that Mr. Justice HENRY in quoting the first clause of sec. 91, entirely omits the important and over-riding closing portion of that clause, and reasons as though it were not there. That, however, in Valin *v.* Langlois was not important, as the question as to the right of Parliament arose there, rather under sec. 41, than under the whole of the first clause of sec. 91. In the City of Fredericton *v.* The Queen, (*Ibid.*, 505), the question was quite otherwise. There the important clause was the opening clause of the 91st section, and, yet, that is absolutely ignored by the learned JUDGE, and he reasons, *first*, as though that clause had no existence ; and, *second*, ignoring the first clause, he entirely misstates the effect of the closing clause of sec. 91. Thus, p. 551,—

" We are bound I think, to conclude that in using the general term, (i. e. trade and commerce), it was not intended to reach the subject specifically provided for in sub-section 9 of 92. It was clearly intended to give the licensing power to the Local Legislatures, because the section so plainly and unequivocally so provides ; but then it is contended the concluding clause of 91 over-rides the specific provision in sub-section 9 of 92, and virtually ignores it, if the general term as employed in regard to trade and commerce includes the subject-matter."

The learned JUDGE does not assent to the correctness of that view ; and, yet, in Valin *v.* Langlois, without considering at all the " over-bearing," " over-riding," " over-ruling " effect of the closing part of the first clause of section 91, particularly in connection with the closing clause of that section, Mr. Justice HENRY laid down the principle more correctly, (p. 62), and so as to include the point involved in the Canada Temperance Act Case ; thus,—

" 'There is but a small minority of the subjects given expressly to the Dominion Parliament that do not affect ' civil rights within the Province,' *and its whole legislation in respect of them is clearly an authorized invasion of the powers of local legislation conferred by the general term ' civil rights in the Province.'* The whole purview of the Act, with a proper consideration of the subjects, is evidence of the policy *to limit local legislation to those ' civil rights in the Province' not included specially or otherwise in the powers given to the Dominion Parliament.*"

But, in the application of the above, within its fair meaning, it is submitted that the learned JUDGE went too far in *limiting the legislative power of the Provinces*, with respect to a subject-matter that may come within one of the more general, or larger, subjects-matter given to Parliament. For as, as has been shown, it may be within the power of the Local Legislatures to legislate with respect to subjects-matter in the 92nd section, that may be perfectly good; and yet such legislation may be "over-borne" or "over-ridden" by the subsequent legislation of Parliament on the wider subject-matter. The learned JUDGE indeed seems to have discovered his mistake in *too greatly limiting* the legislative power of the Local Legislatures, and not seeing his way out of it otherwise, came to another wrong conclusion; thus, (p. 547),—

"If there be not concurrent legislative powers, and the Act, (*i. e.* the Canada Temperance Act), is *intra vires*, then the necessary conclusion is, that all the local legislation on the subject of shop, saloon, tavern, and auctioneers' licenses since the 1st of July, 1867, has been *ultra vires.*"

Thus, jumping from extreme error to extreme error, on the principle that "extremes produce extremes," the learned JUDGE involves himself in another absurdity in suggesting the following fancied difficulty:—

"Under such circumstances," he adds, "it would be interesting to enquire, where there is any law in force restraining the sale of spirituous liquors in counties or cities which have not adopted the Canada Temperance Act, 1878."

See this point, incidently considered by LORD SELBORNE, in L'Union St. Jacques de Montreal *v.* Belisle, and by ALLEN, C. J., *Ex parte* Ellis, cited *supra.* It is matter, also, that is covered by the first of the questions we stated, at the outset of this discussion, and which we propose to make the cases we are citing, and the reasoning from them, answer, with the other questions proposed. We will then show, clearly, how Mr. Justice HENRY has again erred.

We have now to consider the Canada Temperance Act Case before the

JUDICIAL COMMITTEE OF THE PRIVY COUNCIL,

where it appears *nom.* Russell *v.* The Queen, 7 App. Cas, 829. The judgment of the Supreme Court was affirmed, holding that the Act was " within the legislative competency of the Dominion Parliament." The Privy Council also held "That the objects and scope of the Act are general, viz. to promote temperance by means of a uniform law throughout the Dominion, *and relate to the peace, order and good government of Canada, and not to the class of subjects 'property and civil rights.'*"

Mr. *Benjamin*, in this case, claimed that the Local Legislatures had exclusive power to raise money by licenses, and that the Dominion could not interfere therewith by legislating with regard to the commodities which are the subject of licenses. That it was a local matter. That it was also within sec. 13 as to property and civil rights in the Province. The respondent's counsel were,—from the view taken by their LORDSHIPS,—heard only in reference to sub-section 16, " Matters of a local or private nature in the Province." The respondent's counsel contended that " If a matter can only affect the particular locality, directly or indirectly, then it is left to local legislation." That, " If, on the other hand, such private or local matter falls within any of the subjects enumerated in sect. 91, provincial legislation cannot deal with it." The learned counsel also took the position that the case came within the words "regulation of trade and commerce" and also within " Criminal Law." The position was also taken, as was held by the Supreme Court of Canada, that if it came within either of the clauses in sec. 91, it was immaterial if it did come also within one or more of the clauses in sec. 92 ; as these were " over-borne ;" but, as from the view taken by the Privy Council, this did not become material, the counsel were not reported on that point.

As intimated, this case establishes a doctrine far beyond anything that had been decided in the Supreme Court of Canada, relative to the dominant power of Parliament, in matters of conflict between the two legislative bodies. We have before stated the rules from the Parsons Insurance Case. In this case one of those rules has been given its full practical effect. But, in this case, from another principle that has been almost entirely ignored, the second rule in the Parsons Insurance Case was not required to be brought into requisition. And the fact is, the very important doctrine established in Russell *v.* The Queen, seems to have been lost sight of ; probably because the very essence of that case scarcely seemed to have been seriously thought of previously, and the decision has been accepted without due examination, in any public manner having been made, of the very important principle it firmly establishes in connection with these interesting and important questions. This fact is certain, that, if what this case really holds is understood where it ought to be understood, the Executive

Officers in N. B. and Ontario, have, respectively, put most extraordinary language in the opening speech of the Governor of N. B., and in the closing speech of the Governor of Ontario, in connection with the Legislatures of those Provinces, and made those prominent gentlemen give utterance to a great deal of nonsense.

It is proposed now to show, plainly and honestly, exactly what this important case—by far the most important that has yet been decided on the question—really holds. To make this clearer, we will summarize the contention in the courts below. In the Supreme Court of N. B., it was held, by three of the five Judges, that the Act was *ultra vires*, because it was an interference with the right to grant licenses in the Provinces; with property and civil rights, and with matters of a local or private nature in the Province. It was there, not contested, that the Act was an interference with all these things; but, it was claimed, according to numerous decisions in that Court, from Regina *v.* Chandler down, that, if it came also within either of the classes of subjects in the 91st section, the Act was good, no matter how much it might interfere with those in sec. 92. ALLEN, C. J., probably the ablest member of a very weak Court, (delivering the judgment of himself and DUFF, J.), conceded that if it did come within the legitimate meaning of the words, "The Regulation of Trade and Commerce," in the 91st section of the B. N. A. Act, the Act in question was good, no matter how much it might interfere with the classes of subjects named in section 92; but, he concluded, with a good deal of hesitation, that it was not fairly within the meaning of that language. PALMER J., in a later case, took the position, that the Act was within the clauses relating to Trade, and to Criminal Law; but, further than this, his judgment is so unscientifically prepared, it is difficult to tell what he really means as to the difficulties in the case. He ridicules Judge FISHER's instances of interference with property and civil rights in connection with spirituous liquors; but those instances, as well as more important ones, show, clearly, that those different subjects-matter enumerated in the 92nd section, in classes 9, 13 and 16, are, unquestionably, *interfered with by the Act.*

Next, the question came before the Supreme Court of Canada; and there it was again virtually conceded all around that the Act was—as, in fact, cannot seriously be denied—a direct interference with the different sub-sections named; but, it was there held, HENRY J., only, dissenting, that this was immaterial, inasmuch as the Act, coming also within the second clause of the 91st sec., "over-rode," or "over-bore" the local right in the Legislatures.

But, before the Judicial Committee of the Privy Council, the matter is made, by that eminent body, to assume an entirely different aspect. And to make the doctrine, which, in this case—and the very important doctrine, too, that it is,—sufficiently clear; and to show the transparent nonsense in which political writers and speakers, have, recently, been indulging in the matter, who have failed to appreciate recent Privy Council decisions, we will now give a new reading to a portion of the first clause of section 91 of the Act. This, then, without any reference to the important closing part of the clause, which we have previously examined, and without reference to the clause at the close of the 91st section, which we have also examined, provides that Parliament may "make laws for the peace, order and good government of Canada *in relation to all matters* NOT COMING WITHIN THE CLASSES OF SUBJECTS by this Act assigned exclusively to the Legislatures of the Provinces."

All, then, that Parliament is prevented from legislating upon, even by this portion of the clause, are such matters as do not come "*within the classes of subjects*" assigned to the Legislatures. The mistake that has been made, assuming now, as we for the present do, that Russell v. The Queen, is law, in construing this portion of the clause, has been in treating this language, shall not come "within the classes of subjects" assigned to the Legislatures, as being synonymous with "*shall not relate to such classes of subjects.*" This is the important error, (assuming now, as aforesaid), in this tacitly received construction of this language, that Russell v. The Queen removes. And by this case, an Act, no matter how much in its general scope it may interfere with the different subjects named in the different clauses of section 92; if it is an Act, as a whole, (that is, really, the *ratio decidendi* of Russell v. The Queen; for, incontestably, the Canada Temperance Act is a direct interference with, and cutting down of the powers of the Local Legislatures with respect to sub-sections 9, 13 and 16 of section 92), for the peace, order and good government of Canada, which neither of the Local Legislatures could pass, then it is within the power, under the first portion alone of the opening clause of section 91, of the Parliament of the Dominion to pass it. By an examination of the case, we will now make this clear; and, in our examination of this case, for what is intended to be an honest and independent view of the law, we only wonder that, as far as we are aware, it has never, with the important results which it bears in its train, been made clear before. Had it been, all the nonsense about " Provincial autonomy ;" " Federal usurpation," &c., inside of Parliament and the Local Legislatures, and outside of them, never could have been uttered ; and a cry would have gone up *of quite a different character.*

It is admitted at the outset, in the judgment of the Privy Council, delivered by SIR MONTAGUE E. SMITH ; (p. 835), that,—

" The effect of the Act when brought into force in any county or town within the Dominion, is, describing it generally, to prohibit the sale of intoxicating liquors, except in wholesale quantities, or for certain specified purposes, to regulate the traffic in the excepted cases, and to make sales of liquor in violation of the prohibition and regulations contained in the Act, criminal offences, punishable by fine, and for the third or subsequent offence by imprisonment."

Here, then, it is clearly shown, that if this Act, resulting in such consequences, as named, is sustained, then is established the right of Parliament to pass such an Act, the consequences of which, as above shown, will be to interfere with property and civil rights, in, and connected with, spirituous liquors and their sale, in the Provinces ; with the granting of shop, saloon and tavern licenses for the sale of spirituous liquors; and with all such local, private, or municipal rights and powers as are connected with spirituous liquors and their sale in the Provinces. So declaring such Act valid, then, shows a right and power to legislate by Parliament in that and in all analogous cases, so as to interfere with, " over-ride," " over-bear," and " exclude" the legislation of the Provinces in respect to the subjects-matter of the Act as far as they are there legislated upon ; notwithstanding the subordinate powers given to the Local Legislatures in respect to the matters named in the different classes of sec. 92 ;—these all, as far as they are involved in the fair construction of the Act, being over-ridden, over-borne, and excluded by such Parliamentary Act, affecting them.

The principles upon which this important result is reached— a result by the way, of which a large portion of the intelligent public of Canada, seem not to have at all apprehended—are just as in our introductory remarks to this case, we have stated them ; applied there, though, observe, as in the Parsons Case, to test the validity of an Act of the Local Legislature. His LORDSHIP, referring to the rules, (which, in order to meet and dispose of some vicious rules of our JUDGES, relative to the validity of Acts of the Local Legislatures, we have, somewhat in anticipation of our examination of the case, already stated), laid down in the Parsons Insurance Case, says,—

" According to the principle of construction then pointed out, the first question to be determined is, *whether the Act now in question* falls within any of the classes of subjects enumerated in section 92, and assigned exclusively to the Legislatures of the Provinces. IF IT DOES, THEN THE FURTHER QUESTION WOULD ARISE, *viz.* WHETHER THE SUBJECT OF THE ACT DOES NOT FALL WITHIN ONE OF THE ENUMERATED CLASSES OF SUBJECTS IN SECT. 91, AND SO DOES NOT STILL BELONG TO THE DOMINION PARLIAMENT. *But, if the Act does not fall within any of the classes of subjects in sect.* 92, NO FURTHER QUESTION WILL REMAIN, *for it cannot be contended, and indeed was not contended at their Lordships' bar, that, if the Act does not come within one of the classes of subjects assigned to the Provincial Legislatures, the Parliament of Canada had not, by its general power ' to make laws, for the peace, order and good government of Canada,'* FULL LEGISLATIVE AUTHORITY TO PASS IT."

His LORDSHIP, then, after thus laying down these important doctrines, names the three different classes of subjects in the 92nd section of the Act, in consequence of the existence of which it has been so strongly claimed in this Dominion that the Act was *ultra vires*, as *being an interference with the right of the Legislatures to legislate with respect to the subjects-matter named in those classes;* namely the 9th, 13th and 16th; and then proceeds to show—*no! that the Act is not an interference with those subjects-matter, for the very contrary is shown*—but that the Act in question does not " fall within" either of those sub-sections; i. e., *is not such an Act as would be within the competency of the Local Legislature to pass under either of the said sub-sections.*

It is then shown that it does *not come within,* (*it interferes with, pretty clearly, and breaks it down and " over-rides " it*), the clause relating to licenses, as follows,—

"The Act in question is not a fiscal law; it is not a law for raising revenue;" (the 9th class is " licenses in order to the raising of a revenue"); on the contrary, *the effect of it may be to destroy or diminish revenue;* indeed it was a main objection to the Act that in the City of Fredericton *it did in fact diminish the sources of municipal revenue.* It is evident, therefore, *that the matter of the*

Act is not within the class of subject No. 9, and consequently that it could not have been passed by the Provincial Legislature by virtue of any authority conferred upon it by that sub-section."

Attention is also directed to the fact that the power of granting licenses is not assigned to the Provincial Legislatures for the purpose of regulating trade, as, it is thus conceded, the Canada Temperance Act is such an Act, (contrary to the very strong contestation of Judge HENRY, and of all the Judges of the Supreme Court of N. B. in *Ex parte* Grieves), but, " in order to the raising of a revenue for provincial, local or municipal purposes."

The next paragraph, so fully deals with the question, and lays down such important principles, that we insert it entire : thus,—

" It appears that by statutes of the Province of New Brunswick, authority has been conferred upon the municipality of Fredericton to raise money for municipal purposes by granting licenses of the nature of those described in No. 9 of Sect. 92, and that licenses granted to taverns for the sale of intoxicating liquors were a profitable source of revenue to the municipality. It was contended by the appellant's counsel, *and it was their main argument on this part of the case, that the Temperance Act interfered prejudicially with the traffic from which this revenue was derived, and thus invaded a subject assigned exclusively to the Provincial Legislature.* But, supposing the effect of the Act to be prejudicial to the revenue derived by the municipality from license, it does not follow that the Dominion Parliament might not pass it by virtue of the general authority to make laws for the peace, order and good government of Canada. *Assuming that the matter of the Act does fall within the class of subject described in No. 9, that sub-section can in no way interfere with the general authority of the Parliament to deal with that matter.* If the argument of the appellant that the power given to the Provincial Legislatures to raise a revenue by licenses prevents the Dominion from legislating with regard to any article or commodity which was or might be covered by such licenses, were to prevail, the consequence would be that laws which might be necessary for the public good or the public safety would not be enacted at all. Suppose it were deemed to be necessary or expedient for the national safety, or for political reasons, to prohibit the sale of arms, or the carrying of arms, it could not be contended that a Provincial Legislature would have authority, by virtue of sub-section 9, (which alone is now under discussion), to pass any such law, nor, if the appellant's argument were to prevail, would the Dominion Parliament be competent to pass it, since such a law would interfere prejudicially with the revenue derived from licenses granted under the authority of the Provincial Legislatures for the sale or the carrying of arms. Their Lordships think that the right construction of the enactments does not lead to any such inconvenient consequences. *It appears to them that legislation of the kind referred to, though it might interfere with the sale or use of an article included in a license granted under sub-section 9, is not in itself legislation upon or within the subject of that sub-section, and consequently is not by reason of it taken out of the general power of the Parliament of the Dominion.* It is to be observed that the express provision of the Act in question *that no license shall avail to render legal any act done in violation of it, is only the expression,* inserted probably from abundant caution, *of what would be necessarily implied from the legislation itself,* assuming it to be valid."

Their LORDSHIPS next show that no matter how much the Act may interfere with property and civil rights, inasmuch as the Act in question could not have been passed by the Local Legislatures within the proper meaning of those terms, as used in sub-section 13, the Act is within the jurisdiction of Parliament ; concluding their argument on this point, thus,—

"Few, if any, laws could be made by Parliament for the peace, order and good government of Canada, which did not in some incidental way, affect property and civil rights ; and it could not have been intended, when assuring to the Provinces exclusive legislative authority on the subjects of property and civil rights, to exclude the Parliament from the exercise of this general power whenever any such incidental interference would result from it. *The true nature and character of the legislation in the particular instance under consideration, must always be determined, in order to ascertain the class of subject to which it really belongs.*"

The last sentence of the above has a direct bearing on the correct judgment of the Supreme Court of Canada in the Fisheries Case ; which, like the Mercer Escheat Case, as we have shown, has been entirely misapprehended ; the principles on which these cases were decided being simple in the extreme ; and in no way, whatever, breaking down and affecting the rule given in the latter part of the first clause of sect. 91, that, in cases of conflict between the powers of Parliament and of the Local Legislatures, respecting the *bona fide* legislating upon the subjects enumerated in secs. 91

and 92, respectively, the powers of Parliament over-ride; and, as far as may be necessary in the particular case, break down the powers of the Local Legislatures with respect to the matters named in sec. 92, that may be affected by the legislation of Parliament, *bona fide*, within the classes of subjects enumerated in sec. 91. Russell *v.* The Queen establishes the additional doctrine that, unless the Act of Parliament, in question, for the peace, order and good government of Canada, comes within one or other of the sub-sections of section 92, so that the Act could be passed by the Local Legislatures, by virtue thereof, the Act in question is *intra vires* Parliament, no matter how much it may interfere with or destroy the powers of the Local Legislatures to legislate with respect to the subjects-matter named in such sub-sections; just as the Canada Temperance Act, as "would be necessarily implied from the legislation itself," even without it having been expressed in the Act, was held, in the case we are examining, to render all the licenses within the purview of the Canada Temperance Act invalid.

In dealing with the question as to whether the Act "*fell within*," (not interfered with or over-rode), sub-section 16, relative to "matters of a merely local or private nature in the Province," and deciding that it did not, it is observed, that,—

"It was not, *of course*, contended for the appellant that the Legislature of New Brunswick could have passed the Act in question, which embraces in its enactments all the Provinces; *nor was it denied*, with respect to this last contention, *that the Parliament of Canada might have passed an Act of the nature of that under discussion to take effect at the same time throughout the whole Dominion.*"

But it was, "*of course*," as we have seen, very strongly contended in this Dominion, that Parliament could *not* pass "an Act of the nature of that under discussion to take effect at the same time throughout the whole Dominion;" and one of the grounds upon which this strong contention was based, was, that such an Act would *interfere* with the right of the Local Legislatures with respect to matters of a merely local or private nature in the Provinces. A good deal has been made of the statement by the Judicial Committee of the Privy Council, that the case of Russell *v.* The Queen has been misunderstood. It is quite obvious, that, in one direction, it has been egregiously misunderstood. Why, to this very day, it is argued, just as was held by the majority of the Judges in the Supreme Court of New Brunswick, on this same question, and as was urged by counsel in the Supreme Court of Canada, that the Parliament of the Dominion cannot pass an Act the effect of which is to interfere with; to "over-ride," or to "exclude" the legislation of the Local Legislatures; notwithstanding the clear, unequivocal, most extreme holding, on that point, in this same case of Russell v. The Queen. Their LORDSHIPS were so entirely unprepared seriously to consider such an absurd position, that it is not surprising that they *were a little mystified*, (we are not now taking the position that that whole judgment is unmitigated nonsense), as to what the contestation really was, of those, who, to-day, still claim that the Local Legislatures have an absolutely *exclusive* power to legislate with respect to all the subjects-matter in section 92; and that Parliament has no right or power to *interfere*, in its legislation, with any of such subjects-matter. Why, the opening speech of the Lieut. Gov. of N. B., and the closing speech of the Lieut. Gov. of Ontario, at the opening and closing, respectively, of the last session of the Legislatures of those Provinces, were conspicuous for claiming that recent cases went to preserve "*the political autonomy of the Provinces against the dangers which threaten it from Federal encroachments;*" meaning thereby, that those cases had established some very different doctrine from that which is embodied in the latter part of the first clause, and in the closing clause of section 91; and which now, by the first part of such first clause, is shown, *by this case of Russell v. The Queen*, to be established by it as well. To show in what a very different way their LORDSHIPS supposed the contention to be, we give it as stated by themselves. They simply understood the contention to be—

"That, at least in the absence of a general law of the Parliament of Canada, the Provinces might have passed a local law of a like kind, each for its own Province, and that as the prohibitory and penal parts of the Act in question were to come into force in those counties and cities only in which it was adopted in the manner prescribed, or, as it was said, ' by local option,' *the legislation was in effect, and on its face*, upon a matter of a merely local nature."

The learned Board seem to have got that view from a portion of the judgment of ALLEN, C. J., in the Supreme Court of N. B., in which it was held that "An Act which, in effect, authorizes the inhabitants of each town or parish to regulate the sale of liquor, and to direct from whom, for what purposes, and under what conditions spirituous liquors may be sold therein, deals with matters of a merely local nature, which, by the terms of the 16th sub-section of section 92 of the British North America Act, are within the exclusive control of the Local Legislatures." It is no wonder, amid the strange collection of contradictory and absurd views that the different judgments in the case, in the Supreme Court of N. B., contained, that their LORDSHIPS found it difficult to decide what those really meant, and to be candid, made it somewhat difficult to tell what their LORDSHIPS themselves meant. But meeting the very moderate view of the contention, as their LORDSHIPS viewed it, even that is summarily disposed of in the following observations,—

"Their LORDSHIPS cannot concur in this view. The declared object of Parliament in passing the Act is that there should be uniform legislation in all the Provinces respecting the traffic in intoxicating liquors, with a view to promote temperance in the Dominion. Parliament does not treat the promotion of temperance as desirable in one Province more than in another, but as desirable everywhere throughout the Dominion. The Act, as soon as it was passed, became a law for the whole Dominion, and the enactments of the first part, relating to the machinery for bringing the second part into force, took effect and might be put in motion at once and everywhere within it. It is true that the prohibitory and penal parts of the Act, are only to come into force in any county or city upon the adoption of a petition to that effect by a majority of electors, but this conditional application of these parts of the Act does not convert the Act itself into legislation in relation to a merely local matter. The objects and scope of the legislation are still general, viz., to promote temperance by means of a uniform law throughout the Dominion."

Their LORDSHIPS conclude as follows,—

"Parliament deals with the subject as one of general concern to the Dominion, upon which uniformity of legislation is desirable, *and the Parliament alone can so deal with it.* There is no ground or pretence for saying that the evil or vice struck at by the Act in question is local or exists only in one Province, and that Parliament, under color of general legislation, is dealing with a Provincial matter only. It is, therefore, unnecessary to discuss the considerations which a state of circumstances of this kind might present. The present legislation is clearly meant to apply a remedy to an evil which is assumed to exist throughout the Dominion, and the local option, as it is called, no more localizes the subject and scope of the Act than a provision in an Act for the prevention of contagious diseases in cattle, that a public officer should proclaim in what districts it should come in effect, would make the statute itself a mere local law for each of these districts. In statutes of this kind the legislation is general, and the provision for the special application of it to particular places does not alter its character."

Their LORDSHIPS having, then, come to the conclusion that the Act, although it is one that interferes with property and civil rights; with the right to grant licenses, &c., *does not fall within* classes of subjects named in the different sub-sections of section 92, so that the Provinces could pass such an Act; did not find it necessary to enquire whether it did not also fall within one of the enumerated classes of subjects in sect. 91, and so whether it did not still belong to the Dominion Parliament; but, as they refer to it as an Act "for the purpose of regulating trade," their reasoning shows very clearly that they would have so decided, if there had been room left to them, from their somewhat original mode of looking at the matter, for asking such a question. But, having decided, that, although it did, as they show, interfere with and exclude rights and powers of legislation that the Local Legislatures otherwise would have had under different clauses of sec. 92; the Act was, as being within the power of Parliament to legislate for the peace, order and good government of Canada, and not an Act which the Local Legislatures could pass under their powers in the 92nd sect., a valid Parliamentary Act; and that, their Lordships decided, ended the matter, and settled the question, that the local powers, under such circumstances, have to give way to the superior legislative power of Parliament, in such a case. But, in finding it unnecessary to put in force the second part of their rule, they say, that, thereby "they must not be understood as intimating any dissent from the opinion of the CHIEF JUSTICE of the Supreme Court of Canada and other JUDGES, who held that the Act, as a general regulation of the traffic in intoxicating liquors throughout the Dominion, fell within the class of subject, 'the regulation of trade and commerce,' enumerated in that section, and was, on that ground, a valid exercise of the legislative power of the Parliament of Canada."

So, it will now be seen, that, in addition to the doctrine that was previously established, under the latter part of the first clause, and the closing clause, of the 91st section, any *bona fide* legislation by Parliament on the subjects-matter enumerated in sec. 91, was valid, no matter how much such legislation interfered with, or infringed upon, the subjects-matter named in sec. 92; that very remarkable case of Russell v. the Queen, before the Judicial Committee of the Privy Council, establishes the additional doctrine, that, if the subject-matter of the Act does not, *bona fide*, come within any of the clauses of section 92, so that the Local Legislature could pass such Act, then, as an Act passed by Parliament for the peace, order and good government of Canada, it is a valid Act; no matter how much it interferes with; " over-rides," and " overbears" the power of the Local Legislatures with respect to any such subjects-matter in sec. 92; without the necessity of enquiring as to whether or not the Act is in reference to a subject named, specifically, in the 91st section.

That, then, down to this point, is the *ratio decidendi* of all the properly decided cases we have, so far, examined; assuming, as before named, at this stage of our investigation, that Russell v. The Queen is properly decided.

It now remains for us to examine the cases we have not yet examined, which, like the Mercer Escheat case, and the Fisheries case, which we have examined, it is claimed introduce a new rule, or some modification of the rules under which all the cases we have yet examined, rank themselves; at least as regards the validity of Acts of the Local Legislatures within the rules we have stated: the one important point established by Russell v. The Queen being that, because such an Act of Parliament, as was there considered, interferes with, or over-rides, or excludes the power of the Local Legislatures with respect to any of the subjects-matter named in sec. 92, it does not thereby come within such section 92, so as to render it even necessary to enquire whether it does not also come within section 91, and still be *intra vires* Parliament; unless it be an Act which not only interferes with some of the sub-sections of 92, but which, also, under such sub-sections, might have been enacted by the Local Legislatures. We are done with that Privy Council case for the present; but we will return to it again.

During the campaign of February, 1882, in St. John, N. B., connected with the Canada Temperance Act, a leading opponent of that Act, the Editor of one of the leading political journals of Canada, published an editorial, prior to the argument of Russell v. The Queen before the Privy Council, in which he asserted that " the tendency of the recent decisions in the Privy Council is adverse to the constitutionality of the Canada Temperance Act."

The writer was interviewed by a leading representative of the St. John SUN, as to the correctness of this assertion; in answer to which he furnished the SUN with an analysis of the cases reported in the L. R's, down to that time, and showed that the assertion was not well founded. About a week after this, under the inspiration of the leading counsel in N. B., opposed to the C. T. Act, and quoting liberally from an editorial in the Toronto *Globe*, in which it was alleged, that, "in view of what the Privy Council have said, (in the Citizens' Insurance Co. *v.* Parsons), about Provincial jurisdiction in matters of trade, the fate of the Scott Act, now before them on appeal, is, to say *the least* of it, rendered somewhat doubtful;" claimed that the views that the writer had expressed, in the interview named, were not law. In reply to this, the writer furnished the SUN with a strictly accurate analysis of the case of

THE CITIZENS' INSURANCE CO. *v.* PARSONS,

and called attention to the fact that that case, in the Privy Council, was but an affirmation of the holding of SIR WM. RITCHIE, in the Supreme Court of Canada, whose generally correct views, in that Court, on matters relating to Constitutional questions, under the B. N. A. Act, it was claimed could not be impugned. Quoting the language of Mr. Justice TASCHEREAU in that case, as to the holding of the Privy Council, in Cushing *v.* Dupuy, as follows,— "In that case it was contended by the appellant that the provisions of the Dominion Insolvency Act were *ultra vires*, because they interfered with property and civil rights, as well as with the procedure in civil matters, all of which are assigned exclusively to the Provincial Legislatures by the B. N. A. Act. *But that contention was disapproved by their Lordships;*"—it was claimed that, unless the Privy Council reversed their own previous judgments, the constitutionality of the Canada Temperance Act must be sustained ; and to hold otherwise would be to "strike at the root of the great mass of Dominion legislation and judicial decision since Confederation." In fact, if the views about the "political autonomy of the Provinces," that were then fore-shadowed, and which are being so strongly pressed now, were sound, the Parliament, for legislative purposes, would be utterly useless. The anticipations of the Toronto *Globe*, and its contemporary, relative to the result in the Privy Council, as to the validity of the C. T. Act, were, happily, not sustained.

We proceed now to examine this case of The Citizens' Insurance Co. v. Parsons, in the Supreme Court of Canada ; 4 S. C. R. 215. There are two other Insurance cases treated with it, both in the Supreme Court of Canada, and in the Privy Council, to all of which we shall refer so far as may be necessary for the purposes of this examination.

The questions decided in these cases were—

First, That an Ontario " Fire Insurance Policy Act," passed since Confederation, was not *ultra vires*, and was applicable to Insurance Companies, (whether foreign or incorporated by the Dominion), licensed to carry on the insurance business throughout Canada, and taking risks on property, situate within the Province of Ontario ; and *second*, that the legislation on questions, prescribing conditions incidental to insurance contracts, passed in Ontario, relating to property situate in Ontario, was not a regulation of Trade and Commerce within the meaning of these words in sub-sec. 2, sec. 91, B. N. A. Act. From this holding TASCHEREAU and GWYNNE, JJ. dissented.

In both of the Courts below—Queen's Bench, and the Court of Appeal—the Ontario Act, in question, was held *intra vires* the Local Legislature. As the judgment of the Supreme Court of Canada was sustained by the Privy Council, (thus, the whole four Courts holding the Act was not *ultra vires*), with such decisions on the question involved, as we have seen have been so repeatedly delivered by the Supreme Court of Canada and by the Privy Council, it would be a surprise if this case went *contra* to those decisions; more particularly, as we have seen, the case in the Privy Council of Russell v. The Queen, subsequent to the Parsons Insurance case, in extending the power of Parliament to legislate, and in correspondingly limiting the power of the Legislatures, went farther in opposition to the doctrine that was supposed to have been established in the Insurance cases, than any other case that has preceded it. This last remark is peculiarly correct as applicable to the decisions of the Supreme Court of Canada.

If, in this last named Court, the decision had been given on the grounds taken in the case by the Appellants' counsel, (Mr. *Mowat*, Mr. *Bethune*, Mr. *Robinson* and Mr. *Small*), the Toronto *Globe* would have been quite justified in its expectations that the Canada Temperance Act would have been declared *ultra vires ;* and not only would that Act have been so declared, but nearly every other Act of Parliament since Confederation would have shared the same fate; and Parliament would have been virtually powerless for evil or for good.

It must certainly be so apparent to our readers by this time, that the extravagant claims that have been recently so loudly and conspicuously made in favor of a jurisdiction in the Legislatures which they do not possess, are entirely unfounded, that it seems almost like fighting a shadow to pursue the subject further; but, as we wish to get at proper, unquestionable answers to the whole of the questions, with which, at the outset of this examination, we confronted ourselves; we shall make the examination of the questions thoroughly exhaustive, so as to leave no aperture for escape from the conclusions to which we shall simply let the decided cases, and a straight-forward examination of them, bring us; wherever that may be. Certainly, it will not be to sustain any such nonsensical views as were urged for the Respondents in the Supreme Court of Canada, in the cases now before us. It is not, at all, mythical, that such a contention was there made as that to which we have adverted.

Thus, the position was distinctly taken by those very prominent counsel for the Respondents, that, (p. 229),—

"*The Provincial Legislatures are not in any accurate sense subordinate to the Parliament of Canada: each body is independent and supreme within the limits of its own jurisdiction;* so that even if contracts are considered a kind of commerce, they are still governed by section 92, *the powers in which should be read as exceptions to those conferred upon Parliament by section 91 B. N. A. Act.*"

We have, so often, pointed out the utter absurdity of this contention,—persisted in, most pertinaciously, to this very day—and the destructive result that it would have upon, virtually, all the powers of Parliament, if the powers on the subjects-matter in section 92 were "*exceptions*" to the powers of Parliament in section 91, that it is unnecessary to go over the same thing here again.

They emphasize their altogether absurd position, to make it still more distinct and positive, and say,—

"*If the Local Legislature has jurisdiction respecting the subject-matter of insurance contracts at all, it has the most full and ample jurisdiction — plenum imperium—it has sovereign power within its own limits.*"

This, in the other direction, is the exact converse of the equally fallacious holding of the Supreme Court of British Columbia, in the Thrasher Case. That the broad and destructive doctrine that they lay down has not been better established than it has been, they simply attribute to the following reason, evidently using the word " Parliament " instead of " Executive : " (p. 230),—

" The fact that certain powers have been assumed by Parliament hitherto proves little, for the Provinces have not power to disallow those Acts, and can only look to the Courts for defence against the encroachments of the Federal power, whereas Acts passed by the Local Legislatures might be disallowed by the Dominion Parliament."

" Looking to the Courts for defence against " Federal enactments, would seem to be a very reasonable course to pursue. Looking, as we are doing, " to the Courts," to ascertain whether the legislation named is " encroachment," though, seems to settle the matter, very plainly, in the other direction. It is very certain that the cases we are now examining do not help Mr. *Mowat* and his *confreres* in establishing their extreme, and extremely unsound, positions.

The question in this case, simply was, as affects the matter we are investigating, whether there was any subject-matter under which the legislation of the Parliament came, that would oust the jurisdiction of the Legislatures with reference to the legislation by them, making certain regulations about policies of insurance. It was claimed that there was, and that such legislation came within the " Regulation of Trade and Commerce." But the decision simply was that the legislation in question did not come within that subject-matter, and that, being properly within the jurisdiction of the Legislature, there was, therefore, nothing whatever to oust the jurisdiction. There is not a single well decided authority anywhere that holds any different doctrine. The two well decided cases of Reg. *v.* McMillan and *ex parte* Fairbairn, which we have examined, decided years ago in the Supreme Court of New Brunswick, go even farther than these cases we are considering; because, in those cases, there was no doubt, whatever, that the subjects-matter legislated upon by the N.B. Legislature were within a subject-matter that Parliament might have legislated upon. The rule, which we will see, will show what the law is in all such cases, and which we shall evolve from the decided cases and the reasoning thereon ; will, we trust, when we state it, in due course, accurately " define " the powers of the Legislatures in all such cases.

As we have seen in the Fisheries case, that Parliament recognized, by the Fishery Act, legal outstanding rights which the Act was not to affect; so, SIR WM. RITCHIE shows, in these cases, similar "recognition and affirmation," by Parliament, "of the powers of the Local Legislatures," with respect to the matters disputed in the cases. The following is one of the sections quoted by the learned CHIEF JUSTICE, from an Act of Parliament passed as long ago as 1868; 31 Vic., ch. 8, sec. 25, thus, (p. 235),—

"That the provisions of this Act as to the deposit and issue of licenses shall not apply to any Insurance Company incorporated by any Act of the Legislature of the late Province of Canada, or incorporated, *or to be incorporated, under any Act of any of the Provinces of Ontario, Quebec, Nova Scotia or New Brunswick;*" (the italics are by SIR WILLIAM), "so long as it shall not carry on business in the Dominion *beyond the limits of that Province* by the Legislature or Government of which it was incorporated, but it shall be lawful for any *such Company to avail itself* of the provisions of this Act."

SIR WM. RITCHIE, in his judgment, very accurately describes the powers of the two legislative bodies. To show there *are* powers in the Local Legislatures which Parliament has no right to touch, except in so far as legitimate *bona fide* legislation within the subjects-matter of section 91, enables them to do so; taking a strictly analogous position in these cases to that which the same learned and accomplished Lawyer took in the Fisheries Case, and in the Mercer Escheat Case, referring to sub-sec. 10 of sec. 92, he showed, that, clearly, there were subjects-matter there in the Local Legislatures that Parliament had no right to touch, except so far as might be done by legitimate *bona fide* legislation on some one or other of the subjects-matter in sec. 91. As, we submit, it is a perfectly accurate statement of the law as it *is*; avoiding both the absurd extremes that would either render Parliament utterly incapable of legislating, or else, would deprive the Local Legislatures of all power, ("from Scylla to Charybdis"), we give the paragraph entire :—

"If the power to legislate on navigation and shipping and trade and commerce, vested in the Dominion Parliament, necessarily excluded from Local Legislatures all legislation in connection with the same matters, and that nothing in relation thereto could be held to come under local works and undertakings, or property or civil rights, or generally all matters of a merely local or private nature in the Province, or the incorporation of companies with Provincial objects, what possible necessity could there be for inserting the exception 'other than such as are of the following classes as above, '(a. b. c.) ? On the contrary, does not this exception show beyond all doubt, by irresistible inference, that there are matters connected with navigation and shipping, and with trade and commerce, that the Local Legislatures may deal with and not encroach on the general powers belonging to the Dominion Parliament for the regulation of trade and commerce, and navigation and shipping, as well as railways, canals and telegraphs? Can it be successfully contended that this is not a clear intimation that the Local Legislatures were to have, and have, power to legislate in reference to lines of steamers and other ships, railways, canals, and other works and undertakings wholly within the Province, SUBJECT, NO DOUBT, *to the general powers of Parliament over shipping and trade and commerce, and the Dominion laws enacted under such powers*, as, for instance, the 31 Vic., ch. 65 (1868), 'An Act respecting the inspection of steamboats, and for the greater safety of passengers by them', or the Act 46 Vic., ch. 128, 'An Act relating to Shipping.'"

There, again, is the law clearly and correctly stated, and accords with the statement of our view of the law running through the whole of this treatise.

As this is one of the cases so strongly relied on to show the dominant power of the Local Legislature; or, to show, as the learned Counsel themselves put it, that,—"*the powers in which*, (sec. 92), *should be read* AS EXCEPTIONS *to those conferred upon Parliament by sec. 91, B. N. A. Act*," (*ante*); we quote still further from the leading judgment in the case; which, upon the very opposite grounds, on a thoroughly correct principle of law, held that the appeal should be dismissed. Says the learned CHIEF JUSTICE, further; giving the holders of such views very little comfort,—

"No one can dispute the general power of Parliament to legislate as to trade and commerce, *and that when, over matters* WITH WHICH LOCAL LEGISLATURES HAVE POWER TO DEAL, *local legislation conflicts with an Act passed by the Dominion Parliament in the exercise of any of the general powers confided to it*, THE LEGISLATION OF THE LOCAL MUST YIELD TO THE SUPREMACY OF THE DOMINION PARLIAMENT; in other words, that *the Provincial legislation in such a case must be subject to such regulations, for instance, as to trade and commerce of a commercial character, as the Dominion Parliament may prescribe.* I adhere to what I said in Valin v. Langlois, (3 S. C. R. 15), that the property and civil rights referred to, were not all property and all civil rights, but that the terms 'property and civil rights' must necessarily be read *in a restricted and limited sense,* because many matters involving property and civil rights are expressly reserved to the Dominion Parliament, and that *the power of the Local Legislatures was to be subject to the general and special legislative powers of the Dominion Parliament,* and to what I there added; ' But while *the legislative rights of the Local Legislatures are, in this sense, subordinate to the rights of the Dominion Parliament,* I think such right must be exercised, so far as may be, consistently with the right of the Local Legislatures; and, therefore, *the Dominion Parliament would only have the right to interfere with property and civil rights in so far as such interference may be necessary for the purpose of legislating generally and effectually, in relation to matters confided to the Parliament of Canada.*

" I think the power of the Dominion Parliament to regulate trade and commerce ought not to be held to be necessarily inconsistent with those of the Local Legislatures to regulate property and civil rights in respect to all matters of a merely local and private nature, such as matters connected with the enjoyment and preservation of property in the Province, or matters of contract between parties in relation to their property or dealings, although the exercise by the Local Legislatures of such powers may be said remotely to affect matters connected with trade and commerce, *unless, indeed, the laws of the Provincial Legislatures should conflict with those of the Dominion Parliament.*"

Quite ignoring the contention of Messrs. *Mowat, Bethune, Robinson* and *Small,* as we have shown them to have " claimed," (*supra*), and contended, the learned CHIEF JUSTICE makes the following correct distinctions applicable to the causes then before the Court. He adds,—

" I do not understand by the Act now assailed," (the Ontario Insurance Act), "any supreme sovereign legislative power to regulate and control the business of insurance in Ontario, is claimed. As I read the Act, it deals only with this contract of indemnity; *it does not profess to deal with trade and commerce in the sense in which these words are used in the British North America Act.* It is simply an exercise of the power of the Local Legislature for the protection of property in Ontario, and the civil right of the proprietors thereof in connection therewith, by securing a reasonable and just contract in favor of parties insuring property, real or personal, in Ontario, and deals therefore only with a matter of a local and private nature."

It was really, then, not a case of conflicting legislation at all; but a clear case of proper legislation by the Local Legislature of Ontario within its unquestionable power, and not in antagonism with any act of Parliament whatever. There is, however, another point alluded to is this judgment; and an extract containing it will be made in a more suitable place, when we refer to the point of error by Mr. Justice HENRY in the City of Fredericton *v.* Barker, and to which we have already made a passing reference.

Mr. Justice FOURNIER, too, in some parts of the following, is most admirable, while in other parts he comes very closely to the law, particularly as applicable to the facts in the case he was considering. He says, (p. 272),—

"In exercising its power, the Federal Parliament, no doubt, has the right to incidently entertain these matters which are under the jurisdiction of the Provinces, but this power cannot extend any further than to what is just and reasonable and necessary in order to legislate for commercial purposes only. The Federal Parliament could not, therefore, *under the pretence* of legislating on commerce, entirely control a subject-matter which comes under the jurisdiction of the Provinces. *Any legislation having reference to the regulation of commerce must be complete, but it need not necessarily destroy the jurisdiction of the Provinces over that part of the subject-matter* WHICH IS NOT AFFECTED BY SUCH LEGISLATION. If this was not the case, whenever the Federal power in exercise of its authority over commerce, should legislate in such a manner as to indirectly affect property and civil rights, it would follow that all legislation over the subject-matter would belong exclusively to the Federal Parliament, and the legislative power of the Provinces over the same matter would cease to exist."

The further we go in the investigation of the subject the more surprised we are at the continuance, to this day, of such absurd positions as were taken by Mr. *Mowat*, Mr. *Bethune*, &c., in this case. If the evidence were not so overwhelming, as a continuous series of such claims shows it to be, that, on the one hand, one set of men are claiming that Parliament has, virtually, no legislative power at all; while, on the other, there are those of the opposite view, who would adopt such rules of construction as would utterly deprive the Legislatures of all their legislative power, we could scarcely credit it that men of high political, and others of equally high judicial, standing, should continuously disseminate views that partake of the character of puerility itself. We will endeavour to hold the scales of justice, even-handed, between them, and, weighing all the different claims, arrive at a correct decision ; and, removing all of error about those opposing claims, as far as we are able to do so, no matter by whom made; set forth, honestly and faithfully, THE TRUTH !

The learned JUDGE, (FOURNIER), proceeding further, has this admirable passage,—

" In order to reconcile the exercise of these powers, I have arrived at the conclusion, in a case such as the one now under consideration, that the Provincial jurisdiction is only limited by the exercise by the Federal Parliament of its power in so far as the latter is competent to exercise it, *and that the Province can still exercise its power over that portion of the subject-matter over which it has jurisdiction, provided the Provincial legislation does not directly conflict with the Federal legislation.*"

And, seeing, as did the learned CHIEF JUSTICE, (as is also observable in the legislation of Parliament with reference to the Fisheries), that, in this case, also, there is an express recognition and acknowledgment by Parliament, of the right of the Local Legislatures to legislate on the subject-matter of this case, the learned JUDGE comes to the following conclusion :—

" We find, therefore, that the Federal legislation does not in anywise affect the nature of the contract of insurance, nor the conditions forming part of such contract, and that the legislation of Ontario, now under consideration, deals exclusively with that subject,—both legislations deriving their respective powers from different sources, the first from the power of regulating trade and commerce, and the other from their power of legislating over property and civil rights. Why, if the provisions of these laws are neither conflicting nor antagonistic to one another, can we not hold that both are constitutional ? *I must confess that I see between them no conflict, and I see no obstacle to their being carried into operation.*"

Thus, holding that the subject-matter—the legislating as to the conditions of insurance policies by companies doing business in Ontario—did not properly come within the regulation of trade and commerce, as one of the subjects-matter controlled by Parliament, it was obvious that the regulations were simply local in reference to a matter in the Province ; and, thus, expressly, the subject-matter was within the jurisdiction of the Local Legislature. So, thus, applying the rule laid down in this case in the Privy

Council, and repeated by it, and acted on most effectually *and most radically,* in Russell *v.* The Queen, in reply to the first question, "Is this Act one within the competency of the Local Legislature, under any of the subjects-matter in sec. 92 ?" the answer is,—" It is." And, then, putting the second question,—" Does it also come within either of the clauses of sec. 91, so as to over-bear or over-ride the power of the Local Legislature to pass it ?" and the reply is, " It does not." The case, under the discussion, is, clearly, found to be rightly decided under the tests furnished by the Judicial Committee of the Privy Council. More of these "tests" again, under a somewhat different view, and under what might be called a new inspiration.

Mr. Justice HENRY agrees with the learned CHIEF JUSTICE and Mr. Justice FOURNIER in the result to which they arrive, that the Act in question was *intra vires* the Ontario Legislature. But, having previously, incorrectly, held—standing alone in the Court in so doing—that the Canada Temperance Act was *ultra vires* Parliament, while, as a necessary consequence to such holding, there would be no escape for him from holding that the converse was, from his point of view, equally true; and that he would, therefore, necessarily hold that the Ontario Act was *intra vires* the Local Legislature; but, even in holding right, as he does so only as the result of an error in reasoning, we cannot expect to find his reasoning in this case, even, sound. Nor do we so. Take the following. After stating,—"As I have before said, we must construe the whole Act together, and so to give effect, if possible, to every part of it, and reconcile, and ascertain what seeming contradictions the British Act contains;" the learned JUDGE argues thus erroneously :—

" From the peculiar distribution of the legislative powers," he proceeds to say, " and the mode adopted, it was a difficult undertaking to legislate so as to prevent difficulties arising, but they are to be properly resolved only by keeping prominently in view the leading objects intended to be provided for. Looking only at number 26 in the list contained in section 92, we find 'The solemnization of marriage in the Province' is expressly given to the Local Legislatures. No doubt can be entertained that, considering *both* provisions," (the italics are his own), "notwithstanding any other provision of the Act, the intention was to give the solemnization of marriage to the Local Legislatures. I admit that the two cases are not exactly alike, but still it shows that no one part of the Act should alone be looked at."

As intimated by us before, these two subjects of "marriage," and "solemnization of marriage in the Province," contained, respectively, in the 91st and 92nd sections of the Act, have been a great stumbling block in the way of learned JUDGES, who, in their efforts to deal with the principles of construction governing the Act, have tried, if they possibly could, to get some "hard and fast rule or canon of construction" on which to rest. But these subjects, marriage on the one hand, and "solemnization of marriage in the Province," on the other, have been the rock on which they have split. So, as a general rule, they give a wide berth to them, and try to steer clear of them entirely; or, if they do attempt to deal with them, their efforts in doing so are most fantastic. One such attempt we have referred to, that was made by Mr. Justice GWYNNE, in one of the cases we examined. As we have seen, the Act itself lays down just such a "hard and fast rule or canon of construction," by which we are to be governed; and, intelligently examined, there is no necessity of shirking it, on the one hand, nor of indulging in fantastic, ridiculous explanations of it, on the other. Take the rule, now, again, as we have done once before, and apply it to these two subjects-matter, frankly. The rule then, so applied, is "The exclusive power of Parliament, (notwithstanding anything in this Act), shall extend to the subject of marriage, and, *subject to this*," (the meaning of "notwithstanding anything in this Act"), "the exclusive power of the Legislatures extends to the subject of solemnization of marriage in the Province; and, any matter coming within the subject of marriage shall not be deemed to come within the subject of solemnization of marriage in the Province, no matter how much it may *appear* to do so, or how much it *actually* does so, so as to prevent Parliament from effectually legislating on the general subject of marriage."

Where's the difficulty now? Parliament may effectually legislate on the general subject of marriage for the Dominion, and if, in doing so, as an incident to such effectual legislation, it legislates also so as to effect solemnization of marriage in all the different Provinces, by the very language of the Act, it has, expressly, the power to do so. We have already furnished an instance of this, which it is unnecessary here to repeat. Then, having so legislated, the question arises with reference to the Act, under the tests given by the decisions in the Supreme Court of Canada, in reply to the questions proposed in the Privy Council,—"Does the Act in question, (a general Act relating to marriage for the whole

Dominion, incidentally dealing with solemnization of marriage), *fall within any of the classes of subjects enumerated in section 92, and assigned exclusively to the Legislatures of the Provinces?"* (First test from Russell v. The Queen, 7 App. Cas., at p. 836). Assuming now, that, in the Supreme Court of Canada, and as the *ratio decidendi* of their holding in the City of Fredericton v. Barker, the answer would be, (as the Act in that case, while treated as a legislation on the regulation of trade, it was also admitted was an interference with Property and Civil Rights; with Licenses, and with local and private matters in the Province); " Yes, it does 'fall within' a subject-matter named in section 92; or, at least, there is in the Act a legislation on a matter coming within the *classes* (as SIR WILLIAM RITCHIE inadvertently, but, in effect, correctly, quoted the word 'class') of matters of a local or private nature comprised in the enumeration of the classes of subjects by the B. N. A. Act assigned exclusively to the Legislatures of the Provinces."

Then, still following the *rationale* of the holding in the Supreme Court of Canada, in the Canada Temperance Act case, the Privy Council's next test is applied,—Does it also come within either of the subjects-matter in sec. 91 so as to "over-ride" or "over-bear," or "exclude" the legislation of the Local Legislatures to the extent to which Parliament has effectually legislated on any subject-matter enumerated in the 91st section? The reply, again, necessarily, is,—" Yes." And, therefore, by the very language of the Act, it is good legislation, just as much as the Canada Temperance Act is, regulating the Trade or Traffic in Intoxicating Liquors, because it is within the subject of " Trade and Commerce," no matter how much it interferes with " Property and Civil Rights in the Province;" " Tavern licenses in order to the raising of a revenue for local or Provincial purposes," or " Generally matters of a merely local or private nature in the Province." Just as good legislation as legislation by Parliament is, on The Regulation of Trade and Commerce, with reference to *anything* coming within that; or on Navigation and Shipping; Sea Coast and Inland Fisheries; Currency and Coinage; Banks and Banking; Bills of Exchange and Promissory Notes; Bankruptcy and Insolvency; Copyrights; Indians and Indian Lands; Naturalization and Aliens, or any other of the subjects-matter named in sec. 91, no matter how much such legislation, on such subjects-matter, may interfere with, over-ride, over-bear, exclude or supersede the legislation of the Local Legislatures, with respect to Property and Civil Rights; or to Property or Civil Rights; or to matters of a merely local or private nature in the Province; or to any other of the subordinate, inferior, subjects-matter enumerated in section 92.

Now, next, apply to the case we have assumed, the very much stronger answers to the tests in favor of the dominant legislative power of Parliament, as furnished by the Judicial Committee of the Privy Council in the case we are now examining, and commenting on; and as applied by them in the case of Russell v. The Queen, as we have seen was done; and ask the same question with reference to the supposed Act on marriage, for the Dominion, with, as an incident in it, legislation on the "solemnization of marriage," such as we have named; as was asked by the Judicial Committee of the Privy Council with respect to the Canada Temperance Act. Thus, using the very language of the Privy Council,—"DOES THE ACT NOW IN QUESTION FALL WITHIN any of the classes of subjects enumerated in section 92, and assigned exclusively to the Legislatures of the Provinces?" Answering the question, then, as was answered by the Privy Council, in Russell v. The Queen, where an Act regulating Trade and Commerce in the Dominion, in spirituous liquors, which directly interfered with property and civil rights in the Provinces; with the right to grant licenses for local purposes; and with local and private matters in the Province, was, notwithstanding all this, decided *not to be an Act* which "*fell within* any of the classes of subjects enumerated in section 92, and assigned exclusively to the Legislatures of the Provinces;" the answer, in the assumed case of legislation by Parliament on marriage, which has, as an incident, legislation on the solemnization of marriage, is, that it *is not an Act that* "*falls within any of the classes of subjects enumerated in section 92, and assigned exclusively to the Legislatures of the Provinces.*" Then, the language, further, by the Privy Council, is as applicable to the assumed case as to the other, *and to all other cases on the question;* for the rules or canons of construction which they lay down, *are* "hard and fast rules or canons," whether right or wrong, which are generally applicable, and which, on such high authority, are the tests which are to be applied to the cases as they arise. Such language is as follows,—"If it does, then the further question would arise, viz. *whether the subject of the Act does not fall within one of the enumerated classes of subjects in sec. 91, and so does not still belong to the Dominion*

Parliament. But, *if the Act does not fall within any of the classes of subjects in sec.* 92, NO FURTHER QUESTION WILL REMAIN, *for it cannot be contended,* and indeed was not contended at their Lordships' bar, that, *if the Act* does not come within one of the classes of subjects assigned to the Provincial Legislatures, the Parliament of Canada had not, by its general power ' to make laws for the peace, order and good government of Canada,' *full legislative authority to pass it."* (*Supra*).

Passing on, we find, that, as Mr. Justice HENRY has entirely misapprehended the meaning of the B. N. A. Act, the whole of his argument is bad. And, although his vicious reasoning, from the Act, does not, necessarily, in this case, prevent him from agreeing with the decision, correctly arrived at by his learned colleagues, the CHIEF JUSTICE and Mr. Justice FOURNIER; as it caused him to differ with the judgment correctly arrived at, of all his colleagues, in The City of Fredericton v. Barker, yet his judgment is no better in this case, than in that.

Simply wishing to deal, fearlessly and faithfully, with the questions we are examining, with the view of getting at the truth, and the whole truth, whether the effect be to exalt the judgments of SIR WM. RITCHIE, delivered in the Supreme Court of Canada, with the almost total exemption which they present to fairly hostile criticism ; or, relatively, to put some other JUDGES, who have dabbled in a question so far beyond their power as analysts, in a perfectly fair position, is no affair of ours. Claiming the right of fair criticism, and unhesitatingly exercising that right, we shall simply treat the arguments of those with whom we come in contact in our examination of this question, as though we were fairly criticising a book without the remotest conception in the world as to who might be its author :—" Nothing extenuating, nor setting down aught in malice !"

We will, thus, give one short clause more, from the judgment of the same learned JUDGE, Mr. Justice HENRY: (p. 287),—

" I have no doubt," says the learned JUDGE, "that the Dominion Parliament has power to enact general regulations in regard to trade and commerce, *but not to interfere with the powers of the Local Legislatures* in the matter of local contracts, amongst which is properly included policies of insurance against loss by fire on property in the same Province."

The only ground upon which Mr. Justice HENRY would contend that the Dominion Parliament, in enacting "general regulations in regard to trade and commerce," cannot "interfere with the powers of the Local Legislatures" as above, is because such local powers are included in either the *civil rights* or *local or private matters* reserved to the Local Legislatures—"exclusively," if, in the sense in which the word is used, you choose to call it so,—by the 92nd section of the B. N. A. Act. This, as the whole Dominion knows, has so often been contended; and, although its utter, unmitigated, absurdity, has so often been shown, is, *to this very day*, very strongly contended, in Legislative bodies, and in Courts; in Governors' addresses; in political speeches; in legal arguments; in newspaper articles; in pamphlets, and in " letters;"—a very pretentious re-printed one, only the other day. In this treatise, having again and again come in contact with that absurdity; we have again and again exposed it; simply because it is the *radical* error, (the word is not used in a political sense), that has jutted up, so continuously, in the arguments, and in the judgments, in the cases we have been examining. To repeat it *once* more: If Parliament cannot, in enacting "general regulations in regard to trade and commerce," " interfere with the powers of the Local Legislatures ;" then, more than "playing Hamlet with *the part of Hamlet* omitted," it is an attempt to play it *omitting all the parts.* For, if Parliament is excluded, in legislating generally in regard to trade and commerce, from touching *property* or *civil rights*, it is excluded from touching trade and commerce as well; the whole legislation in connection with which consists in legislating upon property and civil rights; or, on property or civil rights. There we leave, in all courtesy, Mr. Justice HENRY and that other quite large class of JUDGES, whose "reasoning" has been like his; with the class of errors of which they have been the unhappy exponents in connection with this question.

Turning now to the dissenting judgments of the learned Judges TASCHEREAU and GWYNNE, who, with SIR WM. RITCHIE, have a much clearer apprehension of the meaning of the B. N. A. Act than Mr. Justice HENRY; but, yet, who, unlike the learned CHIEF JUSTICE, run their comparatively correct view of the Act to too great an extreme; and, in consequence thereof, while giving correct decisions in all such cases as the Canada Temperance Act case; in all such cases as the case we are considering; the Mercer Escheat case, &c., the tendency of their views is to lead them to a wrong decision. It is our design honestly to sift their views, so as to get clear of the chaff of error, and leave us the grain of truth. For, in another sense, there is a *grain* of truth even in the worst judgment of the worst Judge of the worst Court.

Nearly the whole of the judgments of these learned Judges, in this case, are fairly over-flowing with error. Take one or two extracts from the judgment of Mr. Justice TASCHEREAU, which we, preserving the spirit of the judgment, make as short as possible:—

"For it must be admitted," says the learned JUDGE, "that under the B. N. A. Act, *there can be no concurrent jurisdiction* in the matter between the Federal and the local legislative authorities." P. 294.

And again, p. 306,—

"Either the Federal Parliament has no control at all over *Insurance Companies, or it has it supreme, entire and exclusive.*"

The meaning running through all this, is, that with respect to the same subject-matter, there cannot be legislation by both legislative bodies; each, it is claimed, having the "exclusive" right to legislate with respect to the subjects-matter committed to it; each, with respect to those, being "supreme, entire and exclusive." If, therefore, the one body can legislate with reference to Insurance Companies; the other cannot. This is a fair summary of Mr. Justice TASCHEREAU's judgment, outside of those portions of it in which the learned JUDGE shows, correctly,—as he really does show it in parts of his judgment—the nature and extent of the power of Parliament to legislate; and in other portions, as on page 210, he too greatly limits the Federal power. But, aside of these, his idea that on subjects-matter over which either has legislative power, there can be no "concurrent jurisdiction," as he terms it; meaning that the two bodies cannot legislate effectually on the same subject-matter, is an obvious error, which we have pointed out, over and over again. Parliament, legislating within its power in reference to the subject of shipping, can affect ships. The Local Legislature, not interfering with such legislation as Parliament has effectually had on the same subject-matter, ships; can, within its power, legislate on Property; and, in such legislation, can, within its power, affect the same subject-matter, ships. So, as we have shown, as regards the subjects of trade and commerce and licenses.

These instances show that the grounds taken by the learned JUDGE, against each of the legislative bodies being able to legislate, for the reasons alleged, on matters connected with Insurance Companies, was, then, clearly wrong. And the express recognition by Parliament in its Act, of the existence of *a kind* of concurrent legislation existing between both legislative bodies, as also, as we have seen, was the case with the Fisheries Act of Parliament, was perfectly correct; notwithstanding the very strong denial of Mr. Justice TASCHEREAU of the possibility of any such legislative power being in both bodies, and his view of the worthlessness of such Parliamentary admissions. See *Ibid.*, p. 317.

The learned Judge, Mr. Justice GWYNNE, argues, in his judgment, in the same way that Mr. Justice TASCHEREAU has argued in some parts of his. Thus, (p. 329),—

"It it clear that the subject-matter of the Act in question is not one over which jurisdiction is by the B. N. A. Act *given concurrently* to the Provincial Legislatures and to the Parliament. If it were, no doubt the Act would be valid as long and so far only, as it is not repugnant to any Act of the Parliament of Canada. The subject not being one over which jurisdiction is given to the Provincial Legislatures and to the Parliament, must be placed exclusively either under the one or the other."

Here, again, is the too greatly straining of the rule that the *exclusive* power is in Parliament to legislate on all the subjects-matter named in sec. 91. While it is perfectly true in a qualified sense that the "exclusive" power is given to Parliament to legislate on the subjects-matter named in that section; yet, it is equally true, that, in its broadest sense, several of the subjects-matter named in sec. 92, on which the Local Legislatures can legislate, are, directly, within subjects-matter in sec. 91; as instance, as before named, solemnization of marriage as within the wide subject of marriage; and the granting of shop, saloon, tavern, auctioneer and other licenses, as within the wide subject of trade. This, *necessarily*,—and therefore it is not at all singular that it should do so,—*involves a conflict* between the two legislative bodies; and such conflict, when it does occur, is expressly provided for in the Act. Thus, the Local Legislatures can, under the Act, *bona fide* legislate as to licenses, and, although, in one sense, that is legislating on a trade matter; yet, to that extent, *bona fide*, they can do so. So, also, in reference to solemnization of marriage in the Province, though that is a subject clearly within the wider subject of marriage. But, while the Local Legislatures can legislate on all the subjects-matter in section 92, within the legitimate scope of those subjects-matter, and not farther within the subjects-matter in sec. 91 than is necessarily involved in legislating alone on the subjects-matter in sec. 92; as for instance in legislating as to solemnization of marriage, yet no farther than that on the subject of marriage; on licenses, &c., for the purpose of raising a revenue, but no farther than that on the subject of trade; on property and civil rights in the Province, but no farther than that so as to make that a legislation on trade and commerce; on the fisheries, (within the legitimate meaning of the term); on bankruptcy and insolvency; on marriage and divorce; on bills of exchange and promissory notes, or on any other of the subjects-matter enumerated in section 91.

On the other hand, Parliament, under the express language of the Act, and as the *rationale* of the decisions, can, notwithstanding anything in the Act, legislate effectually on the regulation of trade and commerce, no matter how much it may interfere with property and civil rights; with the right to grant licenses, or with matters of a merely local or private nature in the Province: on bankruptcy and insolvency; no matter how much it may interfere with property and civil rights; with licenses, or procedure in civil matters in the courts; and, also, as we have seen, clearly, on marriage, though it may interfere with solemnization of marriage; that great apparent, (as it has been treated), stumbling block in the way of putting in full force the rule, purposely framed for that purpose, as we have seen, that the Act itself furnishes us.

We have before examined some of Mr. Justice GWYNNE's language in this case, and, fairly testing it, have seen, that, carried to its logical sequence, on some of the subjects, at least, in section 92, the Legislatures could not legislate at all. The well decided cases sustain no such position as that.

The learned JUDGE thinks it is impossible that the holding in the cases of Severn v. The Queen; The City of Fredericton v. Barker, and the Citizens' Insurance Co. v. Parsons can be reconciled. From the point of view of the learned JUDGE in the matter it would be as difficult for him to reconcile these cases, as it was for Mr. *Benjamin*, in the Privy Council,—taking the same position as Mr. *Mowat*, Mr. *Blake* and others have taken in the Supreme Court of Canada and elsewhere, that the Local Legislatures, having the "exclusive" power to legislate on all the subjects-matter in section 92, Parliament cannot legislate within any of these subjects-matter—to furnish any reasonable construction of the Act at all; or to show, if Parliament were so limited and confined, how it could possibly legislate at all on the subjects-matter given to it. *Their* absurdities, in the matter, are very apparent.

But, in the three cases named, as they were decided, there is no inconsistency at all. In Severn v. The Queen, whether rightly or wrongly decided, the holding simply was that Brewers' licenses were not included in the classes of licenses named in sub-section 9; and, therefore, by virtue of that clause, the Local Legislatures had no power to legislate in reference to Brewers' licenses. In the City of Fredericton v. Barker, in the Supreme Court of Canada, the holding was that as the legislation was a regulation of trade, therefore, under the provisions of sec. 91, it was *intra vires* Parliament, though it did interfere with Property and Civil Rights in the Province; with the right to grant licenses, or with matters of a merely local or private nature in the Province. The case of Citizens' Insurance Co. v. Parsons held that legislating as to provisions in reference to the conditions in insurance policies, did not legitimately come within the meaning of the term "Trade and Commerce," as used in the 91st section, no more than, in another case, the compelling Commercial Travellers to take out licenses did, so as to render such legislation *ultra vires* the Legislatures. Taking neither the wrong view on the one hand that Parliament has no power, virtually, to legislate at all; nor, on the other hand, that the Legislatures could not, virtually, legislate at all, and there is nothing whatever inconsistent in them; and nothing whatever in them to prevent, (as, in fact, proved to be the case with two of the three cases that did come before them), the Judicial Committee of the Privy Council from sustaining the whole of them.

We will now follow the case we have been considering, in its treatment, by, as they designate themselves,

THE PRIVY COUNCIL BOARD.

The case containing the same question that was so largely discussed in the Court below, and with reference to which, as we have seen, the Court stood three to two, came before the Judicial Committee of the Privy Council, and is reported in 7 App. Cas. 96. That learned body hold, with the learned CHIEF JUSTICE and Justices FOURNIER and HENRY, that the Ontario Act was not *ultra vires* the Local Legislature, on, substantially, the same leading ground upon which it was decided in the Court below, namely :— That the legislation in question was within the clause in section 92, covering property and civil rights; and, therefore, was within the power of the Local Legislature; and the Act in question that was passed with reference to conditions in policies issued by Insurance Companies, was not within the meaning of the terms, "regulation of trade and commerce," in the 91st section; and, therefore, the legislation was not ousted by any power given to Parliament, under the clauses of the 91st section of the Act; and that there was no conflict between the Act in question, and the Insurance Act of Parliament, which expressly recognised in the Local Legislatures the power of legislating with reference to Insurance Companies. In both of these points there is a perfect analogy between this case, and that of Robertson v. The Queen, (The Fisheries case), that was decided in the Supreme Court of Canada. So, this case in the Privy Council is an affirmation of the holding of the Supreme Court of Canada, not only in this case, but in the Fisheries case as well; the point in each case being that it is always a question of construction, the same as in numerous other statutes, as to whether a subject-matter is within certain language or not. The same point, exactly, was involved in several of the earlier cases we have examined; some of which were decided in the Supreme Court of N. B.; and some by the Privy Council. The question in this class of cases is not, then, what shall be done when there is a conflict in the legislation between the two bodies, by the legislation being in respect to, or affecting a matter with reference to which each of the bodies has legislative power; as was the case in Russell v. The Queen; Cushing v. Dupuy, and in a number of other cases; but, rather, whether the subject-matter comes within one or the other of certain clauses, or not. Hence, reasoning in a case,—where the question involved was not one of legislation in which conflicting rights clearly existed, as between insolvency and procedure in courts; between trade and commerce and the right to grant licenses; to legislate as to property and civil rights, or as to matters of a merely local or private nature in the Province; but, only on the question, for instance, whether the right in the property of a fishery was vested in the Dominion by virtue of its right to legislate on the subject of the "Fisheries;" or whether legislation on the narrow subject as to the contents of conditions in Insurance Policies in the particular Province legislating, was within the proper meaning of the term "the regulation of trade and commerce;"—might, as regards the different class of cases named, appear like very incorrect reasoning; and, certainly, would be extra-judicial as applied to the class of cases not then under consideration.

It was thus reasoning from statements in this case,—not so carefully limited, as evidently would have been the case had that very able lawyer, LORD SELBORNE, (formerly SIR ROUNDELL PALMER), delivered the judgment, as he did in some of the earlier cases that we examined,—that led writers for political papers, and others of a similar line of thought, improperly to come to the conclusion that the *ratio decidendi* of The Citizens' Insurance Co. v. Parsons warranted them in coming to the conclusion that in Russell v. The Queen, it would be decided that the Canada Temperance Act was *ultra vires* Parliament. That it was not so decided, but a really more extreme rule being there adopted than had been applied by the Supreme Court of Canada in any case there decided, showed that the reasoning from the Insurance case, that led to the predictions we have named, was wrong.

It is perfectly correct in the class of cases that we are now examining, as we have claimed from the outset, that, when such questions arise, they have to be considered on their individual merits; and, that, giving a proper construction to the words "trade and commerce," as has been done in this class of cases, is not, by any means, to hold, as we have seen some of the learned JUDGES have done repeatedly, because, in case of conflict between the subjects-matter *bona fide* within the clauses in sec. 91 being so legitimately legislated upon by Parliament, though coming in contact with subjects-matter in sec. 92, that, in such case, these latter must yield, so far as they are included in, or are covered or affected by such legitimate legislation within the scope of the subjects-matter in sec. 91; that, therefore, every Act that the Local Legislature may pass must necessarily come within one or the other of the powers of Parliament. In simple fairness, and not, by any means, either as an invidious distinction, or servilely, we would suggest, that, in a thoroughly honest study we have made of the cases during the investigation into which we have gone, we have found, as far as we have been capable of judging, that the learned CHIEF JUSTICE of the Supreme Court of Canada, has, in all his judgments in that Court, on the two different classes of cases named, down to the Canada Temperance Act case, inclusive, invariably drawn the right distinction; and, we think, that, in all of such cases as have gone to the Privy Council, down to that case inclusive, the judgments of that very able lawyer have never been over-ruled; whether, in the Court below, he was with the minority or the majority.

Unless, in the study of this case, as decided in the Privy Council, the point on which we have laid so much stress is constantly kept in view; viz., the particular class of cases within which this case falls, the reasoning is well calculated to mislead. And, it is not at all surprising, applying the reasoning used with reference to one of the classes of cases we have named, to the other entirely different class to which the reasoning was not intended to apply, that the Toronto *Globe* and its *confreres* were led to the incorrect conclusions, as to its far reaching consequences, which they had formed. It is like the case, for instance, of taking SIR WM. RITCHIE's reasoning in such cases as the Canada Temperance Act case, against what we can only truthfully designate as the "absurdities" of the majority of the Judges of the Supreme Court of N. B., and of Mr. Justice HENRY; and, then, taking his judgments in such cases, as,—from these learned JUDGES going too far in depriving the Local Legislatures of power, where there is really no conflict,—he is resisting the reasoning of the learned Justices TASCHEREAU and GWYNNE; and, fancying, as did these learned JUDGES, that the one course was antagonistic to the other. They were entirely different cases, and involved, necessarily, different, but not antagonistic, treatment; because there was a difference, but no antagonism, between the cases. Had the Insurance case followed, instead of having preceded the Canada Temperance Act case, many not bad lawyers, as the phrase goes, would have thought the latter was over-ruled.

To bring out the points as we have named them, as involved in the case, would necessitate our setting out nearly the whole judgment, and that might be found tiresome.

One paragraph we will give, for two reasons; one for the purpose of showing that the next very lengthy paragraph, while containing perfectly sound reasoning as applicable to the case itself; would be entirely wrong, if applied,—as it was not intended to be applied—to the very different class of cases covered by Regina *v.* The Justices of Kings, in the Supreme Court of N. B., under RITCHIE, C. J.; by Cushing *v.* Dupuy, in the Privy Council; and by the Canada Temperance Act case, in the Supreme Court of Canada, and before our highest Appellate Court as well. The other reason, is to show, by a very palpable inaccuracy at the close of the paragraph, that the judgment was not as carefully delivered as it would have been had it been delivered, by, for instance, LORD SELBORNE.

The paragraph, in whole, is as follows, (p. 107):—

"The scheme of this legislation, as expressed in the first branch of sect. 91, is to give to the Dominion Parliament authority to make laws for the good government of Canada in all matters not coming within the class of subjects assigned exclusively to the Provincial Legislature. If the 91st section had stopped here, and if the classes of subjects enumerated in section 92 had been altogether distinct and different from those in sect. 91, no conflict of legislative authority could have arisen. The Provincial Legislatures would have had exclusive legislative power over the sixteen classes of subjects assigned to them, and the Dominion Parliament exclusive power over all other matters relating to the good government of Canada. But it must have been foreseen," (that it was "foreseen," we have seen by the statement we have quoted, from LORD CARNARVON's remarks in the House of Lords), "that this sharp and definite distinction had not been and could not be attained, and that some of the classes assigned to the Provincial Legislatures unavoidably ran into and were embraced by some of the enumerated classes of subjects in sect. 91; hence an endeavor appears to have been made to provide for the cases of apparent conflict; and it would seem that with this object it was declared in the second branch of the 91st section, 'for greater certainty, but not so as to restrict the generality of the foregoing terms of this section,' that, (notwithstanding anything in the Act), the exclusive legislative authority of the Parliament of Canada should extend to all matters coming within the classes of subjects enumerated in that section. With the same object, apparently, the paragraph at the end of sect. 91 was introduced, *though it may be observed that this paragraph applies in its grammatical construction only to No. 16 of sect. 92.*"

That, except the mistake in the criticism, in the italicised part of the paragraph, is a correct statement of the design and effect of the language of the Act; that is, by the first clause, repeated, (we apprehend, with a much fuller grammatical effect than is attributed to it in the above), in the final clause of the section; that, in cases of conflict between Parliament and the Legislatures with reference to the subjects-matter in the 91st and 92nd sections, Parliament is the dominant power, and all *bona fide* legislation by Parliament, within the subjects-matter of section 91, is *intra vires* Parliament; no matter how much it may "over-ride," "overbear," "exclude," or "supersede" the power of the Local Legislatures with reference to any of the subordinate classes in section 92; the so-called "exclusive" legislative authority in reference to which is given to the Local Legislatures; for, not only is this expressly provided for in the first clause of section 91; but, by the closing clause it is also, as we have seen, in effect declared, that no matter how much the subjects-matter in section 91 may come within those in section 92, they shall not be deemed to do so: so, that, notwithstanding anything in the Act, Parliament, legislating *bona fide* on any subject-matter in section 91, *shall have the fullest power and authority to do so,* " notwithstanding anything in " section 92; and notwithstanding that some, at least, of the subjects-matter in section 92, are within the very language of some of those in section 91; yet, *bona fide* legislation by Parliament on subjects-matter in section 91, is not prevented, so far as may be found necessary by Parliament for effective legislation on the subjects-matter in section 91; though such legislation "over-rides," "over-bears," or *entirely destroys,* (as by the Canada Temperance Act; or by a Prohibitory Liquor Act, for instance), the legislative power of the Local Legislatures with respect to the subjects-matter in section 92, that have *bona fide* fallen within the purview of the effectual legislation of Parliament on the subjects-matter in section 91.

That is the law of the passage we have quoted from the Insurance Case, in the Privy Council.

Now comes the next paragraph to which we have referred, which has no bearing at all upon the law as we have above stated it; and has no applicability whatever to the law in such cases as Regina *v.* The Justices of King's; Russell *v.* The Queen; or Cushing *v.* Dupuy. It assumes that all we have alleged, as above, is the clear meaning of the Act, to meet the conflict that the framers of the Act had " foreseen ;" and had, to meet it, made the provisions they did: stating their meaning in clear terms in the closing part of the first clause of the 91st section of the Act, and rendering it more emphatic by stating it again in the closing clause of that section.

All that, then, being conceded in the case we are considering, which was not a question as to whether certain legislation of Parliament was good or not, as to being an interference with local powers, as it was in the cases above named, *in effect,* (because in all of them, admittedly, the questions of clear conflict between the two Legislatures were involved), but whether the Legislatures could legislate in respect to matters within their jurisdiction, though a *forced* construction might possibly bring them within, in some remote sense, some of the clauses in sec. 91. The effect of the paragraph is to show, that, as sections 91 and 92 are framed, the right of the Local Legislatures, *to legislate in the first instance,* that is before Parliament has so legislated on any of the subjects-matter in sec. 91 as to exclude or over-ride such local legislation, is conceded with regard to some, at least, of the subjects-matter of sec. 92, which come, in fact, within the very phraseology of sec. 91.

Take, now, the paragraph which has required the explanation we have given of it; because it, perhaps more than any other portion of the case, has caused the holding in the case to be misunderstood; which holding, as we have seen, simply is, that local legislation as to the conditions in a policy of insurance was not legislating within the term "Trade and Commerce;" and that Parliament itself recognised this fact; as it did in the Fishery Act, that there were other rights outstanding in the Fisheries. Admitting again, at the very commencement of the paragraph " the pre-eminence " which it was designed by the Act to give "to the Dominion Parliament in cases of a conflict of powers," it thus proceeds,—

" Notwithstanding this endeavour to give pre-eminence to the Dominion Parliament in cases of a conflict of powers, it is obvious that in some cases, where this apparent conflict exists, the Legislature could not have intended that the powers exclusively assigned to the Provincial Legislature should be absorbed in those given to the Dominion Parliament."

We have to remind our readers that this applies to a case where it was wrongly contended, in the Court below, by two of the learned Judges, that the Local Legislatures had no power to legislate, even on the subjects-matter named in sect. 92, where these conflicted with the powers in sect. 91. And it is to meet such an error that the judgment in the Privy Council is framed. And it is also necessary constantly to be kept in mind that the reasoning here is not directed against a claim that Parliament cannot override the legislation of the Legislatures, as is provided in and by the opening and closing clauses of section 91; but against a claim, the unsoundness of which from the commencement of this treatise we have insisted on, that, virtually, the Local Legislatures could not legislate at all. And, jumping from the result of this case, which holds they can, it has been perverted—particularly while we were awaiting the decision of the Privy Council in the Canada Temperance Act case,—into making out that it, in effect, holds that Parliament cannot legislate at all. So they jump from extreme to extreme in connection with these noted sections. Thus, in the same spirit, we have Mr. Justice HENRY claiming, in effect, that if it were held that the Canada Temperance Act was valid, this would not only destroy the power of the Legislatures to grant licenses; but it would also declare that such licenses were illegal since Confederation; though during all that time the power of Parliament to over-ride the right of the Local Legislatures to legislate as to licenses, had never been invoked at all. We intend to refer again, more fully, to this illogical view of Mr. Justice HENRY, of the Act, when we get through with our examination of the case we have now under review.

Following the passage we have quoted, the Privy Council continue thus,—

"Take as one instance the subject 'marriage and divorce' contained in the enumeration of subjects in sect. 91; it is evident that solemnization of marriage would come within this general description; yet 'solemnization of marriage in the Province' is enumerated among the classes of subjects in sec. 92, and no one can doubt, *notwithstanding the general language of sect. 91*, that this subject is still within the exclusive authority of the Legislatures of the Provinces."

This, the intelligent reader will not fail to notice, connected with its immediately preceding context, is simply to show, that, because the general language of the term "marriage," in sec. 91, over which Parliament has the "exclusive" power to legislate, is wide enough to include the subject of "solemnization of marriage," a subject-matter within the "exclusive" legislative power of the Local Legislatures—the reader must keep in mind that this stumbling-block "exclusive" is rendered in each case, by the governing language of secs. 91 and 92, a word of limited, qualified meaning—"that it could not have been intended that the powers exclusively assigned to the Provincial Legislatures should be absorbed," ("*swallowed up as a vortex; destroyed.*" Worc.), " in those given to the Dominion Parliament." That is, that because Parliament has the exclusive, dominating, over-riding power, on the general subject of "marriage," which is wide enough to include solemnization of marriage, it must not be supposed that, therefore, the Local Legislature cannot legislate at all, with reference to this subject. This is no answer to the claim, admitted to be well-founded, that Parliament has the over-riding power; but is, in effect, a claim, that, that being the case, does not, necessarily, destroy the subordinate power. It may do so, wholly or partially, after effectual legislation by Parliament, as in the clear case of so destroying the power to license, by the Canada Temperance Act;

but that is only the result of legislation by Parliament, actually and effectually had within a subject matter within its superior cognizance. But, until Parliament has so 'legislated, the Local Legislature can go on and legislate on the subject, for instance, of solemnization of marriage, but no farther within the subject of marriage than that. It can go on and legislate within the subject of such licenses as fall within sub-sec. 9 of sec. 92 " in order to the raising of a revenue for Provincial, Local or Municipal purposes ;" but, no further within the subject of " Regulation of Trade and Commerce," than that. It is on one side of the truth involved in this, that Mr. Justice HENRY errs ; and on the other side of it, Justices TASCHEREAU and GWYNNE : the learned CHIEF JUSTICE, and Mr. Justice FOURNIER with him, in the case below, having been the only JUDGES there who followed, between the two wrong sets of views,—one on the one side, and the other on the other side,—
THE HAPPY MEDIUM LINE OF THE TRUTH.

But all that is there, distorted and misunderstood as it has been, is as far as the poles are asunder from holding that Parliament is not the dominant power, and that when the legislation of the two bodies, under the 91st and 92nd sections, conflicts, the legislation of the Local Legislatures must not give way. The dominant power of Parliament is conceded ; but that concession does not amount to the admission, as Mr. Justice HENRY, from his wrong point of view, and Justices TASCHEREAU and GWYNNE, from theirs, would make it out to be, that thereby the power of the Local Legislatures, was *ab initio*, " absorbed "—" swallowed up as in a vortex ; destroyed !"

We might pursue the matter from this case a little further. In continuance, recollect, of the same line of argument, which we—not as a politician, but simply as a legal analyst—have fairly placed before our readers, in our honest, and, say, patriotic, effort to remove the ignorance and uncertainty in which many of the statesmen, politicians, judges and lawyers of this Dominion have been so apparently hopelessly involved, in connection with the questions we are considering ; the learned JUDICIAL COMMITTEE go on,—

" So, ' the raising of money by any mode or system of taxation' is enumerated among the classes of subjects in section 91 ; but though the description is sufficiently large and general to include ' direct taxation within the Province, in order to the raising of a revenue for Provincial purposes,' assigned to the Provincial Legislatures by section 92, it, obviously, could not have been intended that, in this instance also, the general power should override the particular one."

This is an admirable instance, selected by the Privy Council, to sustain their argument against Justices TASCHEREAU and GWYNNE. True, the power in Parliament "to raise money by any mode or system of taxation" is large enough not only to include direct taxation for general Dominion purposes, but also, as their LORDSHIPS of the Privy Council put it, "for Provincial purposes" as well; but is that reasonable? True, by straining the words you can include that, but isn't it contrary to the very spirit of the Act that that power should, *ab initio*, or at all—as regards that particular subject-matter,—be taken away from the Local Legislatures?

There is no allegation at all that Parliament if it saw fit, for "the peace" of the Dominion, to abrogate the National Policy; and, following England in her so-called "Free Trade" system, obtained the revenue of Canada largely by direct taxation; imposing, as England does, an income tax; that Parliament could not do so. But, that, even in that case, the Local Legislatures could still exercise their right of direct taxation, without at all conflicting with the exercise of a similar right in Parliament. In the dissenting judgment of SIR WM. RITCHIE, (then Mr. Justice RITCHIE), in Severn *v.* The Queen, 2 S. C. R. 101, this very point is considered. In answer to his learned colleagues, who differed with him in that case, he says, on the very point the Privy Council in the case we are examining, were considering.—

"It is said this construction conflicts with the power of the Dominion Government to regulate trade and commerce, and the raising of money by any mode or system of taxation. All I can say in answer to that is that so far, and so far only, as the raising of a revenue for provincial, municipal and local purposes is concerned, the British North America Act, in my opinion, gives to the Local Legislatures *not an inconsistent, but a concurrent power of taxation*, and I fail to see any necessary conflict ; certainly, no other or greater than would necessarily arise from the exercise of the power of direct taxation and the granting of shop and auctioneer licenses specially vested in the Local Legislatures. *It cannot be doubted, I apprehend, that both the Local Legislatures and Dominion Parliament may raise a revenue by direct taxation, and, if so, why may not both a revenue by means of licenses?* There need be no more conflict in the one case than in the other."

This, too, is the view taken of the same matter by the Privy Council, in Dow v. Black, L. R., 6 P. C., 282, referring to clause 2 of section 92, relatively with clause 3 of section 91. Their LORDSHIPS say,—

"They think it must be taken to enable the Provincial Legislature whenever it shall see fit, to impose direct taxation for a local purpose upon a particular locality within the Province. They conceive that the 3rd article of sect. 91 is to be reconciled with the 2nd article of section 92, by treating the former as empowering THE SUPREME LEGISLATURE *to raise revenue by any mode of taxation*, WHETHER DIRECT OR INDIRECT; and the latter as confining the Provincial Legislature to direct taxation within the Province for Provincial purposes."

The reasoning in, and the *rationale* of the Citizens' Insurance Co. v. Parsons, in the Privy Council, are not then,—agreeing precisely with the views of SIR WM. RITCHIE, in the Court below, both in the case itself, and, as quoted above, in Severn v. The Queen,—at all as they have been mistakingly supposed to have been. It was obvious to us, as we pointed out in February, 1882, before the Canada Temperance Act case was decided in the Privy Council, that the Toronto *Globe*, and those of the same line of thought, were wrong, and utterly misunderstood the holding in the case we are considering; and that there was nothing whatever in that case, "the tendency" of which was to show that the Canada Temperance Act was *ultra vires*; and that that Act must, and necessarily would be sustained, unless the Privy Council ignored their reasoning, and reversed their holding, in Valin v. Langlois, and in Cushing v. Dupuy. This, they were very far from doing in the Citizens' Insurance Co. v. Parsons; the holding in which, as the sequel showed, they affirmed, and established, *and extended*, (as we shall see, very much extended), in Russell v. The Queen. So, whether the Citizens' Insurance Co. v. Parsons had preceded or succeeded Russell v. The Queen, the one did not over-rule the other; but the latter case carried the law even still farther than the former.

But, taking the reasoning in the one case, (and, that, not as a whole, but in isolated and distorted passages), used as regards one class of cases, where, on a perfectly correct principle, as we have seen from the start, the power of the Local Legislatures to the legislation in question was sustained; and, applying those isolated and distorted passages to a case, where, in an entirely different class, the legislation of Parliament was sustained, and where the power of the Local Legislatures was "over-borne," "over-ridden," "excluded," and "superseded"—as Mr. *Blake* said could not be done—was not wise: and those political writers, who undertook to be exponents of the Law, succeeded in doing nothing but deceiving their readers and themselves.

It was, then, in the case we are considering, laid down as follows, (p. 109),—

"The first question to be decided is, whether the Act impeached in the present appeals falls within any of the classes of subjects enumerated in sect. 92, and assigned exclusively to the Legislatures of the Provinces; for if it does not, it can be of no validity, and no other question would then arise. It is only when an Act of the Provincial Legislature *prima facie* falls within one of these classes of subjects that the further questions arise, viz., whether, notwithstanding this is so, the subject of the Act does not also fall within one of the enumerated classes of subjects in sect. 91, *and whether the power of the Provincial Legislature is or is not thereby over-borne.*"

There, as has been contended throughout this treatise, is the rule, "a hard and fast one;" given, as the statute furnishes it, as we pointed out at the very outset of this treatise. But, as we have also intimated, in applying this rule,* it is quite another matter; and, there, case after case, as it arises, has to be considered with proper judicial knowledge, and decided on the principles of construction applicable to any similar case—and there are many such cases—arising under any statute, deed or other instrument.

So applied, that is, under "the hard and fast rule" which the Act gives us, the following is perfectly correct. But if misapplied, (as it has been), to affect the force or validity of the rule given, expressly, by the statute itself, it is no wonder that it produces nothing but confusion. The following, properly applied, is exceedingly wise: misapplied, as it has been, it results in confusion and nonsense; so much of which elements abound in many of the foolish arguments and judgments on the intricate questions con-

---

* It will be noticed throughout this treatise how persistently this rule, has, in case after case, been denied or misunderstood; by lawyers who seem to have been utterly unable to grapple with the questions involved; and by Judges, who, though over-flowing with pretension, are so ignorant of law, that, of one of the most ignorant and pretentious of them, it is said, (on the authority of one of his almost equally ignorant, and still more pretentious brother-Judges), that he made the humiliating confession, *that he had never read but one law book in his life*,—Selwyn's Nisi Prius! Fine judgments, certainly, must be expected from a state of facts like that!

tained in the cases we have examined. Their LORDSHIPS say, very judiciously,—

"In these cases it is the duty of the Courts, however difficult it may be, *to ascertain in what degree, and to what extent, authority to deal with matters falling within these classes of subjects exists in each Legislature,* and to define in the particular case before them the limits of their respective powers. It could not have been the intention that a conflict should exist; and in order to prevent such a result, the two sections must be read together, and the language of one interpreted, and, where necessary, modified by that of the other." (Just, for instance, as was done by the Supreme Court of Canada in the Fisheries case, where, altho' the word "Fisheries," was, in an extreme sense, large enough to include the fisheries,—*as property, the riparian rights in the land,*—yet it was held that a fair construction of the different parts of the Act involved no such extreme reading of the word "Fisheries;" and, that, therefore, the riparian rights in the land, were not, by the use of such word, separated from the land itself; of which they were an incident). "In this way it may, in most cases, be found possible to arrive at a reasonable and practicable construction of the language of the sections, so as to reconcile the respective powers they contain, and give effect to them all." (As in the word, "Fisheries," on the one hand; and the word "Lands," on the other, in the case named above in parenthesis; or, in the word "Lands" or "Royalties," on the one hand; and the word "Revenue," on the other, as was done in the Mercer Escheat case). "In performing *this* difficult duty, it will be a wise course for those on whom it is thrown, to decide each case which arises as best they can, without entering more largely upon an interpretation of the statute than is necessary for the decision of the particular question in hand."

And, after the magnificent reasoning, (as a general thing), of SIR MONTAGUE E. SMITH, in *that* case, as applicable to the particular matter for adjudication, their Lordships uttered the exceedingly careful and well-guarded sentence following. They say,—

"Construing, therefore, the words 'regulation of Trade and Commerce,' by the various aids to their interpretation as above suggested, *they would include political arrangements in regard to trade requiring the sanction of Parliament; regulation of trade in matters of inter-Provincial concern, and it may be* that they would include GENERAL REGULATION OF TRADE AFFECTING THE WHOLE DOMINION." (This "*may be,*" was, as we have seen, authoritatively established, as no longer a possibility, or a probability, but an absolute certainty, in Russell v. The Queen—the Canada Temperance Act case,—before the Judicial Committee of the Privy Council). " *Their Lordships abstain on the present occasion from any attempt to define* THE LIMITS OF THE AUTHORITY OF THE DOMINION PARLIAMENT IN THIS DIRECTION. It is enough for the decision of the present case to say, that, in their view, *its authority to legislate for the regulation of trade and commerce does not comprehend the power to regulate by legislation the contracts of a particular business or trade*, SUCH (!) AS THE BUSINESS OF FIRE INSURANCE IN A SINGLE PROVINCE; (!!),* and, therefore, that its legislative authority does not, *in the present case*, conflict or compete with the power over Property and Civil Rights assigned to the Legislature of Ontario by No. 13 of section 92."

AND—THAT—IS—ALL !

And yet it was of this case that one of the great (perhaps, the greatest of the) political Canadian organs wailed out the following false notes,—" In view of what they, (the Privy Council), have said about Provincial jurisdiction, in matters of trade, the fate of the Scott Act, now before them on appeal, is, TO SAY THE LEAST OF IT, *rendered somewhat doubtful ;*" and, away off in the distance, one of the lesser Canadian organs, grinding out its notes, echoes forth, or seems to do so :—" The tendency of the decision in The Citizens' Insurance Company *v.* Parsons, in the Privy Council, is against the validity of the Canada Temperance Act !"

And their readers,—many of them at least,—swallowed this whole. And if the Insurance case had succeeded the Canada Temperance Act case, instead of having preceded it, in the dreadful ignorance and utter inability of those pretentious writers to analize a simple, legal case, there is no doubt that " the great leaders of public thought" would have proclaimed that the decision in the Canada Temperance Act case had been reversed ; as they, in effect, have declared has been done by the later case, in the Privy Council, of the Queen *v.* Hodge—the Ontario License Act case,—yet remaining to be "honestly, and, we trust, intelligently, examined."

Reverting now to an extract we made from the case, and particularly to the part which we put in italics, (*ante*, p. 114),—as to whether, when the subject-matter comes within sect. 92, and is also

---

* See, in the Second Part of this treatise, our criticism on this holding of the Privy Council, in our examination of the principles of construction laid down by them in Dobie v. The Temporalties Board and Russell v. The Queen.

found to come within sec. 91, "*the power of the Provincial Legislatures is or is not thereby over-borne*,"—the "over-ridden," "excluded," or "superseded" of Mr. *Blake*—we will direct attention to the *ratio decidendi* of the cases, and of the reasoning in them, on this point.

For instance, the Canada Temperance Act, and, still more plainly, a Prohibitory Law, would absolutely "exclude" the Provincial Legislatures from legislating with reference to "shop, saloon or tavern licenses," for the sale of spirituous liquors in order to the raising of a revenue for provincial, local, or municipal purposes. The right to legislate on the subject of Fisheries, would only exclude the right to legislate, by the Legislatures, on matters within the sense in which that term "Fisheries" is used in the Act; and would not vest the title in the riparian rights of the land in the Dominion; altho' Parliament could legislate on the "property and civil rights" in the land, as far as such legislation was legitimate legislation within the subject of the Fisheries; and, to that extent, the legislation of the Legislatures relative to the property and civil rights in the land would be over-borne and excluded; the balance of the legislation on the land and its incidents, under property and civil rights, remaining in the Local Legislatures. The right to legislate, by Parliament, on Insolvency, would sweep away, as to property and civil rights; procedure in the courts; local matters, and any other of the subjects-matter affected by Insolvency legislation, the right to legislate on these subjects-matter by the Local Legislatures, as far as they were affected by *bona fide* legislation on the subject of Insolvency; the remainder of legislation, as between those subjects-matter, outside of Insolvency, remaining in the Legislatures. The right in Parliament to legislate for the purpose of raising a revenue by direct taxation, would still leave intact the right of the Local Legislatures to legislate as to the same subject "within the Province in order to the raising of a revenue for Provincial purposes." The right to legislate in Parliament, effectually, on the subject of marriage, so far as such legislation might affect the subject of "solemnization of marriage," would leave the remainder of legislation on such last named subject-matter in the Legislatures. These, for instances, in the consideration of the question, "whether the power of the Provincial Legislature is or is not thereby over-borne," when the subject-matter in sect. 92 also comes within the subject-matter of sect. 91, so that Parliament, in legitimately legislating on the subjects-matter in sect. 91, includes also legislation on more or less of the subjects-matter in sect. 92.

THE PRIVY COUNCIL'S CRITICISM CRITICISED.

We have already stated that among the many mistakes and misreadings of one of the governing clauses in sect. 91; viz., that at the latter end of the section, one such very palpable mistake was made by the Judicial Committee of the Privy Council,—His Lordship, Sir MONTAGUE E. SMITH, delivering the judgment,—in the case we have been examining. After considering, correctly, the effect of the opening clause, as quoted by us, (*ante*, p. 107), they say, in the words, which, in that quotation made by us, we have italicised; thus,—

" With the same object, apparently, the paragraph at the end of sect. 91 was introduced, *though it may be observed that this paragraph applies in its grammatical construction only to No. 16 of sect. 92.*"

In reply, it may, with due deference, " be observed," that this is entirely incorrect.

The 16th clause of section 92, referred to, is as follows,—" 16. Generally all matters of a merely local or private nature in the Province."

The clause at the end of section 91, is,—

" And any matter coming within any of the classes of subjects enumerated in this section shall not be deemed to come within *the class of matters of a local or private nature* COMPRISED IN THE ENUMERATION *of the classes of subjects* by this Act assigned to the Legislatures of the Provinces."

We have already directed attention, *en passant*, to the manner in which the learned CHIEF JUSTICE of the Supreme Court of Canada has dealt with this passage, (see *ante* pp. 63, 64 & 96), using the plural "classes," evidently inadvertenly, but, actually, in the sense of it, correctly, instead of the singular "class," in the phrase "*the class of matters;*" thus treating the enumerated subjects in the 92nd section, as they, in fact, are, as classes of subjects of a local or private nature, &c. The whole first fifteen subjects relate to local or private matters " *in* the Province," or " *to* the Province," or " *of* the Province," or " *for* the Province," &c. Then by the 16th clause, after having named all of these different " classes " of local and private matters in, to, of or for, &c., the Province, there is the more general language as above. But, if this last clause had never been inserted at all, the closing clause of the 91st section, would, then, just as it does now—for, emphatically it does!—*refer to the whole of the fifteen clauses* now standing prior to the 16th. And, grammatically, this is very clear. It is not—" the class of matters of a local or private nature *contained in the 16th clause :*" but it is " the class of matters of a local or private nature, *comprised in the enumeration of the classes of subjects,* by this Act assigned to the Legislatures of the Provinces," The class of matters, &c., comprised *in the enumeration of the classes;* that is, *in the whole sixteen classes of subjects of a local or private nature enumerated in that section.*

This criticism of the criticism is not hyper-criticism! The passage is a most important one in the construction of the two sections; and if, *as alleged by the Privy Council,* " in its grammatical construction"—for *that* is the construction which would govern us in the matter—the clause applies " only to No. 16 of section 92," its force would, in that case, be most materially weakened in itself; and, with such a clause, so interpreted, at the end of the section, the clause at the beginning of the section might be materially weakened ; if, in its effect on the first fifteen classes of section 92, not be altogether neutralized and destroyed. The mistake evidently arose, *first,* from carelessness; and *second,* from the words " local or private nature," used in the closing clause of section 91, having been repeated in sub-section 16 of section 92; and thus the sight and sense of the careless—not to say, stupid—reader, were mislead.

As we shall claim in the *Second Part* of this treatise, that the Privy Council have made another gross, and in *that* instance, *a most serious and far reaching mistake* in their construction of the *first clause* of the 91st section; in order that some of our readers, who may possibly have more awe of "authority" than we have, may not be too much shocked when they find us there attacking and exposing the fallacies of the highest Appellate Court of Canada—*the Judicial Committee of the Privy Council of England*—in two most important Canadian Constitutional cases; to prepare the way for that, we will strengthen ourselves by showing still further than we have done, that they have very grossly erred in respect to the *last clause* of the 91st section, when they so limited such clause " *in its grammatical construction*," (which is the only construction in the matter with which we have to do), " *only to No. 16 of sect.* 92."

Meeting a somewhat wider contention than as above made by

the Privy Council, but including that as well, that very able and talented JUDGE, (as, differing with some of his views, tho' we háve had to do, we must designate him), Mr. Justice GWYNNE, in City of Fredericton *v.* The Queen, 3 S. C. R., at p. 566, says ; as though it were designed to meet the very absurdity in the Privy Council's judgment to which we have directed attention ;—

"The plain meaning of the closing paragraph of the 91st section is, that, notwithstanding anything in the Act, any matter coming within any of the subjects enumerated in the 91st section shall not be deemed to come within *the classes of subjects enumerated in the 92nd section,* however much they may appear to do so."

"It was argued that what was intended by this clause, was, to exclude the subjects enumerated in the 91st section from a portion only of the subjects enumerated in the 92nd section, namely, those only of a 'local or private nature ;' the contention being that the 92nd section comprehends other subjects than those which come under the description of 'local or private,' and so that, in effect, the intention was merely to declare, that none of the items enumerated in section 91 shall be deemed to come within item 16 of sec. 92. If this were the true construction of the clause, it would make no difference in the result, nor would it affect anything in aid of the contention in support of which the argument was used, for the previous part of the 91st section in the most precise and imperative terms, declares, that, notwithstanding anything in the Act ; notwithstanding therefore, anything, whether of a local or private nature, or of any other character, *if there be anything of any other character enumerated in the 92nd section,* the exclusive legislative authority of the Parliament of Canada extends to all matters coming within the classes of subjects enumerated in the 91st section ; *but in truth,* ALL THE ITEMS ENUMERATED IN THE 92ND SECTION ARE OF A PROVINCIAL AND DOMESTIC, THAT IS TO SAY, OF A 'LOCAL OR PRIVATE' NATURE."

And it is, by that last clause, expressly,—" THE CLASS OF MATTERS OF A LOCAL OR PRIVATE NATURE COMPRISED IN THE ENUMERATION OF THE CLASSES OF SUBJECTS," *enumerated in section 92,*—to which the last clause of section 91 does apply ; SIR MONTAGUE E. SMITH and the Privy Council, to the contrary, notwithstanding.

Says Mr. Justice GWYNNE further, (*Ibid.,* 567),—

"The 92nd section, therefore, instead of dealing with the subjects to be assigned to the Local Legislatures in the same general terms as had been used in the 91st section, by placing under the jurisdiction of these Legislatures all matters of a merely local or private nature within the Province, (a mode of expression which would naturally lead to doubt and confusion, and would be likely to bring about that conflict which it was desirable to avoid), *enumerates, under items numbering from 1 to 15 inclusive*, certain particular subjects, *all of a purely provincial, municipal and domestic, that is to say,*

"OF A LOCAL OR PRIVATE CHARACTER,

and then winds up with item No. 16—a wise precaution, *designed, as it seems to me, to prevent the particular enumeration of the 'local and private' matters included in the items 1 to 15* being construed to operate as an exclusion *of any other matter*, IF ANY THERE MIGHT BE, *of a merely local or private nature."*

We have already, *en passant*, called attention to the fact that an abler JUDGE than, apparently, was either of those who sat on the Privy Council Board, when the judgments, the correctness of which we will impugn, were delivered,—SIR WM. RITCHIE,—in repeated references, in a succession of cases, to the construction; that is, of course, to the "grammatical construction;" of the last clause of the 91st section, applies that clause as it only can be applied, SIR MONTAGUE E. SMITH, and the Privy Council, to the contrary, notwithstanding; to, *in the very words of the Act*, "THE CLASS OF MATTERS OF A LOCAL OR PRIVATE NATURE *comprised in the* ENUMERATION *of the classes of subjects*," in the 92nd section.

We shall here repeat but one of these instances we have furnished. The learned CHIEF JUSTICE, in the City of Fredericton v. Barker, 3 P. & B. at p. 540; says,—

"Matters coming within the subjects enumerated as confided to Parliament are *not to be deemed*, (the language of the clause), *to come within* THE MATTERS OF A LOCAL NATURE COMPRISED IN THE ENUMERATION OF SUBJECTS ASSIGNED TO THE LOCAL LEGISLATURES."

Nor do we stop here! But, as we have, in previous instances, so often done, cited the Supreme Court of New Brunswick and *its* "learned" (!) Judges, against themselves; so, now, on the point under consideration, as to whether or not the closing clause of the 91st section, in its grammatical construction, applies only to the 16th clause of the 92nd section, beg to cite the

JUDICIAL COMMITTEE OF THE PRIVY COUNCIL OF ENGLAND, AGAINST THEMSELVES!

Thus, the Privy Council, which, in the case we have cited,

SIR MONTAGUE E. SMITH delivering the judgment, held as we have quoted; in Dow v. Black, L. R., 6 Pr. Col., 282, referring to the question as to whether the subject-matter of the Act in that case came within article 2 or article 9 of section 92, say,—SIR JAMES W. COLVILLE delivering the judgment,—

"Their LORDSHIPS are further of opinion, that the Act in question, even *if it did not fall within the 2nd article, would clearly be a law relating to a matter* OF A MERELY LOCAL OR PRIVATE NATURE *within the meaning of the 9th article of sect. 91 of the Imperial Statute;* and, therefore, one which the Provincial Legislatures was competent to pass, *unless its subject-matter could be distinctly shewn to fall within one or other of the classes of subjects specially enumerated in the 91st section;"* and, therefore, under the operation of the opening and *closing* clauses of the 91st section, might still,—as of "the class of matters of a local or private nature," enumerated in section 92, be taken away from them.

As their LORDSHIPS, then, (SIR JAMES W. COLVILLE their speaker), held, that the 9th clause of the 92nd section is one of that class of *local or private matters* referred to; they hold, that, in the "grammatical construction" of the closing clause of the 91st section, it is *not* confined to the 16th clause, as their LORDSHIPS, (SIR MONTAGUE E. SMITH, their speaker), held; but extends also to the 9th clause.* And, as it no more extends to the 9th clause, (or 10th clause), of the "local and private matters" enumerated in the 92nd section than to any of the other clauses of "local and private matters" in that section, then the criticism of Sir MONTAGUE E. SMITH and his colleagues of the Privy Council is *contra* to the criticism of SIR JAMES W. COLVILLE and his colleagues of the Privy Council, of whom

SIR MONTAGUE E. SMITH WAS ONE!

So, if, by-and-by, in the *Second Part* of this treatise, we undertake to show, (simply exercising a right, as a legal analyst, to fairly examine their judgments to test them as to whether they are right or wrong), that the judgment of SIR MONTAGUE E. SMITH and his colleagues, is no better as to the first clause of the 91st section, than it is as to the last; our sensitive readers will please keep in mind, that, in our view of the closing clause, at

---

* From a critical examination of the case, (Dow v. Black), it is obvious that the clause referred to was the 10th, rather than the 9th. But, that addititional blunder of the Privy Counc I does not, at all, affect their "contradiction of themselves," in the cases, as shown; the reasoning being, precisely, as applicable to the 10th clause as to the 9th.

least, we are supported by quite high authority, as we have been able to cite even
THE PRIVY COUNCIL AGAINST THEMSELVES!

Before passing on to the examination of the politicians' remaining great case—Hodge v. The Queen—there is another matter which we left over for consideration, as intimated, of which we will now dispose. It is in reference to an utter misapprehension by Mr. Justice HENRY, made by him in the case of The City of Fredericton v. The Queen, 3 S. C. R. 547, as to the effect of holding that the Canada Temperance Act is valid. The learned JUDGE says,—

"If there be not concurrent legislative powers and the Act is *intra vires*, then the necessary conclusion is, that all the local legislation on the subject of shop, saloon, tavern and auctioneers' licenses since the first of July, 1867, has been *ultra vires*. Under such circumstances, it would be interesting to enquire, *where there is any law in force restraining the sale of spirituous liquors in counties or cities which have not adopted the Canada Temperance Act, 1878.*"

"The Imperial Act," says again the learned JUDGE," gives to Parliament and the Local Legislatures, *exclusive jurisdiction not contingent upon previous legislation by either.*"

All this is an entire misapprehension, very similar to the mistake, in the opposite direction, of the Supreme Court of British Columbia, in the Thrasher case. They are mislead by treating that word "exclusive," as giving an unrestricted, unqualified, power of legislating with reference to the subjects-matter named, respectively; whereas, as we have seen, it, as used, means nothing of the kind. In connection with the Canada Temperance Act, the law is clear, that, prior to its adoption, the right of the Local Legislatures to legislate as to tavern and other licenses, as named in clause 9, of sect. 92, for the purposes there named, was an unrestricted one; and, where the Canada Temperance Act was not adopted, the law "restraining the sale of spirituous liquors in counties or cities which have not adopted the Act," remained in force as it did before the passage of that Act. But, where that Act came in force; by virtue of the dominant power of Parliament, and the over-bearing, over-riding, excluding and superseding power of the Act, the subordinate power of the Local Legislatures with respect to the subjects-matter in sect. 92, affected by such Act, had to give way; and, as the result, the power of the Local

Legislatures to legislate as to the granting of tavern licenses, &c., was destroyed.

Very much the same position, although not quite so bad as the above, was taken by Mr. *Benjamin*, in the Privy Council, in L'Union, &c. *v.* Belisle, (cited *supra*), where it was contended that the local legislation in that case was *ultra vires* the Local Legislatures, because it was within the subject-matter of Insolvency, one of the dominant subjects-matter of sect. 91, which, therefore, controlled the legislation on local and private matters. To make this out, it was claimed that a general Insolvent Act could be framed that would be wide enough to cover the local matter in question, and, therefore, it was claimed, it was outside of the power of the Local Legislatures. This is very much, from a different point of view, in principle, the same as Mr. Justice HENRY'S fallacy, as above. LORD SELBORNE met Mr. *Benjamin's* contention, thus; (p. 36):—

"Well, no such general law covering this particular association, is alleged ever to have been passed by the Dominion. The hypothesis was suggested in argument by Mr. *Benjamin*, who certainly argued this case with his usual ingenuity and force, of a law having been previously passed by the Dominion Legislature, to the effect that any association of this particular kind throughout the Dominion, on certain specified conditions assumed to be exactly those which appear upon the face of this statute, should thereupon, *ipso facto*, fall under the legal administration in bankruptcy or insolvency. *Their Lordships are by no means prepared to say, that if any such law as that had been passed by the Dominion Legislature, it would have been beyond their competency: nor that, if it had been so passed, it would have been within the competency of the Provincial Legislature afterwards to take a particular association out of the scope of a general law of that kind, so competently passed by the authority which had power to deal with bankruptcy and insolvency.* But no such law ever had been passed; and to suggest the possibility of such a law as a reason why the power of the Provincial Legislature over this local and private association should be in abeyance or altogether taken away, is to make a suggestion which, if followed up to its consequences, would go very far to destroy that power in all cases."

That very effectually disposes of the fallacies of both Mr. *Benjamin* and Mr. Justice HENRY, and states the law quite as we have done in considering the matter. All this is making very easy the answer to the questions which we proposed at the commencement of this treatise, and which seemed so extremely difficult then, from the confusion in which the whole matter was involved, and which we have striven, *lead us where it might,* (and it is going to lead us very much farther, than, when commencing this treatise, we could have possibly anticipated), fairly and honestly, and " we trust, intelligently," to clear away.

The learned CHIEF JUSTICE of the Supreme Court of Canada, in the Citizens' Insurance Co. *v.* Parsons, (cited *supra*), at p. 243, in a few words meets the same point. He says,—

" I do not think the Local Legislatures are to be deprived of all power to deal with property and civil rights, because Parliament, in the plenary exercise of its power to regulate trade and commerce, may possibly pass laws inconsistent with the exercise of the Local Legislatures of their powers—*the exercise of the powers of the Local Legislatures* being in such a case subject *to such regulations* as the Dominion may lawfully prescribe."

The importance of all this will appear clear, when, at the close of the consideration of the cases, we come to state, categorically, the answers to the questions, which, at the outset, we undertook to grapple with; and ascertain, if in our power to do so, whether clear, unqualified answers cannot be furnished to them. We have no doubt now that we shall be able to do so in as clear and satisfactory a manner, as the nature of the subjects involved will admit of. At least, we shall try so to do, and confidently hope to meet with success.

THE ONTARIO LICENSE ACT CASE.

The regular report of this case is just to hand, in the number of the Law Reports for March, 1884 ; Hodge *v.* The Queen, 9 Ap. Cas. 117. The two leading questions involved in this case are two questions of the utmost simplicity; and it is only a matter for surprise that there should have existed a necessity, from the doubts cast about the questions by the utterly untenable judgment of the Ontario Court of Queen's Bench, to have rendered it at all advisable to have taken such simple questions for the disposition of the Judicial Committee of the Privy Council at all. Considering that holding in the Ontario Court of Queen's Bench, and the equally absurd *semble* from another Ontario case we have named, (Regina *v.* Taylor?, that the exclusive power given to Parliament under the 91st section was not exclusive as against the Provincial Legislatures, *but as against the Imperial Parliament,* we are almost forced to the conclusion that there are other Courts in the Dominion of not much higher authority than that extremely weak Court; the Supreme Court of New Brunswick.

The two leading questions involved were, whether the Local Legislatures had power to authorize Commissioners to make certain regulations in the nature of police or municipal regulations of a local character with reference to taverns; and, whether the Legislature itself had power to enact such regulations. The first question, in effect, has been decided over and over again, that a legislative body has such power. Quite a leading case on the question is the Queen v. Burah, 3 App. Cas. 905, in the Privy Council, where such right is clearly established. A similar question came up in the Canada Temperance Act case, with reference to the right of Parliament so to legislate; and where it was decided in the same way, as, as before stated, it has been in a great number of cases. In the somewhat celebrated "Thrasher Case," the Supreme Court of British Columbia held, with reference to the right of the Legislature of that Province to delegate its power to make rules of Court for the Supreme Court there; with other wrong holdings in the case, that it had no such power. They held both points wrongly,—*first*, that the Legislature itself had no power to legislate on that subject; and *second*, if it had, it had no right to delegate that power. On both these points the Supreme Court of Canada decided they were wrong.

One of the questions in that case, (The Thrasher case), submitted to the Supreme Court of Canada, was,—

"If that Legislature can make rules to govern the procedure of that Court, can it delegate this power to the Lieutenant-Governor in Council?"

The answer, rendered on the 18th June last, (1883), to this question, was,—

"The Legislature can make rules to govern the procedure in that Court in all matters, as limited by the preceding answer, *and can delegate* this power to the Lieutenant-Governor in Council."

Clearly, there was no ground for holding otherwise in Hodge v. The Queen.

And there was no greater difficulty involved in connection with the decision of the other question.

Mr. *Kerr* claimed, for the Appellant, that the Legislature was not competent to legislate in regard to licenses for the sale of liquor, and the regulation of licensed houses, as, under the B. N.

A. Act, clause 9 of section 92, they only had that power "for the purpose of raising a revenue." But, if there was any ground for so limiting that clause down to the very exact letter of that language; other clauses gave them much wider scope in reference to that subject-matter, which was merely a local or private matter in the Province;—mere municipal or police regulations. The same question was considered by RITCHIE, C. J., (now SIR WM. RITCHIE), in that quite leading case on the question of legislating by the Legislatures as to Tavern Licenses, of Regina v. The Justices of Kings; (*supra*). In that case, while it was shown that the Legislatures had no power so to legislate affecting licenses, as, substantially, outside of that question, and beyond any power given to them by any other of the clauses of section 92, to make their legislation, real, unquestionable legislation as to trade and commerce; the learned CHIEF JUSTICE there made an exception covering this very simple question in Hodge v. The Queen. He says,—

"We by no means wish to be understood that the Local Legislatures have not the power of making such regulations for the government of Saloons, Licensed Taverns, &c., and the sale of spirituous liquors in public places, as would tend to the preservation of good order, and prevention of disorderly conduct, rioting or breaches of the peace. In such cases, and possibly others of a similar character, the regulations would have nothing to do with trade or commerce, but with good order and local government; matters of municipal police and not of commerce, and which municipal institutions are peculiarly competent to manage and regulate."

To have held, as an incident to the power of the Legislatures to legislate as to Tavern Licenses, in order to the raising of a revenue, that the Legislatures had power to make reasonable regulations, in connection with those licenses, and to include such reasonable regulations in their being acted on, to make them effective, would not have been going very far; but with their wider power to legislate as to Property and Civil Rights in the Province; to municipal institutions in the Province, and, generally to all matters of a merely local or private nature in the Province, it is only singular, after the very sensible view, as quoted, had been taken in the prior case of Regina v. The Justices of Kings, by the very able lawyer, who is now the CHIEF JUSTICE of the Supreme Court of Canada, that either of the Canadian Superior Courts, could have so held as to have left, at any time, the question in the slightest doubt.

The Judicial Committee, on the main point in which we are interested in this discussion, held that such mere municipal or police regulations of a local character did not interfere with the regulation of trade or commerce within the meaning of clause 2 of sec. 91. In so holding, SIR BARNES PEACOCK, in delivering the judgment, says,—

"It appears to their Lordships that Russell v. The Queen, when properly understood, is not an authority in support of the appellant's contention, and their Lordships do not intend to vary or depart from the reasons expressed for their judgment in that case. The principle which that case and the case of the Citizens' Insurance Company illustrate is, that subjects which in one aspect and for one purpose fall within sect. 92, may in another aspect and for another purpose fall within sec. 91."

In Russell v. The Queen, the holding of the Privy Council was, as we have seen, that for the peace, order and good government of Canada, that Act was within the competency of Parliament to pass, and was not within the legislative power of the Local Legislatures. In the Citizens' Insurance Company case, the decision was that local legislation as to the conditions of an insurance policy in a single Province was not legislation on trade and commerce; was within the competency of the Local Legislature, and was not in conflict with any Dominion statute.

The misunderstanding of Russell v. The Queen, referred to, was, probably, contained in the following from the argument of the appellant's counsel :—

"Sect. 91, sub-sect. 2, gives the regulation of trade and commerce to the Dominion. In the case of Russell v. The Queen, it was held that the power to prohibit and regulate the traffic belonged to the Dominion. It is very desirable that legislation on this subject should be uniform ; and this cannot be secured if each Province can pass a licensing act of its own."

This kind of syllogistic argument is unsound. Both the minor premise, and the kind of inferred conclusion, are sophistical. Assuming that it was held in Russell v. The Queen that the power to prohibit and regulate the traffic belonged to the Dominion; that is not necessarily holding—which it would have had to have been, to have sustained the appellant's motion—that *before the Dominion had exercised that power*, legislative powers in the Provinces, which were perfectly good until, by the dominant legislation, *bona fide*, of the Dominion Parliament, within the scope of the powers in sec. 91, has been exercised, the local legislative power under sec. 92, had been "overborne" and "excluded."

Again, whatever objection there may be to the Local Legislatures legislating as to licenses, which was the wide contention in the clause we have quoted, (going far beyond the next preceding sentence which only claimed that they could only legislate as to licenses "for the purpose of raising a revenue"), the express power is given them to do so; and until such power is overborne and destroyed by its being absorbed, where, and to the extent to which it is, *bona fide*, absorbed or overborne by the superior legislation, there is nothing to take such power away. * Hence, their LORDSHIPS well said,—

"It was urged that the decision of this Board in Russell v. Regina was conclusive that the whole subject of the liquor traffic was given to the Dominion Parliament, and consequently taken away from the Provincial Legislature. It appears to their LORDSHIPS, however, that the decision of this tribunal in that case has not the effect supposed, and that, when properly considered, it should rather be taken as an authority in support of the judgment of the Court of Appeal."

Then, no such Act as the valid Canadian Temperance Act having been in force in the locality in question, and the legislation being clearly within the subjects-matter of sect. 92, the Local Legislature had the clear right to make the provisions it did; for, in the language of the Privy Council, such regulations "cannot be said to interfere with the general regulation of trade and commerce which belongs to the Dominion Parliament, and do not conflict with the provisions of the Canada Temperance Act, WHICH DOES NOT APPEAR TO HAVE AS YET BEEN LOCALLY ADOPTED."

And, in the absence of any such Act, there was nothing whatever, in the world—certainly not in any of the properly decided

---

* Since the text of this treatise was written, in a conversation we had with one of the leading and one of the most prominent lawyers of the Dominion, we were astonished to find him taking the position that Hodge *v.* The Queen, in the Privy Council, sustains the position that the Local Legislatures can "exclusively" legislate with reference to tavern licenses ; and, therefore, that Parliament has no power to legislate on any subject-matter so as to interfere with the right of the Local Legislatures to legislate as to tavern licenses It is scarcely necessary for us to say here, we show *that* pretty plainly in the text of our treatise, that such a position is transparent nonsense ! It is, however, astonishing, and the instance we here give, is another proof of it how general and wide spread such absurdities of construction, throughout the Dominion, are to this day.

cases on analogous questions— to have justified the question being raised; much less to have justified one of the Superior Courts of the Dominion in holding the Act *ultra vires;* and, after it had been correctly decided, to have justified the carrying of so extremely simple a case for the decision of the Judicial Committee of the Privy Council of England. The Supreme Court of Canada, under its able CHIEF JUSTICE, assuredly could and would have decided that question quite as well.

Yet the holding in that simple case has been dreadfully magnified and distorted. Two clauses in the judgment have been prominent for this purpose. One, that to which we have referred, as to the misimpression as to the effect of Russell *v.* The Queen, in its having been supposed,—if, really, any one ever supposed such nonsense!—because the Canada Temperance Act was declared *intra vires* Parliament, so that, where the Act was adopted the right to grant licenses was destroyed; that, therefore, *where it was not adopted at all,* the same result was produced. As though, the misimpression referred to did not relate to that, but rather to the thoroughly correct and general understanding of that Act that it was *intra vires* Parliament; and, as such, deprived the Legislatures of the power to legislate as to licenses when and where such Act was adopted.

The other of the clauses in that judgment which has lead to error, and in consequence of which the power of the Local Legislatures relative to that of Parliament, in cases of conflict between the two bodies in the subjects-matter for legislation, has been, in popular and political, and even in legal, circles, greatly magnified, is the following :—

"It appears to their LORDSHIPS, however, that the objection thus raised by the Appellants is founded on an entire misconception of the true character and position of the Provincial Legislatures. They are in no sense delegates of or acting under any mandate from the Imperial Parliament. When the British North America Act enacted that there should be a Legislature for Ontario, and that its legislative assembly should have exclusive authority to make laws for the Province, and for Provincial purposes in relation to the matters enumerated in section 92, it conferred powers not in any sense to be exercised by delegation from or as agents of the Imperial Parliament, *but authority as plenary and ample, within the limits prescribed by section* 92, as the Imperial Parliament, in the plenitude of its power possessed and could bestow. *Within these limits of subjects and area the Local Legislature is supreme, and has the same authority as the Imperial Parliament, or the Parliament of the Dominion,*"—now mark what follows!—"*would have had* UNDER LIKE CIRCUMSTANCES, *to confide to a municipal institution or body of its own creation authority to make by laws or resolutions as to subjects specified in the enactment,* and with the object of carrying the enactment into operation and effect."

This paragraph is very plain, but laymen, or ignorant or careless lawyers or judges, misapprehending it, and misapplying it, are led astray. It was made use of in answer to the claim, under the maxim, "*delegatus non potest delegare,*" that the Local "Legislatures" were simply delegates themselves and not Legislatures; and, therefore, could not delegate their delegated power. Then, is simply shown, that they are "Legislatures," and as such have as full legislative power, *within their "limits of subject and area,"* as the Dominion Parliament or the Imperial Parliament itself; namely, within *that limit,* supreme legislative power. But, what that limit is, there is here,—as that is not the subject, in this branch of the case, under consideration,—not the slightest attempt at stating. But, misapplying the language in the case,—as though it were used in the other branch of it,—and distorting it, to make out, in cases of conflict between Parliament and the Local Legislatures, on the subjects-matter in sections 91 and 92, within the jurisdiction, respectively, of the two legislative bodies, that, in respect to those subjects-matter, Parliament and the Local Legislatures were equally "supreme;" and, therefore, neither should yield to the other; and, hence, that Parliament was not, in cases of conflict, the dominant power, was entirely wrong. And the great amount of talking and writing that there has recently been, both in Parliament and the Local Legislatures and out of them, under such a misconception of the meaning of the language used by their LORDSHIPS of the Privy Council, in this, and in some of the other late cases we have examined, has, simply, no better foundation than appears in these exceptionally strong instances we have quoted.

We have now fully and fairly examined all the cases in the Courts of ultimate appellate jurisdiction—the Fisheries cases; the Mercer Escheat case; the Insurance cases; the Ontario License case, &c.—which, it is claimed, have broken into the rule of construction in the Act as explained by us at the beginning of this treatise; but it still stands intact, with an additional feature to which we have adverted, and to which we shall recur again; the effect of which may be to greatly enlarge, instead of to lessen, the power of Parliament in its legislation for the peace, order and good government of Canada.*

---

* Before the above was reached by the printer, after the whole treatise had been completed by us, we observed a newspaper report of a case in the Province of Quebec, which is further confirmation of the correctness and justness of our remarks in the text. In a judgment recently delivered in the Practice Court, at Montreal, by Mr. Justice MATHIEU, that Judge is reported as having taken the "*firm ground*" "that the Provinces retained and retain, *the sovereign power*, except those (? that) which they have expressly renounced to the Dominion." And it is also said that the judgment of the Privy Council in the Queen *v.* Hodge was cited; "their LORDSHIPS declaring the absolute independence, in their sphere, of the Provincial Legislatures." And, in this utter distortion, as we have shown, of the language used in the case by the Privy Council, the following is given as the very natural deduction;—"In the United States there was *only one* sovereign power. HERE THERE ARE TWO. *The powers of the Dominion were only exclusive in this sense:* that the Provinces could not levy taxes for Federal purposes." It was, obviously, quite time that an attempt were made to deal with those questions scientifically, and to strip them of the great amount of absurdity and distortion that has accumulated about them. Mr. Justice MATHIEU's treatment of the subject is, decidedly, *a la Loranger!*

SECOND PART.

In addition to those cases which we have examined, there are two other Privy Council cases which we shall now examine.

The first of these cases is The Attorney General for Quebec v. The Queen Insurance Co., 3 App. Cas., 1090. This was a case where the Act of the Legislature of Quebec required certain classes of Insurance Companies to take out licenses; the payment therefor to be made by affixing stamps to the policies issued; imposing a penalty for the contravention of the Act.

The questions were as to whether this was a license act within the 9th clause of sect. 92 of the B. N. A. Act; and, if not, whether it was direct taxation under the 2nd clause. The Court below held that it was neither; and, on appeal to the Privy Council, their judgment was sustained.

Mr. *Benjamin*, who, unsuccessfully, argued so many of these appeal cases, where he has sought to sustain the power of the Local Legislatures as against Parliament; defeated so often, and, finding the construction of the Act against him on that point, claimed that sections 91 and 92 "were self-contradictory and very difficult of construction." As a rule, he fought very shy of those governing clauses in section 91. Without calling on the other side, their LORDSHIPS held that the Act was neither a license act, nor an act for direct taxation; and they held the act was *ultra vires* the Local Legislature. In coming to this conclusion it was simply a construction of the language used in the Act, such as often occurs in questions of construction of statutes; deeds, or other instruments; like a number of the other cases we have examined; the holding in which has been distorted into that of holding that they were cases of conflict between Parliament and the Legislatures, as between subjects-matter in sections 91 and 92, decided in favor of the Local Legislatures; when, in fact, they were nothing of the kind.

DOBIE v. THE TEMPORALITIES BOARD.

This case, which is reported 7 App. Cas., 136, is one where an attempt was made by the Quebec Legislature to alter an Act that was in force in the Provinces of Ontario and Quebec prior to Confederation; and which was sustained by the Court of Queen's Bench of that Province. Their LORDSHIPS of the Privy Council, holding that such an Act could only be passed by Parliament, and not by the Legislature of either Province, or by the conjoint legislation of both, reversed the judgment.

In this case their LORDSHIPS say :—

"There is no room in the present case for the application of those general principles of constitutional law which were discussed by some of the Judges in the Courts below and which were founded on an argument at bar. There is really no practical limit to the authority of a Supreme Legislature except the lack of executive power to enforce its enactments. *But the Legislature of Quebec is not supreme; at all events it can only assert its supremacy within those limits which have been assigned to it by the Act of* 1867."

There is no mistaking the application of this language, as, right in the teeth of this, has been so extensively done in the case of the similar language, and the different application of it there, which was used in Hodge v. The Queen.

The distinction is taken between this case and that of The Citizens' Insurance Co. v. Parsons, showing that the Act in that case was a mere local Act which "merely prescribed that certain conditions should attach to every policy entered into or in force for insuring property, situate within the Province, against the risk of fire." Then, repeating that the rule laid down in that case for testing "the validity of an Act of the Provincial Legislature is to consider whether the subject-matter of the Act falls within any of the classes of subjects enumerated in sect. 92. *If it does not* THEN THE ACT IS OF NO VALIDITY. If it does then these further questions may arise, viz. 'whether, notwithstanding that it is so the subject of the Act, it does not also fall within one of the enumerated classes of subjects in sect. 91, and whether the power of the Provincial Legislature is or is not thereby overborne;'" they decided that it did not fall within any of the classes of subjects enumerated in section 92; and, that, therefore, it was invalid.

Here, again, it was contended, and the plausibility of the argument was admitted, that the Act was within class 13 of section 92, "Property and Civil Rights in the Province," but LORD WATSON, in delivering the judgment, said, — "It has failed to satisfy their Lordships that *the statute impeached* by the Appellant, *is a law in relation to property and civil rights within the Province of Quebec,"* and it was, as intimated, held, that "The Parliament of Canada is therefore the only Legislature having power to modify or repeal the provisions of the Act of 1858."

And, yet, unquestionably, that Act *did affect, and was in reference to* property and civil rights in the Province of Quebec.

THE PRIVY COUNCIL TESTS EXAMINED.

This brings us now to a fuller examination than we have yet made, of the tests proposed by the Privy Council in the case of Russell *v.* The Queen ; which were very strongly acted on in that case.

From the stress, that, in political circles, has been laid—by those who are extreme advocates for much more greatly enlarged rights of legislation in the Local Legislatures than a proper construction of the B. N. A. Act will admit of—on the statement in the case of Hodge *v.* The Queen, that the holding of the Privy Council in the case of Russell *v.* The Queen had been misunderstood ; we might reasonably have expected that a fair examination of this latter case, would have shown the adoption in that case of some rule or test that would have established such enlarged rights of legislation in the Local Legislatures ; as, it was assumed, it had been decided in that case that they possessed. But, on a fair examination of that case, we confess our surprise to find the adoption of a test there, originally applied in another case for a very different purpose; the effect of which seems to be to have increased the legislative power of Parliament far beyond what was established in any of the decisions in the Supreme Court of Canada ; maligned, as that Court has been, for its wrongly alleged extreme holdings in the matter, in favor of the legislative power of Parliament as against that of the Local Legislatures. As we have seen, from the statement made in Hodge *v.* The Queen itself, all that was there meant, was, that when it was fancied that because that case of Russell *v.* The Queen decided that the Canada Temperance Act was valid, that that implied, even where such Act had not been adopted at all, that the power of the Local Legislatures with respect to licenses for the sale of spirituous liquors was taken away; was a mistake, not at all justified by any holding in that case.

The tests named, which we are about fairly to examine, were stated and applied in the Citizens' Insurance Co. *v.* Parsons. Again, as we have seen, in Dobie *v.* The Temporalities Board; and, still again, in Russell v. The Queen. As the rules or tests laid down by our highest Appellate Court, are, of course, authoritatively to govern all other Courts in the construction of the B. N. A. Act, and as we cannot dispel doubts that we have as to the accuracy of the tests, and as to the soundness of the rules, as they have been recently applied, with which we are supplied by the Judicial Committee of the Privy Council, we propose to consider the rules or tests pretty fully, with a view of ascertaining the meaning that is to be attached to them, and the effect that their adoption must have upon the legislation of Parliament and of the Local Legislatures; and, for this purpose, we shall freely re-quote much, which, in another connection, we have already quoted.

In the examination of these tests we quote from Russell v. The Queen, 7 App. Cas., at p. 836, as follows,—

"The general scheme of the British North America Act with regard to the distribution of legislative powers, and the general scope and effect of sections 91 and 92, and their relation to each other, were fully considered and commented on by this Board in the case of the Citizens' Insurance Co. v. Parsons. According to the principle of construction there pointed out, the first question to be determined is, whether the Act falls within any of the classes of subjects enumerated in section 92, and assigned exclusively to the Legislatures of the Provinces. If it does, then the further question would arise, viz., whether the subject of the Act does not also fall within one of the enumerated classes of subjects in section 91, and so does not still belong to the Dominion Parliament. But *if the Act does not fall within* any of the classes of subjects in section 92, no further question will remain, for it cannot be contended, and indeed was not contended at their Lordships' bar, that, if the Act does not come within one of the classes of subjects assigned to the Provincial Legislatures, the Parliament of Canada had not, by its general power ' to make laws for the peace, order and good government of Canada,' full legislative authority to pass it."

It will be noticed, that, in this case, the tests are proposed to determine the validity of an Act *passed by the Parliament of the Dominion*. This, it can be easily seen, is a very different matter from applying precisely the same tests to determine as to the validity of an Act passed *by the Local Legislature*. In this latter case, it will be seen from our entire examination of the question, that, as the Legislatures obtain their power to legislate by the 92nd section, subject to their having such power over-ridden by the effectual *bona fide* legislation on any of the subjects-matter in section 91, by Parliament; it is quite clear, in such case—*i. e.* as regards all legislation by the Local Legislatures—that the question *first*, "whether the Act in question falls within any of the classes of subjects enumerated in section 92," if answered in the negative, ends the matter. For, as they get all their powers of legislation by virtue of that section, " if the Act in question do not fall within any of the classes of subjects enumerated in section 92," clearly they have no power to pass such an Act. And, *second*, if it do fall within one of the classes of subjects enumerated in section 92, then the second question would arise; viz., whether the subject of the Act does not also fall within one of the enumerated classes of subjects in section 91, and so does not still belong to the Dominion Parliament. If, then, notwithstanding it may have fallen within one of the classes of subjects enumerated in section 92, if it also falls within one of the enumerated classes in section 91, so as to belong to Parliament; again, clearly, as we have seen, the Local Legislatures would be ousted of such legislation.

But, applying the same tests to determine whether the legislation of Parliament is valid or not, is quite another thing; and pre-supposes the existence of another element which is not contained in connection with the question as to the legislative powers of the Local Legislatures. If it is true, as is expressly stated in the quotation we have made, that " If the Act does not fall within any of the classes of subjects in section 92, *no further question will remain ;* " and, that, " *It cannot be contended* that, if the Act does not come within one of the classes of subjects assigned to the Provincial Legislatures, the Parliament of Canada had not, by its general power ' to make laws for the peace, order and good government of Canada' full legislative authority to pass it ;" then we have an exceedingly simple rule ; and all that will be necessary, in order that we may be able intelligently to apply it, will be, simply, to ascertain what their LORDSHIPS mean by the language, " If the Act does not come within one of the classes of subjects assigned to the Provincial Legislatures ; " and, that, we are able to do by their holding in the two cases of Dobie *v.* The Temporalities Board, and Russell *v.* The Queen ; where such tests were applied. The deduction from those cases, on the point, is, then, that the meaning of the words, " If the Act does not come within one of the classes of subjects assigned to the Provincial Legislatures," is, simply,—" If the Act is not such an one, as by virtue of one of the classes in section 92, might be passed by the Local Legislature." That, then, would leave the statement even more simple and unmistakeable, and open to less possibility of being " misunderstood," than even the comparatively clear way that their LORDSHIPS have put it. Extended then, as regards the power of Parliament to pass an Act, according to that rule, it would stand thus,—"Parliament, for the peace, order and good government of Canada, can pass all Acts except those which the Legislatures, by virtue of the clauses in section 92, can pass." This, of course, is the deduction, from the application of the first test, without any reference to the further enlarged powers of Parliament, and the relatively circumscribed powers of the Local Legislatures by the application of the second test. If so simple a test as that named, is the true one; that all Acts that the Local Legislatures cannot pass, Parliament can pass ; it, certainly, does appear singular that a Court under the able leadership of the present CHIEF JUSTICE of the Supreme Court of Canada has never acted on that rule; nor even discovered its existence.

True, there are expressions in the City of Fredericton *v.* The Queen, 2 S. C. R., 557, which we have already quoted, precisely similar to the language contained in the Privy Council's first test ; but the *rationale* of that case, really is, that the Act was *intra vires* Parliament, not because the Local Legislatures could not pass such an Act; but, because it was within the power of Parliament to pass it, as a legislation on trade and commerce ; and, therefore, it was immaterial how much the subject-matter of the Act might come within, interfere with, or over-ride any of the subjects-matter enumerated in sect. 92; as Parliament, by virtue of its over-riding power, could still pass it.

The language of Judge TASCHEREAU,—similar to what we have seen is the effect of the Privy Council's first test, as applicable to the legislation of Parliament—is, as follows,—

" It is clear that the Canada Temperance Act, 1878, could not be enacted by the Provincial Legislatures, for the simple reason, that they have only the powers that are expressly given to them by the B. N. A. Act, and that the said B. N. A. Act, does not give them the power to effect such legislation. This . . seems to be admitted by all the learned JUDGES of the Court below who have held this Act to be *ultra vires* of the Dominion Parliament. Well, it seems to me, *the admission that the Local Legislatures could not pass such an Act implies an admission that the Dominion Parliament can do so. Once the power of legislation over a certain matter is found not to vest in the Provincial Legislatures, the question is solved, and that power necessarily falls under the control of the Dominion Parliament*, subject, of course, to the exigencies of our Colonial status."

That clearly states the result of the application of the Privy Council's first test, as to whether the Act in question is one within the power of Parliament to pass it;—"*If it is an Act that the Local Legislatures cannot pass*, then, subject to the exigencies of our Colonial status, *Parliament can pass it*." That is the clear effect of the language of Mr. Justice TASCHEREAU; and, we submit, it is the equally clear holding of the Judicial Committee of the Privy Council. If it can possibly be stated more distinctly, Mr. Justice TASCHEREAU repeats,—

"*If this Temperance Act would be ultra vires of the Provincial Legislatures, because the B. N. A. Act does not give them the power to enact it, I fail to see why it is not intra vires of the Dominion Parliament.*"

But, then, the learned JUDGE goes on to argue in the case, as we have before seen, precisely as did the learned CHIEF JUSTICE, (who, as a significant fact, we might observe, neither in this case nor in any other, has laid down the principle as laid down, unmistakeably, by the Privy Council, in the cases named), that "under the words, ' regulation of trade and commerce,' the B. N. A. Act expressly gives the Dominion Parliament the right to this legislation," though " it may, *it is true*, interfere with some of the powers of the Provincial Legislatures;" for, says the learned Judge, further,—" Sect. 91 of the Imperial Act clearly enacts that notwithstanding anything in this Act; notwithstanding that the control over local matters; over property and civil rights; over tavern licenses for the purpose of raising a revenue, is given to the Provincial Legislatures, the *exclusive* legislative authority of the Dominion extends to the regulation of trade and commerce, and this Court has repeatedly held that the Dominion Parliament has the right to legislate on all matters left under its control by the Constitution, though, in doing so, it may interfere with some of the powers left to the Local Legislatures."

And, as we have seen, the whole strength of that case in the Supreme Court of Canada is the emphatic holding, that, being legislation on the regulation of trade and commerce, it was good no matter how much it might interfere with property and civil rights in the Province; with the right to legislate as to licenses, and with local and private matters in the Province.

Mr. Justice GWYNNE, too, after discussing the question as to its relation to an Act within the regulation of trade and commerce; and, therefore, good, no matter how much it may interfere with the local and private matters enumerated in the clauses of the 92nd section, also takes the same position as did Mr. Justice TASCHEREAU, and as covered by the Privy Council's first test. Thus, the learned Judge says, (p. 573),—

"The Act, then, being *ultra vires* of the Provincial Legislatures, as dealing with a subject not exclusively assigned to the Provincial Legislatures, *cadit questio, for that point being so determined, it follows*, by the express provision of the B. N. A. Act, *that it is within the jurisdiction of the Dominion Parliament.*"

But, what we allege has never yet been held by the Supreme Court of Canada, is, that, with reference to an Act of Parliament, it is necessarily *intra vires* Parliament, because it is an Act that the Local Legislature of a Province cannot pass. That they have never yet held that a simple answer of "No," to the question, "Is that such an Act as the Local Legislature can pass?" is equivalent to the answer of "Yes," to the question,—"Is it such an Act as Parliament can pass?" Unless the language of the Privy Council is unintelligible, we think that is what they hold in the two cases named; Dobie *v.* The Temporalities Board, and Russell *v.* The Queen. We do not think we have mis-stated the Privy Council in the matter any more than we have mis-stated Justices TASCHEREAU and GWYNNE, whose express language we have quoted as above. And yet, with the fullest deliberation, and the greatest deference, we cannot bring our reasoning to the assent that the test named, as to the powers of Parliament to legislate, is the correct one. And, because we think the rule is corrupt, in order to thoroughly test it, we now propose to follow it, historically,

FROM ITS INCEPTION IN THE PRIVY COUNCIL.

In L'Union St. Jacques de Montreal *v.* Belisle, L. R., 6 P. C., 35, there is an informal statement of the principle from which the tests are derived. In that case, to which we have before referred in tracing out the law on the main point of this investigation, there was a claim made that an Act of the Legislature of Quebec, relative to the appellants—a building society—was an Act relating to insolvency, and therefore, was *ultra vires* the Local Legislature.

It was decided otherwise; their LORDSHIPS in the judgment, delivered by LORD SELBORNE, saying,—" Clearly this matter is private; clearly it is local, so far as locality is to be considered, because it is in the Province, and in the City of Montreal." That, then, brought it within one of the clauses of sect. 92; and it is then declared that *the Act of the Local Legislature* is valid unless it is qualified by something in sec. 91; which section, it is stated, "qualifies it undoubtedly, if it be within any one of the different classes of subjects *there specially enumerated.*" And, after quoting the closing clause of sec. 91 as establishing that point, their LORD-SHIPS add,—" But the *onus* is on the respondent to show that this, being of itself of a local or private nature, does also come within one or more of the classes of subjects *specially enumerated* in the 91st sect." It was, then, as we have before seen, held, that it did not come within either of the classes of subjects enumerated in sect. 91; and, hence, was *intra vires* the Local Legislature.

Here, then, are the tests in embryo; but they are tests *not as to the validity of an Act of the Dominion Parliament;* but, as we have seen,—a very different thing,—as to the validity of an Act of the Local Legislature. The tests clearly applicable to that case where they were so applied, were, then; *first,* Does it come within sec. 92? If not, there is an end of it, for the Local Legislatures only have power to legislate with respect to matters enumerated in sect. 92. But, if it does come within sect. 92, does it also come within sect. 91? If not, then it remains. If it do come within one of the clauses in sect. 91,—unless, indeed, we might add, it is one of the classes of subjects, which, expressly, by its nature, is brought to a certain, limited, defined extent, within one of the clauses in such section,—then it is qualified by section 91; the manner and extent of the qualification varying with the circumstances of the case, as we have before pointed out.

In Dow *v.* Black, *Ibid.*, 282, where it was claimed, in the Privy Council, after having been so held in the Court below, (the Supreme Court of New Brunswick), that the Act in question, enacted *by the Local Legislature* of the Province, was *ultra vires,* as being legislation on a subject-matter—that of a railway extending beyond the Province—out of the jurisdiction of the Local Legislature, it was held that the Act in question was *intra vires* the Legislature as being legislation on the subject of direct taxation in the Province; but, if not within that subject-matter, it was still good as relating to a merely local or private matter in the Province within the 9th article (properly the 10th) of the 92nd sect. Here, again, the tests, which are clearly appliable, as we have seen, to a statute enacted *by the Local Legislatures*, were applied, and more distinctly so than in the previous case; although not then regularly formulated as they have since been. However, in effect, they were applied when their LORDSHIPS held that the Act in question was "a law relating to a matter of a merely local or private nature within the meaning of the 9th article of sect. 92, of the Imperial statute; and, therefore, one which the Provincial Legislature was competent to pass," (the first test); "unless" (the second test) "its subject-matter could be distinctly shown to fall within one or other of the classes of subjects specially enumerated in the 91st section." "This view," their LORDSHIPS add, "is in accordance with the ruling of this tribunal in the recent case of the L'Union St. Jacques de Montreal *v.* Bélisle, decided on the 8th of July, 1884."

In neither of the cases, so far, it will be observed, where the tests were introduced and established, is the slightest intimation given that the tests are also appliable to the decision as to the validity of an Act of Parliament; involving, as that does, as we have seen, additional and very different considerations.

In the next case; Attorney-General for Quebec *v.* The Queen Insurance Co., L. R., 3 App. Cas., 1097, which was the case where an Act of the Quebec Legislature, providing that stamps should be affixed to certain insurance policies, was in question; and where it was held, by the Judicial Committee of the Privy Council, that such Act was *ultra vires*, as being neither legislation for direct taxation, nor as to licenses under the 9th clause of sect. 92; but a Stamp Act. As this, too, was an Act of the Local Legislature; to decide that, only involved an application of the first test;—Does this come within either of the clauses of sect. 92? If not, it is clearly *ultra vires*, and the next test is unnecessary.

THE MASTER OF THE ROLLS, in delivering the judgment, said,—

"The sole question their LORDSHIPS intend to consider is whether or not the powers conferred by the 92nd section of the Act in question are sufficient to authorize the statute which is under consideration?"

Then, they add, noticing a distinction we have previously pointed out, with reference to the powers of the Local Legislatures being qualified; over-ridden, or left undisturbed, by their coming within the classes of subjects enumerated in sect. 91; just according, as, from the nature of the subjects-matter of the clauses in sect. 92, and the nature of the legislation by Parliament, they may be affected,—

"It is not absolutely necessary to decide in this case how far, if at all, the express enactments of the 92nd section of the Act are controlled by the provisions of the 91st section, because it may well be that so far as regards the two provisions which their Lordships have to consider, namely, the sub-sections 2 and 9 of the 92nd section, those powers may co-exist with the powers conferred on the Legislature of the Dominion by the 91st section. *Assuming that to be so*, the question is, whether what has been done is authorized by those powers."

And, having found that it was not; even without the assumption as above, in the simple case as to the validity of an Act by a Local Legislature; no further test was necessary to be applied. This, however, is still very different from holding that, arising out of such an answer to that question, Parliament would have had the right to have passed *that Act in question;* which, in this case, was simply an Act providing that insurance policies *in a single Province*, (Quebec), on being issued should have stamps attached. Unless the meaning of the language used by the Privy Council, which we have previously quoted, and to which, in due course, we will recur again, has been "mistaken" by us in some quite inexplicable way; then, according to that language, equally as according to the language, which, in the same connection, we quoted from Justices TASCHEREAU and GWYNNE, *the Legislature of Quebec, not having been competent to pass that Act, Parliament could do so;* for, according to all that, "If the Act does not fall within any of the classes of subjects in sect. 92, no further question will remain," (7 App. Cas., 836), i. e. as to the right of Parliament to pass it; "for,"—without any reference to whether it comes within any of the clauses of section 91, or not,—"*it cannot be contended*, and indeed was not contended at their LORDSHIPS' bar, that, *if the Act does not come within one of the classes of subjects assigned to the Provincial Legislatures*, the Parliament of Canada had not, by its general power 'to make laws for the peace, order and good government of Canada', *full legislative authority to pass it.*" (*Ibid.*) This, mark, is a result from the application of the first test, —"Does the Act now in question fall within any of the classes of subjects enumerated in section 92, and assigned exclusively to the Legislatures of the Province?" "If it does, then, the further question would arise, viz., whether the subject does not also fall within one of the enumerated classes of subjects in sect. 91, *and so does not still belong to the Dominion Parliament?* But, if the Act does not fall within any of the classes of subjects in sec. 92, *no further question will remain, for it cannot be contended that the Parliament of Canada had not . . . full legislative authority to pass it!*"

And having thus decided that the Act in question did not come within the power of the Local Legislature to pass it; if there is any virtue in language that seems to be too clear to admit of its being said that one is "mistaken," when he treats it as plain English; the inevitable conclusion from the adoption of the tests proposed, is, that the holding of the learned Judicial Committee of the Privy Council,—our highest Appellate Court,—is, that a statute such as was passed by the Quebec Legislature rendering policies of insurance liable to a Stamp Act, *in that single Province*, was within the exclusive jurisdiction of the Parliament of the Dominion. Because, to test the validity of an Act of Parliament, it is declared, and expressly held, in Russell *v.* The Queen, and in Dobie *v.* The Temporalities Board, that you must first ask the question, does the Act of Parliament in question fall within either of the classes of subjects in sect. 92 ? If not, no further question will remain, and the Act will be within the legislative power of Parliament. But if it does fall within either of the classes of subjects in sect. 92, then the further question will remain,—Does it not also fall within one of the classes of subjects in sect. 91, and so still belong to Parliament ? But, in the Attorney General of Quebec *v.* The Queen Insurance Co., in reply to the first question,—on the doctrine upon which, rests, in the Privy Council, their holding in Dobie *v.* The Temporalities Board and in Russell *v.* The Queen,—the Privy Council have found that the subject of that Act does not fall within section 92; therefore it does fall within the power of Parliament; and the new doctrine is thus established by the Privy Council, and by the fair and plain application of their tests, that Parliament can pass *the identical Act* that was, in the case under consideration, held *ultra vires* the Quebec Legislature. If there is any escape from this deduction *we* look in vain to find it. Their language, on the point, seems quite as plain as that from Mr. Justice TASCHEREAU and Mr. Justice GWYNNE; which language, by the way, having been used by these learned Judges in the City of Fredericton *v.* Barker, before the Judicial Committee decided the case of Russell *v.* The

Queen,—which latter case was, indeed, in effect, an appeal from the former,—their language seems almost adopted by the Privy Council, as an affirmation of their views therein expressed from the judgments of the learned Judges named. And their language was : By Mr. Justice TASCHEREAU,—

"Well, it seems to me, the admission that the Local Legislatures could not pass such an Act implies an admission that the Dominion Parliament can do so. *Once the power of legislation over a certain matter is found not to rest in the Provincial Legislatures, the question is solved, and that power necessarily falls under the control of the Dominion Parliament.*"

And, again,—

"If this Temperance Act would be *ultra vires* of the Provincial Legislatures because the B. N. A. Act does not give them the power to enact it, I fail to see why it is not *intra vires* of the Dominion Parliament."

And Mr. Justice GWYNNE, of the same Act; (to repeat), says,—

"The Act, then, being *ultra vires* of the Provincial Legislatures, as dealing with a subject not exclusively assigned to the Provincial Legislatures ; *cadit questio, for that point being so determined, it follows, by the express provisions of the B. N. A. Act, that it is within the jurisdiction of the Dominion Parliament.*"

If this is law ; and if the holding of the Privy Council on the tests upon which they decided, in the two cases named, as to the power of Parliament to legislate, is an affirmation of the views we have quoted ; we have, then, exceedingly simple rules to determine many of the questions of conflict arising under these two sections. But, *if it is law (?)* the advocates of the "Provincial autonomy" idea have strangely erred in fancying that the recent decisions of the Privy Council have tended to establish enlarged powers in the Local Legislatures, relatively with those of Parliament. For, if it is true, as the Privy Council have laid it down, as shown, that every Act which does not fall within one of the clauses of sec. 92, *so that it could be passed by the Local Legislature,* Parliament can pass ; (for, as we have seen, it really comes to that); then it is quite clear, that, not only could Parliament pass the Quebec Act, "regulating the contracts of insurance in a single Province,"—for that was what that Act really did ; regulating the issuing of insurance policies in a single Province ; and held bad on the ground of its being a stamp Act, and neither a license Act, nor an Act for direct taxation ; but, still, "a regulation as to the contract of insur-

J

ance in a single Province,"—but they can pass other acts relating to property and civil rights ; relating to the issuing of licenses ; and to numerous other questions, in cases, and in a Province or Provinces, that scarcely any one had, previously, for a moment, imagined was within the competency of Parliament! Certainly, no holding of the Supreme Court of Canada ever went as far as that!

But, if applying the tests given us, in the two cases named, to the Act in the Attorney General of Quebec v. The Queen Insurance Co., which was an Act that the Legislature of Quebec could not pass; and, therefore, "without any further question being asked," was *intra vires* Parliament; legislating, as we see it would then be, by Parliament, as to the regulation of "the contracts of a particular business or trade, such as the business of insurance in a single Province ;" does not such holding trench pretty closely on the doctrine in the case of The Citizens' Insurance Company v. Parsons, in which the Judicial Committee of the Privy Council say; (7 App. Cas. 113),—

"Construing therefore the words 'regulation of trade and commerce' by the various aids to their interpretation above suggested, they would include political arrangements in regard to trade requiring the sanction of Parliament, *regulation of trade in matters of inter-Provincial concern, and it may be that they would include general regulation of trade affecting the whole Dominion.* Their Lordships abstain on the present occasion from any attempt to define the limits of the authority of the Dominion Parliament in this direction. It is enough for the decision of the present case to say, that, in their view, *its authority to legislate for the regulation of trade and commerce does not comprehend the power to regulate by legislation the contracts* OF A PARTICULAR BUSINESS OR TRADE, SUCH AS THE BUSINESS OF FIRE INSURANCE IN A SINGLE PROVINCE?"

And, if, in their powers to regulate " matters of Inter-Provincial concern," so as to " include general regulations of trade affecting the whole Dominion," Parliament had not the power to legislate as to the conditions of policies of insurance "in a single Province," we are rather at a loss to know under what particular power it will come that Parliament can legislate with reference *to stamps on Policies of Insurance in a single Province.* But, as we have seen, if we have been logical, while the Citizens' Insurance Co. v. Parsons decides they can't do the one; the Privy Council's own tests, applied to the Attorney General for Quebec *v.* The Queen Insurance Co., show that they can do the other. But how such a contrary result is produced, simply, because, in the one case, the Local Legislature has the power to pass the Act, and, in the other case, has not, we quite fail to understand. We certainly are driven very strongly to question the soundness of the rules laid down by Justices TASCHEREAU and GWYNNE as quoted; and the soundness of the tests on which the Privy Council acted in these recent cases mentioned.

We might, here, well enquire, is not this another palpable, unquestionable, instance of a decision of

THE PRIVY COUNCIL AGAINST THEMSELVES?

In the Citizens' Insurance Co. *v.* Parsons, 7 App, Cas. 109, the question was as to the validity of an Act of the Local Legislature; and therefore, the tests foreshadowed in the first two Privy Council cases we have examined, were applicable. As intimated, we only see ground for questioning the correctness of those tests when they are applied, in an entirely different way from what they were, in one of the cases named, by LORD SELBORNE; and, in the other, by SIR JAMES W. COLVILLE. To test the validity of an Act of the Local Legislature, they are clearly sufficient; to test the validity of an Act of Parliament, we are very strongly impressed with the fact, notwithstanding that that authoritative Board have laid down otherwise, that they are, simply, as a matter of fact, nothing of the kind. And, that, no matter by what body decided, cases decided on such grounds, are not, therefore, well decided cases.

The tests then applied to the Act of the Local Legislature in the Citizens' Insurance Company *v.* Parsons were quite in accord with the doctrine established in the first two Privy Council cases we have examined; and the principle reiterated in the following, from the former case, covers the questions connected with the validity of *Acts of the Local Legislatures;* thus,—

"The first question to be decided is, whether the Act impeached in the present appeals falls within any of the classes of subjects enumerated in section 92, and assigned exclusively to the Legislatures of the Provinces; *for if it does not, it can be of no validity, and no other question would then arise.* It is only *when an Act* OF THE PROVINCIAL LEGISLATURE *prima facie* falls within one of these classes of subjects that the further questions arise, viz., whether notwithstanding this is so, the subject of the Act does not also fall within one of the enumerated classes of subjects in section 91, and whether the power of the Provincial Legislature is or is not thereby over-borne."

Having then decided, on these tests, that the Act was within section 92, and did not, also, come within either of the clauses in section 91, their LORDSHIPS concluded as follows, —

"It becomes unnecessary to consider the question how far the general power to make regulations of trade and commerce, when competently exercised by the Dominion Parliament, might legally modify or affect property and civil rights in the Provinces, or the legislative power of the Provincial Legislatures in relation to those subjects; questions of this kind, it may be observed, arose and were treated of by this Board in the cases of L'Union St. Jacques de Montreal v. Belisle, and Cushing v. Dupuy."

Down to this stage, then, in the Privy Council cases, it will be observed that the tests have been stated in reference to *Acts of the Legislatures only*, and applied to them; and not, so far, by the remotest hint, to Acts of Parliament; which, as we have seen, involve entirely different considerations; and, we beg to submit, with all possible deference and respect, require tests quite the reverse. More reasonable and logical tests, we apprehend, are those furnished us by the decisions of the Supreme Court of Canada. Summarizing them just here, before going further, we would again say that the tests are, as to an Act of the Local Legislature, just as decided in the Privy Council cases where we have seen that those rules or tests have been acted on; viz.,—

First:—Does the Act of the Local Legislature fall within either of the classes of local and private subjects enumerated in the 92nd section? If not, that is an end of it, as that section fully covers the outside of all their legislative powers. But if it does fall within any of the classes of subjects enumerated in section 92, then the next question arises:—

Second:—Does it also fall within any of the classes of subjects enumerated in section 91, and if so, is, or is it not, thereby overborne, and rendered nugatory? The answer to this last question, depends, as we have seen in our previous discussion of it, as to whether the subject-matter of the Act comes any further within the subjects-matter of the 91 section, (before Parliament has legislated effectually on the subject-matter in the 91st section, affected by the Act of the Local Legislature), than the subject-matter of the Act may legitimately do; for instance, on solemnization of marriage, but no further than that within the subject of marriage; on trade licenses within clause 9 of section 92, but no further than that within the subject of trade and commerce; on property and civil rights, but no further on that so as to make it a legislation, *bona fide*, on trade and commerce; on bankruptcy and insolvency; on naturalization and aliens, or on any of the other subjects from which Provincial legislation is excluded by the operation of the language in section 91.

Then, after Parliament has legislated, *bona fide*, within the subjects-matter of section 91, so that such *bona fide* legislation has come within the subjects-matter of section 92; the result of such legislation, would, as we have seen, depend upon the relative subjects-matter. Thus, an Act on the regulation of trade by Parliament, might take away from the Local Legislature all power to legislate with reference to certain classes of licenses. Legislation on fisheries, might, *bona fide*, affect and overbear, as far as such legislation was legitimate legislation on the subject of the fisheries, the local right to legislate, as so affected, on property and civil rights; legislation on the subject of marriage, might, as we have seen, lessen or affect the right of the Local Legislature to legislate with reference to the subject of solemnization of marriage. So, again, as we have also seen, Parliament might legislate with reference to direct taxation, and leave unaffected the right of the Local Legislature to legislate with reference to the same subject-matter.

But, on the other hand, we would respectfully submit, that it is reasoning backwards, and not fully reasoning at that, in order to ascertain whether an Act of Parliament is good, to ask the question—Could the Local Legislature enact it? For, we submit, and we think there is no difficulty in furnishing instances of it, (one of which we think is furnished us by the Privy Council's own case of the Attorney General for Quebec v. The Queen Insurance Co., which we have examined; somewhat ironically, perhaps, to detect the weakness, in the tests proposed by the Privy Council as to the validity of an Act of the Parliament), that there *are* Acts which the Local Legislatures cannot enact, and which the Parliament of the Dominion cannot enact either.* In all such cases, then, it is

---

* While this work is going through the press, we are in receipt of the report of Reed v. Mousseau, 8 S. C. R., 408, where a majority of the Supreme Court of Canada, held, that an Act of the Legislature of Quebec, providing that a duty should be imposed on papers filed in the Courts, payable in stamps, was *ultra vires* that Legislature, as not being direct taxation. In so holding, they follow the Attorney General of Quebec v. The Queen Insurance Co, above ci ed. As

obvious, that the question being asked, Can the Local Legislature pass it? and, being answered in the negative, does not show that such an Act could be enacted by Parliament. Then, if that is so, there is no escape from the conclusion, that, upon the grounds on which they have put them, the case of Dobie v. The Temporalities Board, as far as it decides that the Act there in question was *intra vires* Parliament, (for, in holding that, they really acted *extra judicially*, as *that* was not the question before them in that case); and upon which, (*not extra judicially*), they decided the case of Russell v. The Queen; have been wrongly decided; and the rules or tests there laid down are completely fallacious. We will again, by-and-by, examine those cases still more closely than we have yet done. What, we would submit, are the tests to be applied in order to decide whether an Act is *intra vires* Parliament, or not, are questions that have to be proposed in quite different order, and of a very different nature, from those named by the Judicial Committee of the Privy Council in the cases to which we have just referred. The tests, we apprehend, as we have shown, very fully, in the first part of this treatise; from the Act itself; from the well-decided cases of the Supreme Court of Canada under it; and from the whole current of the Privy Council's own decisions, down to that point, where, we beg to submit, (mistaking those early laid down rules as tests of the validity of an Act of the Local Legislature, for an equally good test of the validity of an Act of Parliament), they have gone astray, and have laid down rules and tests which are utterly delusive and which will have to be abandoned as entirely unsound; are as follows,—Does the Act in question, *bona fide*, and as legitimate legislation on the subjects-matter in question, come within any of the subjects-matter enumerated in, or covered by section 91; that is to say all matters not coming within section 92, and on the enumerated subjects in section 91, whether they come within the subjects-matter in section 92 or not? If so, then

---

the Privy Council have held that the right to legislate by Parliament, on the regulation of trade and commerce, does not extend to the regulation of a particular trade, such as that of fire insurance in a single Province; on the same principle, they would hold, that the right, in Parliament, to legislate for "the raising of money by any mode or system of taxation," would not include the right to raise money by imposing a stamp tax on papers filed in the Cour s in a single Province. And assuming, as we do, that they will affirm the judgment of the majority of the Court in Reed v. Mousseau, we will then,—the Privy Council themselves being, again, the Judges, *against themselves*,—have another instance furnished us of the falsity of their position that "it cannot be contended that Parliament had not full legislative authority to pass" an Act, simply because such Act was not within the competency of the Provincial Legislature.

that is good legislation within the power of Parliament, under the express language of the Act.

That, we take it, as between sections 91 and 92 of the Act, covers the whole ground; though, to pursue the course of reasoning of the Supreme Court of Canada, in the Canada Temperance Act case, in which another difference appears between their holding and that of the Privy Council, it may be further put thus:—That Act in question, (the C. T. Act), is a legislation on subjects which come within the classes of matters of a local or private nature comprised in the enumeration of the classes of subjects assigned exclusively to the Legislatures of the Province; such as property and civil rights; shop, saloon, tavern and other licenses for the sale of intoxicating liquors, and local and private matters. It is legislation with reference to those matters and affects them most materially and directly; but as it is, also, *bona fide* legislation regulating the traffic, (from the *Italian* " *tratta*," to trade), in intoxicating liquors, it is, therefore, a legislation on the regulation of trade; and however much such legislation, therefore, interferes with, over-rides, over-bears, excludes or supersedes the right of the Local Legislatures to legislate on the subjects-matter affected, that does not affect the validity of the Act, for, " *notwithstanding* anything in the Act," (B. N. A. Act), the exclusive legislative authority of the Parliament of Canada extends to all matters coming within the regulation of trade and commerce; and any matter coming within the regulation of trade and commerce, shall not be deemed to come within the subject of licenses; of property and civil rights, or of local and private matters in the Province; no matter how much it may appear to do so, nor how much it may actually do so, so as to interfere with or prevent Parliament from *bona fide* passing an Act regulating the trade or traffic in intoxicating liquors.

It is with no desire to indulge in mere captious criticism that we pursue this matter further. We have proposed to discuss the questions in connection with our subject fairly and honestly, and with our utmost intelligence; and, if, in so carrying out the design, we find—*as we do find*—a series of decisions by our very highest Appellate Court, the Judicial Committee of the Privy Council, which we think are unsound; and, followed to their logical sequence, most pernicious, and calculated to destroy—not the powers of Parliament to legislate; but to greatly increase those powers in a manner in which we believe the framers of the Act never for one moment contemplated would be the result of the Act;—but very much of the legislative power of the Act, exclusively given to and vested in the Local Legislatures. So, it seems to us, that while such men as Messrs. Blake, Mowat, Judge HENRY, &c., have been pressing utterly unsound arguments, the effect of which would be, as we have shown, virtually to strip Parliament of any power of effective legislation; and while the political papers have been exulting over the result of such cases as the Mercer Escheat case; the Fisheries case; the Ontario License case, and even the Parsons Insurance case, with the questions of mere detail under the Act, which the decisions in these cases, and in the Ontario Streams case as well, (as far as we can tell, from the newspapers' reports, of what is involved in it; the report of the case, neither in the Supreme Court of Canada, nor in the Privy Council, being yet to hand),* involve, they have entirely lost sight of, or failed to appreciate, the fact, that, in the Parsons' Insurance case, itself, coupled with the holding of the same learned Board that decided that case, in Dobie v. The Temporalities Board, and in Russell v. The Queen, the law has been carried—if it be law, which we very much doubt—far, far beyond any holding in the Supreme Court of Canada relative to the legislative powers of Parliament under the 91st section of the Act.

Coupled with the point we have been considering,—which has reached its *ultima Thule* in Russell v. The Queen, where, as we have seen, it has been directly held, that, if *in reference to an Act of Parliament*, the question be asked, Could the Local Legislature pass the Act? the reply be in the negative, the matter is settled; for that it cannot then be contended, that Parliament could not pass the Act which was without the competency of the Local Legislature,—there is another question running closely into it, but which we will endeavour to keep apart from it, until we have more fully discussed the question we are now considering.

The principle, then, as we have intimated, in an earlier part of this treatise, which lays at the bottom of the rule of construction, which, in Russell v. The Queen, has been fully developed, is this: By the first clause of the Act, it is provided, that, for the peace, order and good government of Canada, Parliament, in addition to

---

* Since the above was written, the report of the case in the Supreme Court of Canada is to hand: McLaren v. Caldwell, 8 S. C. R, 435. As this is not a case of construction under the B. N A. Act at all, it has still less force as affecting the question of the relative powers of Parliament and the Legislatures than the other cases named, and seems to involve no question of importance connected with the matters we are discussing in this treatise.

the right of legislating on the subjects specified in the 91st section, whether they come within the classes of subjects enumerated in section 92, or not, has also the right to legislate "in relation to all matters not coming within the classes of subjects by this Act assigned exclusively to the Legislatures of the Provinces."

Hence, the Privy Council argue,—under that portion of the clause which gives Parliament the right to legislate on all subjects-matter not given to the Local Legislatures, without any reference to the other portion of the clause at all,—if, to the question, Can the Local Legislatures *pass the Act in question?* the reply be in the negative, then it cannot be contended that Parliament by virtue of its general power to legislate for the peace, order and good government of Canada, could not pass it. But, if the reply be in the affirmative, the question will then remain,—Does the Act not also come within the subjects-matter enumerated in section 91, and so still belong to Parliament? Putting in force, then, in Dobie *v.* The Temporalities Board, the principle, as above named, from the first portion of that clause, they find that the right to pass an Act relating to property and civil rights in the Province, is not in the Local Legislature, because property and civil rights in another Province are inseparably involved with those in the legislating Province; and they hold that not only cannot one of these Provinces, under such circumstances, effectively legislate in such case; but that the conjoint operation of both Provinces is equally futile. That, then, was the whole question before them, but as the legitimate consequence of their reasoning in the case, although to that extent *extra judicial*, their conclusion really was, as fully developed in Russell *v.* The Queen; that, as the power of legislation was neither in the one Province, nor in the both of them; it was, therefore, in the Parliament of the Dominion. Yet, they might logically have held both of the first propositions, and yet the third remain untrue; unless, indeed, we accede to their deduction from the first portion of the first clause of the 91st section, that all powers of legislation not in the Local Legislatures, alone, or collectively, are in Parliament. But, that, which the Privy Council have rather assumed than proved, though they say *it cannot be contended otherwise*, is the very thing we very gravely question; and we must say it, frankly and honestly,—being, in honesty, fairly forced to do so,—we emphatically deny to be correct; the good foundation for which denial we think we will be able, unanswerably, to establish.

But, the result of their reasoning in Dobie v. The Temporalities Board, is to sustain the right of Parliament,—without bringing the subject-matter within either of those subjects enumerated among the over-riding subjects of section 91 at all,—to legislate with reference to property and civil rights in the Province, entirely outside of any of the subjects-matter in section 91, simply by grouping the property and civil rights in one Province, with the property and civil rights in another Province. This is exactly what has been done by the Judicial Committee of the Privy Council in Dobie v. The Temporalities Board. Then, if, on their holding that all Acts that the Local Legislatures, alone, or conjointly, cannot pass, can be passed by Parliament; and, hence, if, as in the case named, by simply grouping the property and civil rights in the one Province with the property and civil rights in another Province, Parliament could pass that Act, and Parliament can, as it hence can, legislate almost indefinitely on the subjects of property and civil rights in the Provinces; the power of the Local Legislatures, under such circumstances, over such important subjects-matter as property and civil rights, is not worth much. Not only so; but, if by simply grouping two or more Provinces together, an Act relating to property and civil rights in those Provinces is *intra vires* Parliament, and Parliamentary legislation is as effective in reference to those subjects-matter in the Provinces as is held in Dobie v. The Temporalities Board; the principle does not stop there; but, carried to its legitimate sequence, it sweeps away almost every vestige of legislative power that the Legislatures possess. For, if the principle applies to property and civil rights in the Provinces, by simply grouping two or more Provinces together, so that the Act could not be passed by one of the Provincial Legislatures, nor by two or more conjointly; by simply adding two Provinces together, Parliament, by the same principle, could as well legislate on the solemnization of marriage; on procedure in civil matters in the Courts; on municipal institutions; on licenses, outside of trade and commerce; and, on virtually all the other subjects in section 92, as it could on property and civil rights, under the holding in Dobie v. The Temporalities Board.

Yet, in the Citizens' Insurance Co. v. Parsons, as we have seen, their LORDSHIPS, in reference,—*not to the special subject-matter, exclusively, under the 92nd section of the Act, placed within the legislative control of the Local Legislatures*,—but to one of the dominant subjects-matter placed within the exclusive legislative power of Parliament; (that as to their right of legislating as to the great sweeping subject in commercial communities, " the regulation of trade and commerce ;" were, in their anxiety not to trench, improperly, on the rights of the Local Legislatures to exercise their full powers of legislation, careful to lay down the doctrine that those wide, sweeping words, must be construed simply to mean— *" Political arrangements* in regard to trade requiring the sanction of Parliament ; regulation of trade *in matters of inter-provincial"* (*i. e.* meaning between the Provinces, generally, of the Dominion) " *concern,* and *it may be* that they would include general regulation of trade *affecting the whole Dominion ;"* the only limitation, however, which their LORDSHIPS would, as a matter of abundant caution, then authoratively attach to the power of Parliament to legislate on that subject, was to hold, merely, that " its authority to legislate for the regulation of trade and commerce does not comprehend the power to regulate by legislation the contracts of a particular business or trade, *such as the business of fire insurance in a single Province."*

For the purposes of that case all that was necessary to decide was that the legislation of the Local Legislature as to the conditions of a fire insurance policy, did not fairly come within the words " regulation of trade and commerce ;" and, therefore, there was no actual necessity for their LORDSHIPS then going beyond that. Otherwise, doubtless, had it been necessary to have acted on the rules they subsequently adopted, as we have seen, and they had then reasoned from the principles established in Russell *v.* The Queen, instead of defining the powers of Parliament to legislate on the regulation of trade and commerce, with the limitation on such powers, as named ; the doctrine would then have been established, as acted on in Dobie *v.* The Temporalities Board, and as plainly declared in Russell *v.* The Queen, that it is only such Acts on any subject-matter, whatever, as are actually within the power of the Local Legislatures, (subject, too, to the over-riding power of Parliament where these come within the subjects-matter of the 91st section), that Parliament is precluded from passing. And, hence, any Acts, without any further question, affecting property and civil rights in the Provinces ; the granting of licenses ; local and private matters generally; or, in fact, any of the classes of local and private matters, whatever, enumerated in the 92nd section, that the Legislatures of the Provinces, either alone, or conjointly, cannot pass; Parliament, by virtue of the power in the first portion of the opening clause of the 91st section " to make laws for the peace, order and good government of Canada, in relation to all matters not coming within the classes of subjects by this Act assigned exclusively to the Legislatures of the Provinces," can pass.

Here, then, their LORDSHIPS, in the Citizens' Insurance Company v. Parsons, reasoning from the one point of view, relative to the right of Parliament to legislate with reference to a subject-matter expressly in their power, while careful to lay down the principle, that their right, in that case, does not extend to legislating with reference to the business of fire insurance in a single Province, carefully refrain from claiming, from that point of view, that Parliament can legislate at all on that (*their own express*) subject-matter, except in the broad, general, inter-Provincial way that they have named. Yet, their reasoning in Dobie v. The Temporalities Board, and in Russell v. The Queen, from the entirely new point of view in these cases, being applied to the case of The Citizens' Insurance Co. v. Parsons, would at once have shown that their exceedingly careful limitation was unnecessarily guarded ; because, on that ground, as it was a subject with reference to which no special power was given the Local Legislatures at all, Parliament could legislate—excluded, only, on the new theory, by the actual powers of the Local Legislatures to legislate—in any other than the narrowest way.

Yet, again, while even in the one case, from the one point of view, on such a subject as trade and commerce, which is exclusively given Parliament, that body *is excluded from legislating on the business of fire insurance in a single Province ;* in the other case, from the other point of view, where it is not a question of legislating upon a subject-matter specially given Parliament at all ; but, simply, acting on the *assumed incontrovertible position* that Parliament can enact all Acts out of the competency of the Local Legislatures, the very reverse conclusion is reached, as we have seen, in that case of the Attorney General for Quebec v. The Queen Insurance Co., (on an application of those rules to that case), that Parliament *can legislate on the business of fire insurance in a single Province !"* And, in the same way, reasoning first from the one point of view, and then from the other, in reference to the same subject-matter, you reach the same ridiculous, contradictory conclusions in reference to hosts of subjects ; which, like co-relative tests in addition and subtraction, should, on the contrary, produce precisely the same co-relative results.

And, now, in our examination, chronologically, of the cases bearing on the particular point we are considering, we return again to Russell v. The Queen, 7 App. Cas., 829. And, looking at the question we are now considering, together with one to which we shall refer hereafter as being the foundation for the conclusion of the Privy Council, that, if the reply to the question as to whether the Act can be passed by the Local Legislature be in the negative, there can be no contention about the power to enact it being in Parliament; we will, more closely than we have yet done, examine the case on that point in the Court below—the Supreme Court of Canada; 3 S. C. R., 505.

Mr. *Lash*, Counsel for the Appellants, there said, with reference to " property and civil rights in the Province,"—

" I do not understand that the Respondent contends that by virtue of those powers, the Legislature could have passed this Act, but they say it is an interference with such powers. *The Appellants contend that this fact does not affect the general powers of Parliament, as if there be such interference the powers of the Local Legislatures must give way.*

The Privy Council, it will be remembered, place no stress on this in their decision, holding, as we have seen, that the Local Legislature not having the power to pass the Act, there is no further question to be asked, and Parliament can pass it.

Then, Mr. *Lash*, in reply to the claim that the matter of the Act came within class 16 of sect. 92, relating to matters of a merely local or private nature in the Province, does not deny this, but says,—

" To this it is answered, that by the latter part of sect. 91, it is expressly provided that any matter coming within sect. 91, shall not be deemed to come within the class included in sub-section 16 of sect. 92."

And, to the same effect, is Mr. *Maclaren*, (who, we doubt not, must have been astonished at the course on the argument which the Privy Council pursued; passing over, as they did, the really strong point in the case), also for the Appellants ; thus,—

" The Appellants chiefly rely on sub-sections 2 and 27 of sect. 91, as giving power to the Dominion Parliament to pass the Canada Temperance Act. . . It is said that this Act interferes with the exclusive control given to the Local Legislatures over municipal institutions in the Province, and matters affecting civil rights and property. My contention is that the Dominion Parliament has full power to legislate upon all matters strictly within its jurisdiction *no matter what effect it may have on classes of matters comprised in those assigned by sec. 92 to the Legislatures of the Provinces ; and I base my contention on the concluding lines of sect. 91. Where there is an apparent conflict, in so far as it is a bona fide regulation of trade and commerce, the local interest must give way."*

All this shows, very clearly, the admission, on the part of the Appellants that there is a conflict in authority : that the subject-matter of the Act *does come within* different classes of the matters of a local and private nature enumerated in sect. 92.

Then, too, the very foundation of the contention for the Respondent was, that the Act was a legislation in relation to matters coming within different classes of sect. 92, which, as will be observed, was, in effect conceded ; and, it was further contended, that, *bona fide*, the Act did not come within the term "regulation of trade and commerce ;" and, therefore, it was claimed, being, as was virtually conceded on all sides, an Act relating to matters coming within different classes of the subjects enumerated in sect. 91, that it was *ultra vires* Parliament.

So, too, the learned CHIEF JUSTICE of the Supreme Court of Canada, in his able judgment, admits the whole contention, that, on the point, was conceded by the Counsel for the Appellants; that the subject-matter of the Act did come within the subjects-matter of sect. 92, and that the Act did conflict and interfere with the local rights of legislation in reference to such matters. The following shows that his judgment was to cover that very point of concession. Thus, says the CHIEF JUSTICE ; (p. 540),—

"In my opinion, if the Dominion Parliament, in the exercise of and within its legitimate and undoubted right to regulate trade and commerce, adopt such regulations as in their practical operation *conflict or interfere with the beneficial operation of local legislation, then the law of the Local Legislature must yield to the Dominion law*, BECAUSE MATTERS COMING WITHIN THE SUBJECTS ENUMERATED AS CONFIDED TO PARLIAMENT ARE NOT TO BE DEEMED TO COME WITHIN THE MATTERS OF A LOCAL NATURE COMPRISED IN THE ENUMERATION OF SUBJECTS ASSIGNED TO THE LOCAL LEGISLATURES. In other words, the right to regulate trade and commerce is not to be over-ridden by any local legislation in reference to any subject over which power is given to the Local Legislature."

Here were the clear claim and concession :—that the subject-matter of this Act was the regulation of trade and commerce, and that it did "come within" classes of matters of a local nature enumerated in sect. 92. It was, very plainly, never dreamt by that astute lawyer, SIR WM. J. RITCHIE, that the Act would have been good merely because the Local Legislatures could not pass it, as a whole ; nor, on any other ground than that though the Act was "in conflict and interfered with the beneficial operation of the local legislation," it came within the provision that being legislation, *bona fide*, on a subject-matter within section 91, it was good, "notwithstanding anything in the Act ;" under the latter part of the first clause, and the last clause, of that section.

Mr. Justice FOURNIER agreed with this judgment.

So, too, the dissenting judgment of Mr. Justice HENRY was based not only on the contention, that the Act was not within the regulation of trade and commerce, but that if declared valid it would be over-riding the powers of the Local Legislatures as to their right of legislation on the subjects-matter of sec. 92. We make the following extract on the point from the judgment of that learned JUDGE ; (p. 556),—

"If it be finally decided that the provision for the 'regulation of trade and commerce' over-rides the power of the Local Legislatures in the matter of licenses, I see no impediment in the way of legislation, in regard to matters affecting in the remotest way trade and commerce, that would not merely restrain and control, but completely nullify, the Local Legislative power in respect of 'civil rights and property' and other important interests."

That learned JUDGE evidently thought that if the Act were sustained it would be sustaining the "making laws," by Parliament, "in relation to matters coming within the classes of subjects by the Act assigned exclusively to the Legislatures of the Provinces ;" quite unaffected by the consideration that the Act was one, which, *of course*, could not be passed by the Local Legislatures.

And, Mr. Justice TASCHEREAU, although giving expression to the views as quoted by us ; still, admitting that the Act is an interference with the legislative powers of the Local Legislatures, under section 92, falls back upon the same position, taken, as we have seen, by the learned CHIEF JUSTICE, that, notwithstanding that, the Act being a regulation of trade and commerce within the meaning of section 91, the legislation by Parliament is still good under the latter part of the first clause of the section. Thus ; (p. 558),—

" Then, it seems to me, that under the words 'regulation of trade and commerce,' the B. N. A. Act expressly gives the Dominion Parliament the right to this legislation. *It may, it is true, interfere with some of the powers of the Provincial Legislatures*, but section 91 clearly enacts, that, notwithstanding anything in the Act, *notwithstanding that the control over local matters, over property and civil rights, over tavern licenses, for the purpose of raising a revenue, is given to the Local Legislatures*, the exclusive legislative authority of the Dominion extends to the regulation of trade and commerce, AND THIS COURT HAS REPEATEDLY HELD, *that the Dominion Parliament has the right to legislate on all the matters left under its control by the Constitution*, THOUGH, IN DOING SO, IT MAY INTERFERE WITH SOME OF THE POWERS LEFT TO THE LOCAL LEGISLATURES."

And the whole of the five Judges in the Supreme Court of New Brunswick, who, in Ex parte Grieves, (supra), held that the Act was *ultra vires* Parliament,—not to trouble the reader with any further quotations from their judgments,—all took the position, which, then, no one seriously questioned, that the Act was a legislation with reference to various subjects or matters *within* THE CLASSES *of local and private matters enumerated in section* 92, (that advisedly, SIR MONTAGUE E. SMITH, and the Privy Council, to the contrary notwithstanding), and assigned to the Local Legislatures.

As we have seen in our examination of the Privy Council cases, (once more to repeat it), in all the cases preceding Dobie v. The Temporalities Board, where the rules of construction were laid down, they were cases where the question arose as to the validity of the Acts of the Local Legislatures; and the tests there, quite properly proposed, were, *first*, Does the subject-matter legislated upon come within any of the clauses of sec. 92 ? If not, that ended the enquiry, as the Local Legislatures received all their powers under that section; and, therefore, if the subject-matter were not included in that section, obviously the Act was *ultra vires* the Local Legislature. But, if the answer were in the affirmative, then the next question arose as to whether the Act did not come within the 91st sect., and, if so, whether it was or was not thereby over-borne? That was the state of affairs down to the Citizens' Insurance Co. v. Parsons, where, as we have seen, the question was still as to the validity of an Act of the Local Legislatures; for which these tests were adapted. To make the first of these tests applicable to the almost opposite case of an Act of Parliament; the test, as we have seen, is utterly worthless, unless we assume, if the reply to the question as to whether the Act in question comes within the 92nd section, be in the negative, that the power then exists in Parliament to pass the Act, *be it on what subject it may, and without any enquiry as to what subject it is on.* But, in order to make that test of any value as to an Act of Parliament, *we must assume* THAT, *in its entirety ; without any limitation or qualification.* And this, we find, was actually the result of the holding in Dobie *v.* The Temporalities Board. There, acting on this, as it appears to us (because, the assumption, we take it—and that, without any doubt ; or, otherwise we would not presume to do, as we now very strongly do ; question, as a matter of principle, the correctness of such holding by a Court of such high authority— *is* an utterly unsound one) utterly unsound assumption, in holding that as to two Provinces, because, they neither separately, nor conjointly, could pass an Act relating to property and civil rights in those Provinces,* therefore Parliament could do so.

And in Russell *v.* The Queen, the principle established,— though, really, *extra judicially* so, in Dobie *v.* The Temporalities Board,—is affirmed ; and assumed, without being demonstrated, as beyond the possibility of contention. " LAW is the very reason of the thing," and that which is not reason is not law, no matter from whom the declaration of what is law, proceeds !

We give, again, the statement of their LORDSHIPS in Russell *v.* The Queen, (p. 836), showing clearly, in this connection, that that old, and as we respectfully submit, utterly inapplicable test to this entirely different case from that in which that test was a legitimate one, was actually applied and established. After a reference to the case of the Citizens' Insurance Company *v.* Parsons, in which it will be remembered the test was as to the validity of an Act of the Local Legislature, their LORDSHIPS say,—

" According to the principle of construction there pointed out, the first question to be determined is, *whether the Act now in question* falls within any of the classes of subjects enumerated in sect. 92, and assigned exclusively to the Legislatures of the Pro-

---

* It will be observed that we have raised no question on the points decided by the Privy Council, as to the competency of the Legislatures, alone or conjointly, to pass such Acts as that in question, in Dobie *v.* The Temporalities Board ; although we think their holding on those points, is open to the gravest doubt. For the present, however, we prefer confining ourselves to the contention. that, even admitting the correctness of their holding on those points, the test they have proposed as to the validity of Acts of Parliament is, still, an unsound one.

vinces. If it does, then the further question would arise, viz. whether the subject of the Act does not also fall within one of the enumerated classes of subjects in sect. 91, and so does not still belong to the Dominion Parliament. But if THE ACT does not fall within any of the classes of subjects in sect. 92, no further question will remain, *for it cannot be contended*, and indeed was not contended at their Lordships' bar, that IF THE ACT does not come within *one of the classes of subjects assigned to the Provincial Legislatures*, the Parliament of Canada had not, by its general power ' to make laws for the peace, order and good government of Canada,' full legislative authority to pass it."

Surely, no language can be more distinct; positive, and *unmistakeable* than *that!*

Then, after stating the three subjects-matter under which it was contended the " legislation fell," viz., the 9th, 13th and 16th sub-sections; as to licenses; property and civil rights, and local and private matters generally, their LORDSHIPS go on to show that "*the Act,*" or "*the matter of the Act,*" as they convertibly call it, is not within either of those classes of subjects ; so, that, under either of them, the Local Legislature *could pass the Act*. Thus, (p. 837),—

" *The Act in question* is not a fiscal law. IT *is not a law for raising revenue.* Indeed, it was a main objection to the Act that in the City of Fredericton it did in point of fact diminish the sources of municipal revenue. It is evident, therefore, that *the matter of the Act* is not within the class of subject No. 9, *and consequently that it could not have been passed by the Provincial Legislature* by virtue of any authority conferred upon it by that section."

Again,—" It was contended by the appellant's counsel, and it was their main argument on this part of the case, that the Temperance Act interfered prejudicially with the traffic from which this revenue was derived, and thus invaded a subject assigned exclusively to the Provincial Legislature. But, supposing the effect of the Act to be prejudicial to the revenue derived by the municipality from licenses, it does not follow that the Dominion Parliament might not pass it by virtue of its general authority to make laws for the peace, order and good government of Canada. Assuming that *the matter of the Act* does not fall within the class of subjects described in No. 9, that sub-section can in no way interfere with the general authority of the Parliament to deal with the matter."

Their LORDSHIPS also go on to show that *the Act in question* did not " fall within" either of the other classes of subjects enumerated in sec. 92.

We make a few additional extracts from their LORDSHIPS' judgment. Having shown, as above, that the Act directly affected the matter of licenses and reduced the revenue therefrom, their LORDSHIPS, on that point, further say,—

" It is to be observed that the express provision of the Act in question that no licenses shall avail to render legal any act done in violation of it, is only the expression, inserted probably from abundant caution, of what would be necessarily implied from the legislation itself, assuming it to be valid."

Here, then, is the clear admission of the fact, as is apparent from the Act itself, that the Act is a direct interference with and overriding; a total destroying, of the power to legislate as to the *granting of licenses* for the sale of liquor. Is this not a legislation " relating to matters coming within " the 9th clause of section 92 ? What, in the world, else, is it ? Is it not, being an Act preventing the sale of *liquor*, an Act relating to matters of *property* in liquors ? If not, what in the world is it ? Being an Act to make licenses nugatory, and to prevent *the sale* of liquors, is not that legislating in reference *to the civil rights* of citizens to get licenses, and, under them, to sell liquor ? If not, what in the world is it ?

" In however large a sense these words," (property and civil rights), their LORDSHIPS go on to say, " are used, it could not have been intended to prevent the Parliament of Canada *from declaring and enacting certain uses* (civil rights) OF PROPERTY, *and certain acts* (civil rights), *in relation to* PROPERTY, to be CRIMINAL and wrongful."

Certainly not ; and, therefore, the Act provides, under the 91st section, 27th clause, that " *The Criminal Law*" is within the jurisdiction of Parliament ; and, " notwithstanding anything in the Act," the' exclusive authority of Parliament extends to all matters coming within the criminal law ; and, " any matter coming within criminal law shall not be deemed to come within property and civil rights," to prevent effective legislation by Parliament on the criminal law.

Just so the Statute ! Just so, the holding, in principle, of the Supreme Court of Canada ! But, the very opposite is the manifestly incorrect holding of the Judicial Committee of the Privy Council ! With all deference !

And, yet, then, they do admit, after all, it *is* a legislation as to property and civil rights? But, being so, on their own test, that is not to be justified by its being legislation on criminal law; but, as regards their theory, it must stand or fall, on the single ground, that, because it is an Act *dehors* the power of the Local Legislatures to pass, therefore it is a perfectly good Act within the power of Parliament. Their LORDSHIPS, even, must not be allowed to abandon their ground in that way, and when driven to the admission that the Act is a legislation on property and civil rights, to escape by showing that it is also legislation on a criminal law. If they rely on the test above named, that the Act is to be decided to be good because the Local Legislature cannot pass it; they must not be allowed, when they find that ground falling beneath their feet, to sustain themselves on ground the soundness of which cannot successfully be questioned ; and, to uphold their newly manufactured, destructive, and utterly unsound test, to fall back on the other that the Statute gives, and which is one as unquestionable as it should always have been unquestioned !

True, again, it is, that, as their LORDSHIPS observed,—"Few, if any, laws could be made by Parliament for the peace, order and good government of Canada which did not in some incidental way *affect property and civil rights;* and it could not have been intended, when assuring to the Provinces *exclusive legislative authority on the subjects of property and civil rights,* to exclude the Parliament *from this general power,* (that is, *of passing Acts in relation to matters of property and civil rights*), whenever *any such incidental interference would result from it."*

No!—with all courtesy and respect—Certainly not! And, therefore, the Imperial Parliament, while giving to the Local Legislatures *general* "EXCLUSIVE legislative authority on the subjects of property and civil rights," made the express provision in the Act, that, notwithstanding such exclusive power was given, generally, to the Local Legislatures, "exclusively to legislate on property and civil rights ;" with respect to twenty-nine classes of large and general subjects, Parliament should have the right to legislate with respect to *them,* even though they did come within property and civil rights; and no matter how much such legislation, on such twenty-nine large and general specified subjects-matter, should come within property and civil rights, "it shall not be deemed to do so ;" leaving all other powers, (except where affected by other parts of the Act, as by the 41st sect. as to Election Courts, under the decision of Valin v. Langlois), subject, under the express phraseology of the Act, to the "exclusive" power of the Local Legislatures to make laws as to property and civil rights, as well as to the others of the subjects-matter enumerated in sect. 92. But, that clause from their LORDSHIPS' judgment is very far from establishing the disputed doctrine, held by them to be indisputable, that, if, in reply to the question as to any Act of Parliament,—Can the Local Legislatures pass it, either alone, or conjointly?—the answer be in the negative, then, Parliament can pass it.

Their LORDSHIPS continue, with this extraordinary statement,—

"It was not, of course, contended for the Appellant that the Legislature of New Brunswick could have passed the Act in question, which embraces in its enactments all the Provinces; *nor was it denied, with respect to this last contention, that the Parliament of Canada might have passed an Act of the nature under discussion to take effect at the same time throughout the whole Dominion.*"

Well, if this latter clause is not a surprise to our intelligent Canadian readers, then the extraordinary doctrine established by the Judicial Committee of the Privy Council, in Dobie v. The Temporalities Board, and in Russell v. The Queen, has not been *astounding* to ourselves;* and, on this latter point we are neither doubtful nor reticent. Why, if their LORDSHIPS read, at all, (which they assume to have done), the judgments delivered in the Supreme Courts of New Brunswick, and of Canada, they surely could not avoid knowing that the great contention was that Parliament *could not pass* that Act; because it was an interference with,

---

*When we had the truth forced upon us in this investigation, so, that, do what we could, we could not escape it, that a Court which we have always looked upon with such deference, almost amounting to awe; certainly, a Court looked upon by us so as to cause us to receive their judgments as unquestionably correct,— had delivered such judgments as they have delivered, in Dobie v. The Temporalities Board, and in Russell v. The Queen, *we were astounded!* For a time we were undecided what course to take. This treatise was well under way, before, in investigating the cases exhaustively, the truth was forced upon us, so that we could not resist it, that the judgment of the Judicial Committee of the Privy Council on the validity of the Canada Temperance Act, was even worse than the judgment which we had previously thought was the worst judgment we had ever examined, (and we have critically analized many thousands of judgments— over three thousand in one treatise alone, we once wrote), *i e.* the judgment, on the same question, of the Supreme Court of New Brunswick. We thought we would have to stop the work and abandon it, so monstrous were these governing decisions from our Appellate Court. But, after much thought, we decided otherwise. We resolved "to take the bull by the horns," (even though that were John Bull himself), and wrestle with it to the death! We have done so; and, we apprehend, the death is not with us. "PALMAM QUI MERUIT FERAT!"

and a legislation upon, (and the Privy Council expressly admit, as we have shown, that it was so, to some extent, and in some way, at least), "matters coming within the classes of subjects by the Act assigned exclusively to the Legislatures of the Provinces"—*the very words of the Act*, as we shall see more particularly, directly. And, as we have shown, herein, very plainly, it was admitted on all sides, with scarcely an exception, that the Act was a legislation on those local and private matters; property and civil rights, &c., &c.; and that the Act could not have been passed but for the saving clauses at the beginning and end of the 91st section : saving clauses, however, which their LORDSHIPS, by their extraordinary holding, shut themselves out from deriving any benefit from ; the doctrine established by their LORDSHIPS in Dobie *v*. The Temporalities Board, and in Russell *v.* The Queen, having to stand without *that* aid, or else not continue to stand, as establishing doctrines of sound law, at all !

No ! " It was not, *of course*, contended for the Appellant that the Legislature of New Brunswick could have passed the Act in question, which embraces in its enactments all the Provinces ;" but, *it is contended*,—and that very strongly, notwithstanding their LORDSHIPS have alleged it could not be contended,—that *that* did not enable the Parliament of Canada to pass the Act. Their LORDSHIPS *assumed* that the one involved the other ; but they simply assumed, we beg to claim, one of the most unmitigated fallacies that a rural Justice of the Peace, of the most illogical kind, could have assumed ! They assumed it ; but they utterly failed to demonstrate it !

" New Brunswick could not pass the Act ; therefore Parliament could," is not, necessarily, a logical sequence. New Brunswick could not pass an Act to raise a revenue for Provincial purposes from tavern licenses in New Brunswick, and Nova Scotia : Could Parliament do it ? New Brunswick could not pass an Act on solemnization of marriage, pure and simple, for New Brunswick and Nova Scotia : Could Parliament do it ? New Brunswick could not pass an Act as to the riparian rights on unnavigable streams, in non-tidal waters, for New Brunswick and Nova Scotia : *Could-Parliament-do-it ? ?* New Brunswick could not pass an Act for the sale of the public lands belonging to New Brunswick and Nova Scotia : Could Parliament do *that ?* New Brunswick could not pass an Act on the solemnization of marriage in the Province, containing clauses in no way connected with that subject, on the subject of marriage. Could Parliament enact a law *bona fide* on solemnization of marriage, with clauses added relating to the subject of marriage? Ontario could not pass laws relating to escheat in Ontario and Quebec: Could Parliament do that? Quebec could not pass a law regulating the procedure in civil matters in Ontario and Quebec: Could *not* Parliament do that? Ontario could not legislate with reference to property and civil rights in Ontario and Quebec : *Could not* Parliament do *that ?* If not, why not? Our highest Appellate Court,—the Judicial Committee of the Privy Council, in Dobie *v.* The Temporalities Board,—*say it can ;* and that is authority unquestionable, at least for us :—is it not ?

But, if Parliament can legislate for Ontario and Quebec on property and civil rights,—classes reserved for the "exclusive" legislation of the Local Legislatures by section 92,—why cannot it legislate on procedure in all or any of the Courts in those Provinces as well? another of the subjects so reserved for the exclusive legislative authority of the Local Legislatures. And, as we have seen in Parsons *v.* The Citizens' Insurance Co., on the subject of trade and commerce, Parliament was to have, as its special, peculiar, kind of power, the right to legislate *generally for the Dominion,* if Parliament can legislate on the subjects of property and civil rights and procedure in the Courts, by virtue of that wonderfully ridiculous (with all deference !) holding in Dobie *v.* The Temporalities Board, and in Russell *v.* The Queen ; why, in the name of common sense, can it not legislate on such subjects for the three Provinces of Ontario, Nova Scotia and New Brunswick ; or, as for that, for the whole Dominion as well ?

Well, if it could, by virtue of its general power to make laws for the peace, order and good government of Canada, do that, because the Provinces alone, or conjointly, could not do it, is it not *a little singular* that a special power should have been found necessary to enable Parliament to do that for three of the Provinces, Ontario, New Brunswick and Nova Scotia, (absolutely excluding Quebec from being so operated upon), in reference to these very subjects of property and civil rights and procedure in the Courts, as is specially provided in section 94 of the B. N. A. Act? Surely that could scarcely have been done *ex abundanti cautela,* as a kind of declaration of a common-law right such as is established by our Highest Court of Appeal in Dobie *v.* The Temporalities Board, and in Russell *v.* The Queen !

Were there ever cases in this world, decided before, where the *reductio ad absurdum* was more applicable than to the carefully considered, authoritative cases of Dobie *v.* The Temporalities Board, and Russell *v.* The Queen, as decided by that august body, the Judicial Committee of the Privy Council of England? It surely would not be deemed contempt of Court, if committed within their unquestioned jurisdiction, to say, that such decisions in law are equalled only by their criticism of the grammatical construction of a sentence!

We might add, that the judgments of the Privy Council have been received by us, simply because they are the judgments of the Privy Council, without any regard whatever to their merits or demerits; and, absolutely, without investigation or question. Even their extremely faulty criticism of the grammatical construction referred to above, of the closing clause of section 91 of the Act, has been quoted, and tacitly accepted, by, for instance, so able a lawyer as Sir Wm. Ritchie, as though on all questions, even as to a simple matter of grammar, the Privy Council must be treated as infallible. In the same way the doctrines in Dobie *v.* The Temporalities Board, and in Russell *v.* The Queen,—despite their absolutely destructive tendencies, and the almost total annihilation of the legitimate powers of the Local Legislatures that the application of such doctrines involves,—have been accepted as correct in principle as they are assumed to be binding as authority.

"Of course, recognising as I do that the Bishop possesses a discretion in this matter, I most fully admit that he is vastly more capable of exercising it well than I am. But the way he does exercise it is subject to criticism—even by those less competent than himself; in the same way *as the opinions and sentences of this Court,* MAY, AND OUGHT TO BE, AND ARE, *criticised by laymen.*" Per Bramwell, L. J., in Reg. *v.* Bishop of Oxford, 4 Q. B. Div. 556, in Court of Appeal of England.

THE PRIVY COUNCIL'S JUDGMENTS FURTHER CRITICISED.

It is almost painful, (a kind of, as *Byron* would call it, "pleasing pain"), in the excessively ridiculous aspect in which their views are presented, to follow them further.

Their ignorance; (to be perfectly candid and strictly just); actual, stupid, stolid, ignorance, of the matter they are examining, when we consider that *that* is our highest, authoritative, Appellate Court, is positively painful!

Our readers, in the perfectly fair and unquestionably correct analysis we have furnished of the case in its successive stages,—so plain and so simple are the points involved!—can easily see, that, what was mainly contended, on the one part, was that the Act was a legislation, by Parliament, "*in relation to matters coming within the classes of subjects by this Act* (the B. N. A. Act) *assigned exclusively to the Legislatures of the Provinces*," such as property and civil rights in the Provinces; the granting of licenses; municipal institutions; and, generally, matters of a local or private nature in the Provinces. To this, it, in effect, was answered,—Yes, we admit that, but it is also an effectual, *bona fide*, legislation, by Parliament, on "*matters coming within the classes of subjects enumerated in section* 91;" namely, the regulation of trade and the criminal law; and, therefore, by the closing part of the first clause of the 91st sect., the legislative power in connection therewith, is—"notwithstanding anything in the Act"—still with Parliament; for, also, by the last clause of the 91st section, " any matter coming within" trade and commerce, or the criminal law, "shall not be deemed to come within the class of matters of a local or private nature" (such as property and civil rights in the Provinces; the granting of licenses; municipal institutions, or, generally, local and private matters) "comprised in the enumeration of the classes of subjects by this Act assigned to the Legislatures of the Provinces," so as to prevent Parliament from effectually, *bona fide*, legislating on the subjects of the regulation of trade and commerce and the criminal law.

While that—we think simply and clearly stated, so that a child might understand it—was the main contention; it was also claimed, by those resisting the Act, that, even assuming Parliament itself had the power to legislate on the subject-matter of the Canada Temperance Act; the Act committed certain matters of a legislative kind to localities where the Act was to be brought into operation; and, therefore, was bad, on the ground that Parliament had no right to delegate its legislative power to the different localities.

It will scarcely be credited that the Privy Council were as utterly ignorant as so many children,—in the case in which they were to lay down principles of construction of the most far-reaching kind, and in which, (if those principles, from their utter absurdity, and entire impracticability, were not, as they are, rendered virtually inoperative, as principles), is involved, as they are laid down, the complete destruction of the "political autonomy" of the Provinces,—of the simple points stated above, that were involved in the case. But credited, or not; astounding as the fact was, even to ourselves, when it was forced upon our minds; so, that, in this investigation, it was impossible for us to avoid or ignore it; the *fact* is most lamentably apparent in every part of their judgment.

After the complete fallacy, as exposed by us, which they have committed in the first part of the following clause; and the entire mis-statement of which they are guilty in the latter part of the clause, thus,—

" It was not, of course, contended for the appellant that the Legislature of New Brunswick could have passed the Act in question, which embraces in its enactments all the Provinces; *nor was it denied*," (just fancy that; when it WAS THE VERY THING, *in every stage of the case, from beginning to end*, THAT WAS DENIED), " with respect to this last contention, that the Parliament of Canada might have passed an Act of the nature of that under discussion to take effect at the same time throughout the whole Dominion ;" (that's simply horrible!); their LORDSHIPS, to the surprise of none others more than ourselves, who, in *their* judgments, looked for wisdom; not for folly; go on with this utter nonsense; (p. 840),—

"'Their LORDSHIPS understand the contention to be that, in the absence of a general law of the Parliament of Canada, the Provinces might have passed a local law of a like kind, each for its own Province, and that, *as the prohibitory and general parts of the Act in question were to come in force in those counties and cities only in which it was adopted in the manner prescribed, or, as it was said*, BY LOCAL OPTION, *the legislation was in effect, and on its face, (that's really dreadful!), upon a matter of a merely local nature.*"

And to make less excusable the ignorance of their LORDSHIPS of what was really involved in the case, they had before them, in the argument of Mr. *Benjamin*, on that point, the following; (*Ibid.*, p. 831),—

" Even if the Dominion Parliament possessed the powers which it assumed to exercise by this Act, *it had no power to delegate them and to give local authorities the right to say whether the provisions of the Act should be operative or not.*"

This was simply the argument in the Supreme Courts of New Brunswick and Canada, from the maxim "*Delegatus non potest delegare;*" and, it is quite obvious, from the brief statement of Mr. *Benjamin's* argument, and the references to clauses 9, 13 and 16, made by him that he took all the positions before the Privy Council, that were taken in the Courts below; but, the reporter of the Privy Council, evidently puzzled with the nonsense of their LORDSHIPS' judgment, makes Mr. *Benjamin's* position to harmonize with it; and, right in the teeth of what that able man claimed, as quoted above, makes him, also, give away his whole case, by this simple statement, that no counsel employed in the case in these Provinces will credit that he was simple enough to have made, as follows:—

"*If it* (the Act) *applied to the whole Dominion without local option it would then be in the power of the Dominion Parliament.*"

Mr. *Benjamin*, having thus been got to have made such a fool of himself, as such a statement would—contrary to the fact—show him to have been; Mr. Chief Justice ALLEN, of the Supreme Court of New Brunswick, is operated on by their LORDSHIPS, and by the distortion of an isolated passage from his judgment, is made responsible for similar nonsense. (*Ibid.*, p. 840.)

The statement quoted from the judgment of ALLEN C. J., as the explanation of their LORDSHIPS having derived their extraordinary view of what was contended in the case, against the validity of the Act, is as follows; (p. 841),—

"*Had this Act prohibited the sale of liquors, instead of merely restricting and regulating it,* I should have had no doubt about the power of Parliament to pass such an Act; but I think an Act, which in effect *authorises the inhabitants of each town or parish to regulate the sale of liquor and to direct for whom, for what purposes, and under what conditions spirituous liquors may be sold therein,* DEALS WITH MATTERS OF A MERELY LOCAL NATURE, *which,* by the terms of the 16*th sub-section of sect.* 92, *of the British North America Act,* ARE WITHIN THE EXCLUSIVE CONTROL OF THE LOCAL LEGISLATURE."

This is quoted, by their LORDSHIPS, from The Queen v. The City of Fredericton, 3 P. & B. 188, for the purpose of showing, as they have stated, that it was admitted that Parliament could have passed such an Act as the Canada Temperance Act, "to take effect at the same time throughout the whole Dominion;" but that such legislation was bad because of the "local option" clause which it contained. The very extract they give for that purpose, shows ALLEN C. J. took no such nonsensical position at all. It shows, on the contrary, that he admitted that had the law been an absolutely prohibitory law, it would then have been *intra vires* Parliament; but, he claimed, that merely restricting and regulating the sale of liquor was without the competency of Parliament; that an Act "authorizing the inhabitants of the towns and parishes to regulate the sale of liquors;" and an Act directing " *by whom*," (*for whom*, they quote it, but that is a mis-quotation), " *for what purposes, and under what conditions, spirituous liquors may be sold therein*, deals with matters OF A MERELY LOCAL NATURE, which, within the 16th sub-section of sect. 92, of the B. N. A. Act, ARE WITHIN THE EXCLUSIVE CONTROL OF THE LOCAL LEGISLATURES!"

And that plain contention, which, as we have previously seen, was a part of Chief Justice ALLEN's general contention,—which, again summarized, was, that if the Act were a *bona fide* regulation of trade and commerce, within the meaning of class 2 of section 91, the Act was valid; but, the learned CHIEF JUSTICE claimed, that, for the reasons he gave, the Act was not a *bona fide* regulation of trade and commerce, within that sub-section; and, therefore, as he claimed, in the very paragraph which their LORDSHIPS have quoted, and which is undeniably correct, that the Act, then, was legislating upon local and private matters in the Provinces, within the meaning of sub-section 16 of section 92; and, that, therefore, ALLEN, C. J., claimed, the Act was *ultra vires* Parliament. And it is quite obvious, that, if we admit, as ALLEN, C. J., claimed, that an Act *regulating the traffic in intoxicating liquors* was not, on the grounds he put it, or on any other grounds, an Act *regulating the trade in intoxicating liquors;* then, there is no escape from the fact, that the Act being a legislation on matters " coming within the classes of matters by this Act (the B. N. A. Act) assigned exclusively to the Legislatures of the Provinces," was *ultra vires* Parliament, and void. But, as we have shown, almost *ad nauseam*, because it *did* come within the regulation of trade and commerce, it was *intra vires* Parliament, " notwithstanding anything in the Act," though it did come within various classes of subjects enumerated in section 92; because, "any matters coming within any of the classes of subjects enumerated in section 91, *shall not be deemed* to come within " the local and private matters enumerated in section 92, &c.

Their LORDSHIPS singularly omit *the very next words* from the judgment of Chief Justice ALLEN; which, if they had quoted them, would have made more apparent their strange perversion of his language and position, than is done by the passage which they did quote. That language is as follows; (3 P. & B. 188),—

"I admit that these provisions of the 99th section* of the Canada Temperance Act may be said to be regulations for the trade in liquors; but looking at the declared object of the Act and the manner in which it is intended to be put in operation, *I cannot think that it is such a regulation of trade and commerce as is contemplated by the British North America Act.* IF THESE ARE NOT MATTERS OF A MERE LOCAL NATURE IN THE PROVINCE, I AM UNABLE TO SAY WHAT WOULD BE SO, IN RESPECT TO THE SALE OF LIQUOR."

There is the whole contention of ALLEN, C. J., in a nut-shell. And, yet, it was *that* clearly-stated contention that has been so greatly distorted by their LORDSHIPS, that that was an admission —to quote again their very language—"*that the Parliament of Canada might have passed an Act of the nature of that under discussion to take effect at the same time throughout the whole Dominion;*" but that that, in the case in question, could not be done because of the "local option" clause in the Act. It *is* wonderful that such nonsense has escaped exposure until now!

To show what a mere phantom they thought they were fighting, we give an extract from their LORDSHIPS' judgment, next succeeding the passage they quoted from the judgment of ALLEN, C. J., as above quoted. Their LORDSHIPS say; (p. 841),—

"Their LORDSHIPS cannot concur in this view. The declared object of Parliament in passing the Act is that there should be uniform legislation in all the Provinces respecting the traffic in intoxicating liquors, with a view to promote temperance in the Dominion. Parliament does not treat the promotion of temperance as desirable in one Province more than in another, but as desirable everywhere throughout the Dominion. The Act, as soon as it passed, became a law for the whole Dominion, and the enactments of the first part, relating to the machinery for bringing the second part into force, took effect and might be put in motion at once and

---

*This section, (pp. 105-107, Dominion Acts, 1878), has no relation, whatever, to the "Local Option" clause in the Act; which is contained in the "*First Part*" of the Act, extending from *Ibid.*, pp. 82 to 104 inclusive. Section 99, is *the whole of the "Second Part" of the Act*, which makes all the minute provisions *of a local nature* to be in force where the Act is adopted, regulating the sale for medicinal purposes, &c.; which Mr. Chief Justice ALLEN claimed rendered the Act *ultra vires* Parliament, on his assumption that the Act was not within the clauses in the 91st section; the regulation of trade, or the criminal law.

everywhere within it. It is true that the prohibitory and penal parts of the Act are only to come into force in any county or city upon the adoption of a petition to that effect by a majority of electors, *but this conditional application of these parts of the Act does not convert the Act itself into legislation in relation to a merely local matter."*

And, having effectually battled with the mere myth—a creature of their own imagination—that was the only difficulty which stood in their way; their LORDSHIPS added, that "The objects and scope of the legislation are still general, viz., to promote temperance by means of a uniform law throughout the Dominion."

And, that is the case, which, as we have clearly shown, (we apprehend so clearly that no reader of any intelligence can misunderstand it), *establishes* a principle of construction, foreshadowed, and in effect acted on, in Dobie v. The Temporalities Board; which, logically applied, if in its peculiar kind of absurdity it were capable of being so applied, would sweep away, virtually, all the legislative power which the B. N. A. Act confers on the Local Legislatures!

We have already intimated, that, in the exercise of our right of criticism, we will treat all matters coming before us as though we were honestly, and impartially, criticising a mere literary work, the author of which to us was entirely unknown; and, though we have told the truth plainly, and expressed our honest views unmistakeably; *that* is exactly what we have done in our examination of those judgments of the Judicial Committee of the Privy Council of England; the ultimate Appellate Court of the Dominion of Canada. But, in doing so, we are constrained now to say, on deliberation, that, were not the proofs on the face of the judgment to the contrary, we should have thought that that judgment could not have been prepared by that Board at all, or by any of the Judicial members of it; but, that, more probably, it was prepared by some ignorant secretary of the Board, without its having come under their LORDSHIPS' subsequent examination at all. In charity to such a high Appellate Court as that, we should have constrained ourselves to have come to that conclusion. But, the report itself, deprives us of even that charitable view.

But, even on that charitable view of the judgment, had it been open to us, their LORDSHIPS must, at least, have fixed the basis on which the judgment was to be framed; which basis, as we have seen, they obtained by the misapplication of the tests in the earlier

Privy Council cases, (where such men as LORD SELBORNE were to be found acting), that were applied to determine as to the validity of Acts of the Local Legislatures, to those Acts of a very different character, and involving very different tests; viz., Acts of the Parliament of the Dominion.

Thus, as we have shown, from a quotation, which we re-quoted to make their whole position and contention clearer, their LORD-SHIPS lay down the principle that "IF THE ACT" of Parliament "DOES NOT FALL WITHIN any of the classes of subjects in sect. 92, *no further question will remain, for*" (they add, to prove this), "IF THE ACT DOES NOT COME WITHIN *one of the classes of subjects assigned to the Provincial Legislatures,*" "*it cannot be contended,* and indeed was not contended at their LORDSHIPS' bar, *that the Parliament of Canada had not,* BY ITS GENERAL POWER" (*merely that, notice!*) "' *to make laws for the peace, order and good government of Canada,*' FULL LEGISLATIVE AUTHORITY TO PASS IT."

That is the rock on which they have split! The blunder which they have committed; which has led them hopelessly astray!

THE RESERVED POINT NOW CONSIDERED.

Now let us see how it happened. This is the matter so closely connected with that which we have been considering, which we desired to keep apart from it until we had disposed of *that*, (see ante, pp. 152 and 157); and which we have so kept apart. We will now make this other additional point clear.

We have seen how very grossly the Judicial Committee have failed in their criticism of the last clause of the 91st section, in its grammatical application to the classes of local and private matters enumerated in section 92; quoting, as we did, on that point, the Privy Council against themselves. We have also seen how they have mis-applied, to Acts of Parliament, tests, which, in all the cases preceding Dobie *v.* The Temporalities Board, had been properly applied to Acts of the Local Legislatures; and have fully pointed out the differences existing in the two cases. Now, we will make their blunder, in such a mis-application of those tests, more apparent; which blunder arises from their equally as gross misconstruction of the first clause of section 91.

They say,—*If the Act* (of Parliament) *does not fall within any of the classes of subjects in section* 92, no further question need be asked." "*If the Act of Parliament, does not come within one of the classes of subjects assigned to the Provincial Legislatures,* the Parliament of Canada had . . full legislative authority to pass it." That, observe, is what they say. The result of such an absurd position we have already fully shown. *We now say*, that, when their LORDSHIPS make those assertions, in the paragraph quoted, *they make them without the slightest authority in the world !*

True, they are the Appellate Court of the Dominion of Canada, under some circumstances. For, the appeal from the Supreme Court of Canada is taken, not as a matter of *right*, but merely exists in the Privy Council as a matter of *favor*. But they are our *highest* Appellate Court. Then, for us, from their judgments, their is no appeal. But, if they do as they have done in Dobie *v.* The Temporalities Board, and in Russell *v.* The Queen, establish principles which are utterly nonsensical ; and, which, from the peculiar kinds of absurdity attaching to them, render them, as principles, valueless, and incapable of being applied ; notwithstanding even *their* decision, such judgments are not Law, nevertheless. If they twenty times over decreed that, if *they* chose to call a horse's tail a leg, it would make it a leg ; it would *not* make it a leg, nevertheless ! If, for a hundred years, the highest Appellate Courts of England wandered off from the correct tests as to what constitutes a partnership ; and only came back to the truth a few years ago, when the House of Lords, in Cox *v.* Hickman, brought back the law to the point from which, a hundred years before, it had wandered away from the principle laid down in the Civil Law, that " The contract of partnership is nothing otherwise than the contract of agency ;" during the whole of that hundred years, the cases which we had on the subject of partnership *were not* LAW. And, so, again, if the Appellate Court of Canada—the Judicial Committee of the Privy Council of England—choose, authoritatively, to say two-and-two are eight ;" " two-and-two" remain four, still, notwithstanding !

Precisely so, when they made the not true statements as quoted above, on which we have been animadverting. " *If the Act of Parliament* DOES NOT FALL WITHIN *one of the classes of subjects assigned to the Provincial Legislatures, then Parliament has the full legislative authority to pass it,*" is not law, in the sense in which the Judicial Committee of the Privy Council use that language, and apply it, in Dobie *v.* The Temporalities Board, and in Russell *v.* The Queen. This we say advisedly.

Where do they get that language ? They profess to find it in the British North America Act ; but find it there they most certainly do not. It is an utter perversion by them, of the language there, to claim anything of the kind.

If the British North America Act provided that if an Act of Parliament did not fall within one of the classes of subjects assigned to the Local Legislatures, Parliament had the power to pass it; then, assuredly, the Privy Council's law in Dobie *v.* The Temporalities Board, and in Russell *v.* The Queen, would have been perfectly good law. But, if that had been the provision, as the Privy Council claim, that, by the first portion of the first clause of the 91st section, it is; then, all the machinery provided in the Act for disposing of cases of conflict when they arise, would have been unnecessary; for no such conflict could ever have arisen. The Local Legislatures, then, would have been, expressly, limited and confined to the passage of such Acts, (literally *such Acts*, as the Privy Council treat it), as come within those classes of subjects in section 92; so, that, under that section, they could pass such Acts; and *all other Acts* would have been within the competency of Parliament. Then, with that simple provision, the closing part of the first clause of section 91, and the last clause of that section, and all the enumerated subjects-matter in section 91 would have been unnecessary; because the simple test would *then* have been, just as the Privy Council have *now* made it; that, all Acts, with the exception only of just such Acts as the Local Legislatures could pass under section 92, whatever they might be, greater or less, would have gone to Parliament. True, that, while simplifying the matter in one way, would have greatly complicated it in another, considering the nature of some of the subjects given to the Local Legislatures by that section; but, with the very elastic rules of construction that the Privy Council have applied to the present Act, applied to that, and the difficulties that would have existed in the imaginary Act, (which, however, is the Act as created by the Privy Council, and not by the Imperial Parliament), would have been easily surmounted.

In sober seriousness, then, the British North America Act makes no such provision as that *if the Act of Parliament does not fall within one of the classes of subjects named in section 92, it is within the Legislative competency of Parliament.*

What, in the clause named, it does provide, is, that it shall be lawful for Parliament "to make laws *in relation to* TO ALL MATTERS *not coming within the* CLASSES OF SUBJECTS *by this Act, (the*

B. N. A. Act), *assigned exclusively to the Legislatures of the Provinces."**

That is a very different thing from the Privy Council's statement of it. *That*, (we are treating now, mark, as they have done, only of the first part of the first clause of the 91st section, relied on by the Privy Council), *excludes Parliament from legislating on all matters* COMING WITHIN THE CLASSES OF SUBJECTS assigned to the *Legislatures*, (the plural, mark!), *of the Provinces*. Assigned "*exclusively*," so, too, is the language of the Act. Then, that excludes Parliament from legislating on property and civil rights ; on local and private matters ; on licenses for revenue purposes, and on all the rest of the subjects named in sect. 92. Hence, as Parliament is excluded from legislating on property and civil rights ; as property and civil rights are of the classes of subjects assigned exclusively to the Local Legislatures ; and as Dobie v. The Temporalities Board, and Russell v. The Queen are cases in which legislation in relation to matters which do come "*within the classes of subjects*," &c., viz., property and civil rights, as we have shown ; to say nothing of the latter case being also, as is too clear for question, a legislation relating to local and private matters in the Provinces, *these cases are wrongly decided,*

AND ARE NOT LAW!

It remains now, from the Act itself, where it is much better stated, than is done in the horrid perversion of it, by the Privy Council, to state what the law is.

The Act then provides:—

First,—That it shall be lawful for Parliament to make laws for the peace, order and good government of Canada, *in relation to all matters not coming within the classes of subjects by the Act assigned exclusively to the Legislatures of the Provinces ;* and

Second,—Without restricting the right of Parliament to make laws for the peace, order and good government of Canada, as above named, in relation to all matters not coming within the classes of subjects by the Act assigned exclusively to the Legislatures of the

---

*See *ante*, p. 9, *et seq.*, for our construction of this clause, entirely irrespective and independent of the holding of the Privy Council in the cases under examination. "The first part of the clause is clear. By it, Parliament has the power 'to make laws for the peace, order and good government of Canada in relation to all matters not coming within the classes of subjects assigned exclusively to the Legislatures of the Provinces.' Here, then, Parliament is allowed to legislate, only, for the purposes named, *on the matters that do not come within* THE CLASSES OF SUBJECTS assigned to the Legislatures ;" &c., &c.

Provinces; Parliament may, notwithstanding anything in the Act, exclusively make laws in relation to all matters enumerated in section 91, whether these come within the subjects-matter enumerated in sect. 92, or not; and if any matters enumerated in sect. 91 do come within those enumerated in section 92, they shall not be deemed to do so, so as to prevent the effectual, *bona fide*, legislation by Parliament, on the subjects-matter enumerated in section 91.

Then, it now remains, merely, for us,—summarizing from our entire discussion,—categorically to answer the questions we placed before us at the beginning of this treatise, (see *ante*, p. 7); and, making the answers as much of the nature of definitions as the nature of the case will admit of, we say, as the law under the Act, all the badly decided cases in the Privy Council, or elsewhere, to the contrary, notwithstanding :—

1. The Local Legislatures have the right and power, in the first instance, (i. e., before Parliament has effectually legislated so as to affect the particular subject-matter in section 92), to legislate on all subjects-matter enumerated in the 92nd section, within these subjects-matter, not farther on them within the subjects-matter enumerated in section 91. For example, the Local Legislatures can legislate on the solemnization of marriage, but no farther than that within the subject of marriage; on licenses, &c., under the 9th sub-section; but no farther than that, on that subject, within the subject of regulation of trade and commerce; on the subject of property and civil rights, but no farther than that to make it a legislation on trade and commerce; on bankruptcy and insolvency, or on any of the other subjects-matter enumerated in section 91; &c., &c.

2. Parliament has the right and power to legislate for the peace, order and good government of Canada, on all matters not coming within the classes of matters enumerated in section 91; and effectually and *bona fide* on all subjects-matter enumerated in section 91, no matter how much such effectual and *bona fide* legislation on such subjects-matter in section 91, may come within, interfere with, over-ride, over-bear, destroy, supersede or exclude the right and power of the Local Legislatures to legislate on the subjects-matter enumerated in section 92.

3. After Parliament has so effectually and *bona fide* legislated on the subjects-matter in section 91, as to have affected the subjects-matter in section 92, the Local Legislatures have the right and power to legislate on the subjects-matter enumerated in section

92, (not farther within the subjects-matter enumerated in section 91, as aforesaid), so far as such subjects-matter in section 92 remain unaffected, or not over-ridden and superseded by the effectual and *bona fide* legislation of Parliament on the subjects-matter in section 91. For instance, legislation by Parliament on direct taxation under class 3 of section 91, would leave intact direct taxation under class 2 of section 92 ; legislation by Parliament under sub-section 2 of section 91, under such an Act as the Canada Temperance Act, or under an absolutely Prohibitory Law, would, virtually, take away all power from the Local Legislatures to legislate as to shop, saloon and tavern licenses for the purpose of raising a revenue for local purposes ; legislation on bankruptcy and insolvency, and on other subjects enumerated in section 91, would take away from the Local Legislatures, property and civil rights in the Provinces, so far as these were brought within, or were affected, or over-ridden, by, the *bona fide* legislation, by Parliament, on such subjects-matter in section 91.

The above is the deduction as to the THE LAW, from the Act itself, and from all the well decided cases under it, whether decided in the Supreme Court of Canada, by the Privy Council, or elsewhere ; which, manifestly,

DO NOT INCLUDE

Dobie v. The Temporalities Board, nor Russell v. The Queen, as decided by the Judicial Committee of the Privy Council of England ; and which cases we think we have shown, honestly and unanswerably,

ARE NOT LAW.

Admitting the above to be a correct statement of the law, as between Parliament and the Legislatures, under sections 91 and 92 of the Act, questions for the Courts like those in the fisheries cases ; in the *causes celebre*, the Mercer escheat case; the Parsons' insurance case ; the Ontario license act case, and in other similar cases, will continue to arise ; but these questions come within the ordinary rules as to construction ; and, as they arise, have to be treated as analogous cases are treated in other instances. So, too, questions may arise as to the effect of legislation by Parliament on subjects-matter in section 91, *bona fide* affecting subjects-matters in section 92 ; as to the greater or less extent to which these latter may have been affected by such legislation : this, as we have seen, being greatly dependent on the relative subjects-matters in the particular case. Such questions are not more difficult than many other questions of law which are continually arising, and which have to be disposed of by the Courts; and under the intelligent leadership of the able head of the Supreme Court of Canada,

WILL BE MORE INTELLIGENTLY DEALT WITH

by that Dominion Court, with one of the ablest lawyers in America at its head, than by a body, incapable, as it seems, of doing any better, as far as we are concerned, than delivering such ridiculous judgments as those in Dobie v. The Temporalities Board and in Russell v. The Queen;—

THE JUDICIAL COMMITTEE OF THE PRIVY COUNCIL OF ENGLAND, who, when they hear appeals from the Supreme Court of Canada, hear them not as of right, but in a kind of illegitimate way, called "*as of favor !*"

THE VALIDITY OF THE DOMINION LICENSE ACT OF 1883, UNDER THE TESTS.

And, now, in closing, we would simply apply the tests with which we are supplied by the Privy Council of England, in Russell v. The Queen; and by the wiser judgment of the Supreme Court of Canada, in the City of Fredericton v. Barker, to the Dominion License Act of 1883.

By what we think, as we have plainly intimated, is the absurd Privy Council test, the Act is undoubtedly good; from the fact, alone, that the Local Legislatures could not pass it, being an Act for the whole Dominion; which is, as we have seen, according to the Privy Council, equivalent to a declaration that. Parliament can pass it. And, therefore, assuming that the Privy Council's test is a sound one; or, adopting it as an authoritative statement of the law, the License Act of 1883 would be *intra vires* Parliament. But, we confess that we shall be somewhat surprised if the Privy Council themselves do not abandon their rule, which, we think we have clearly shown, is utterly unsound and worthless.

By the wiser tests furnished by the Act, and developed by the Supreme Court of Canada in the City of Fredericton v. Barker, the Act is question being a general Act for the regulation of traffic in intoxicating liquors, for the "peace and order" of Canada, is an Act regulating trade, and is as valid as the Canada Temperance Act; the Fisheries Act; or the Insurance Act—which two latter Acts have been already fully considered, with the cases under them, in this treatise. As these latter two Acts contained clauses expressly reserving the rights of the Local Legislatures, so the Act under consideration has a clause, (the 2nd sub-section of section 7), expressly reserving the right of imposing "a tax" (it is called "*in order to the raising of a revenue;*" which is, in effect, but another way of designating a license for that purpose; the effect intended under the B. N. A. Act being thus accomplished. That concedes the right, call it by what name you please, reserved to the Local Legislatures, to raise the revenue for local purposes contemplated to be raised under sub-section 9 of section 92. So, the question as to the over-riding of that section is eliminated from the case. Besides that, under the 16th clause of section 92, any mere local or private regulations, of the nature of municipal or police regulations, not inconsistent with the Dominion Act, and not over-ridden by it, would remain intact. Such questions as these are very simple ones. No more difficult, in fact, than are the very simple questions in the Mercer escheat case; the fisheries case; the Parsons' insurance case; &c., &c.

As far as these cases justify the portion of the speech of the Lieut.-Gov. of N. B., at the opening of the Legislature of that Province, which we have inserted at the beginning of this treatise, in the face of what we have shown is the *rationale* of the decisions in the Privy Council cases of Dobie v. The Temporalities Board and of Russell v. The Queen, that passage can stand, and have the effect to which it may be entitled, but no further than that. So, too, as far as the principles that are developed in these cases justify the statement put in the closing speech of the Lieut.-Gov. of Ontario, in his closing speech to the Legislature of that Province, it, too, can stand and have that effect to which it is entitled. It is as follows,—

"*By the confirmation of Provincial jurisdiction over the liquor traffic, to which I referred at the opening of the House*, the way was laid for further legislation on the subject, and I was glad to find that, by the bill to which I have assented, you have done all that seems at present practicable for further mitigating the evils of intemperance by imposing greater restriction on the sale of liquor, and severer penalties for the violation of our license law."

We placed at the fore-front of this treatise, quotations which we thought apt, from *Shakspeare* and Lord Justice BRAMWELL, as a fair indication of the course we should pursue in dealing, "fearlessly and faithfully," with all questions that might come in our way, in this investigation after LAW, and after TRUTH. And, now, looking back upon the plain, unhesitating manner in which, "calling a spade a spade," we have dealt with the cases we have investigated, and with those who have figured in them; we place at the end of this treatise, as

NOT AN INAPT CONCLUSION,
a quotation from the the utterance of an out-spoken citizen of the United States—the Rev. T. DeWitt Talmage; which is as follows:—

"*Those who are in editorial chairs* and in pulpits *may not hold back the truth.* King David must be made to feel the reproof of Nathan, and Felix must tremble before Paul, *and we may not walk with muffled feet lest we wake up some big sinner! If we keep back the truth* what will we do in the day when the LORD rises up in judgment, and we are tried not only for what we have said *but for what we have declined to say?*

"In unrolling the scroll of PUBLIC WICKEDNESS *I first find incompetency for office. If a man struggle for an official position for which he has no qualification, and win that position, he commits* A CRIME *against* GOD *and against society!* It is no sin for me to be ignorant of medical science, but if, ignorant of medical science, I set myself up among professional men and trifle with the lives of people, then the charlatanism becomes positive knavery. It is no sin for me to be ignorant of machinery, but if, knowing nothing about it, I attempt to take a steamer across to Southampton, and through darkness and storm I hold the lives of hundreds of passengers, then all who are slain by that shipwreck may hold me accountable. . . . .

"*We have had judges of courts who have given sentence to criminals in such inaccuracy of phraseology that the criminal at the bar has been more amused at the stupidity of the bench than alarmed at the prospect of his own punishment.*

"I ARRAIGN INCOMPETENCY FOR OFFICE AS ONE OF THE GREAT CRIMES OF THIS DAY IN PUBLIC PLACES."

POSTSCRIPT.

From the intimations I have received as to the demand for this work, I have felt myself warranted in having an edition issued very much larger than is usual, in this Dominion, for works of this class. If, notwithstanding this fact, the present edition should be soon exhausted, as it now seems probable that it will be, and the issuing of a second edition should become advisable, I propose, in addition to discussing all further Canadian Constitutional cases that may have been decided in the Supreme Court of

Canada, and by the Judicial Committee of the Privy Council, to take up all the remaining cases in the different Provinces of the Dominion, (Ontario, Quebec, Nova Scotia, P. E. Island, &c.), decided under the B. N. A. Act, 1867; and, subjecting them to the same course of impartial and independent criticism that I have applied to the cases I have examined, by means of the crucible of criticism, separate the gold from the dross; as I have striven to do in the present edition; I trust not altogether without success.

J. TRAVIS.

Saint John, N. B., June, 1884.

www.ingramcontent.com/pod-product-compliance
Lightning Source LLC
Chambersburg PA
CBHW032147160426
43197CB00008B/799